Global Linguistics:
An Introduction

Our gratitude goes also to Sabine Christopher-Guerra, Ioana Agatha Filimon, Sabrina Mazzali-Lurati, Rudi Palmieri and Gergana Zlatkova who read and commented parts of the manuscript in its successive stages of development.

Last, but not least, we wish to thank the editors at Mouton de Gruyter, in particular Marcia Schwartz and Monika Wendland, who provided sure and patient guidance throughout the editorial process.

Marcel Danesi, University of Toronto

Andrea Rocci, University of Lugano

Global Linguistics:
An Introduction

by
Marcel Danesi
Andrea Rocci

Mouton de Gruyter
Berlin · New York

Mouton de Gruyter (formerly Mouton, The Hague)
is a Division of Walter de Gruyter GmbH & Co. KG, Berlin.

♾ Printed on acid-free paper which falls within the guidelines
of the ANSI to ensure permanence and durability.

Library of Congress Cataloging-in-Publication Data

> Danesi, Marcel, 1946—
> Global linguistics : an introduction / by Marcel Danesi and Andrea Rocci.
> p. cm. — (Approaches to applied semiotics ; 7)
> Includes bibliographical references and index.
> ISBN 978-3-11-021405-5 (hardcover : alk. paper)
> ISBN 978-3-11-021406-2 (pbk. : alk. paper)
> 1. Intercultural communication.   I. Rocci, Andrea.   II. Title.
> P94.6.D36   2009
> 303.48′2—dc22
>
> 2009009108

ISBN 978-3-11-021406-2

Bibliographic information published by the Deutsche Nationalbibliothek

The Deutsche Nationalbibliothek lists this publication in the Deutsche Nationalbibliografie; detailed bibliographic data are available in the Internet at http://dnb.d-nb.de.

© Copyright 2009 by Walter de Gruyter GmbH & Co. KG, D-10785 Berlin
All rights reserved, including those of translation into foreign languages. No part of this book may be reproduced or transmitted in any form or by any means, electronic or mechanical, including photocopy, recording, or any information storage and retrieval system, without permission in writing from the publisher.
Printed in Germany.

Preface

In a world where telecommunications technologies have made it routine for people of different linguistic and cultural backgrounds to interact on a daily basis, the risk for conflict based on misunderstanding has increased significantly. It goes without saying, therefore, that the need to understand the forms and meanings of the language used in such interactions has become an urgent one. The study of such use can be pigeonholed, for the sake of convenience, under the rubric of *global linguistics*, defined tentatively as the study of how the native languages of speakers influence the outcomes of intercultural interactions.

Although much has been written on language in intercultural communication, relatively little effort has been expended to integrate the research and the theories in a textbook fashion. As instructors of a course on the topic of linguistic aspects of intercultural communication at the University of Lugano, we have always, in fact, had to prepare our own handouts, tailoring them to meet the needs of our students. We soon realized that these could be integrated into a manual with a broader focus.

This book constitutes, in effect, our reworking of those materials into a systematic introduction to a field that, as mentioned, we wish to call "global linguistics". Actually, The term was suggested to us by one of the students taking the course. Later we found that G. Leech (2004) used incidentally the same phrase in discussing whether it is "time to invent a new branch of the discipline" dealing with the rapid changes that languages and language use are undergoing due to globalization. In fact, global linguistics, as we envisage it, overlaps only in part with this idea, focusing more specifically on language use in the countless intercultural communication contexts created by the globalization of the economy, the increased mobility of individuals and the worldwide reach of electronic media. We sincerely hope that this book will pique the interests of all students to investigate the crucial role that native languages play in global communicative contexts. We also hope that the idea of a "global linguistics" will be accepted by our colleagues and fashioned into a full branch of our discipline.

Six chapters make up this text, each one identifying the thematic and methodological issues and areas to be covered by a so-called global linguistics. The first one presents a general overview of language, intercultural communication, and language contact. The second chapter examines the nature of speech in intercultural settings, focusing on dialogue, conversation, discourse and the meaning of messages. The third, fourth, and fifth chapters look respectively at the relation between communication and culture from various theoretical and methodological angles. These chapters discuss, in a basic fashion, how the various systems of language come into play in shaping the understanding (or misunderstanding) of messages in intercultural communication. The final chapter takes into account the relations that exist among language, culture, and worldview looking specifically at the presupposition that words are more than carriers of information. They are, in effect, culture-specific evaluative artifacts that condition users to anticipate events in the world as necessary or "logical." Breakdowns in communication are traceable to the differential evaluative effects that words have on their users.

In a world where instant global communication has become a mundane reality, the appeal on the part of humanitarians, politicians, and other people committed to the elimination of conflict and hostility among peoples through meaningful intercultural dialogue will end up being little more than lip service, unless it is accompanied by a rational scientific understanding of the role language plays in such dialogue. This text will hopefully provide a point-of-departure for gaining such understanding. It can be used by those committed to promoting intercultural understanding in the workplace, in society, and in other contexts.

We have composed it so that a broad readership can appreciate the fascinating and vital work going on in the whole area of intercultural communication studies, most of which is often too technical for general consumption. Our ultimate objective is to impart a basic understanding of how intercultural communication works in practical situations and why it often breaks down.

We are grateful, first and foremost, to all our students. They have given us constant feedback and have encouraged us to put into a textbook format the ideas presented in class. We are especially indebted to Eddo Rigotti, the director of the course, and our guiding intellectual light, who not only has inspired us with his many insights into the salient features of intercultural communication, but also given us unwavering support and advice in putting our ideas into print. We would also like to express our deep gratitude to Sara Greco Morasso who worked with us in the design of the course materials and compiled the first version of the lecture notes from which this book originates. Without her early efforts much of the interactions that sparked this book would have been lost in the vagaries of memory.

Contents

Preface ... v

Chapter 1: Language in the global village
1. Introductory remarks ... 1
2. Intercultural communication ... 3
3. Language ... 11
4. Speech ... 24
5. Linguistics ... 33

Chapter 2: Speech
1. Introductory remarks ... 45
2. Dialogue ... 46
3. Conversation and discourse ... 49
4. Speech functions ... 57
5. Meaning ... 67
6. Utterances ... 82

Chapter 3: Communication
1. Introductory remarks ... 95
2. Human communication ... 96
3. Action and its representation in language ... 105
4. Interaction ... 113
5. Verbal communication ... 124
6. The relational dimension ... 129

Chapter 4 : Culture
1. Introductory remarks ... 137
2. What is culture? ... 138
3. Culture, perception and cognition ... 149
4. Conceptual calquing ... 157
5. Intercultural contact ... 161
6. Cultures in context ... 169

Chapter 5: Argumentation
1. Introductory remarks — 173
2. Discussions: freedom and responsibility — 174
3. Discussions: plausibility and relevance — 177
4. Reasoning — 181
5. Reasonableness — 193
6. Arguments in context — 200
7. Culture-bound and universal components of argumentation — 203
8. Intercultural Fallacies — 212

Chapter 6: Global Linguistics
1. Introductory remarks — 217
2. The Whorfian Hypothesis — 218
3. Noise versus interference — 227
4. Intercultural Competence — 243
5. Concluding remarks — 248

References — 251
Index — 269

Chapter 1
Language in the global village

> *Transport of the mails, transport of the human voice, transport of flickering pictures—in this century as in others, our highest accomplishments still have the single aim of bringing people together.*
>
> Antoine de Saint-Exupéry (1900–1944)

1. Introductory remarks

The emergence of homo sapiens as a species dependent on culture (and not just nature) for its survival coincides with the advent of language in the species. Without it, the ability and disposition to think and plan consciously, to transmit learned skills to subsequent generations knowingly, to promote social relationships in a continuous fashion, and to modify the environment creatively would likely never have materialized. In effect, language has made it possible for humans everywhere to explore the world abstractly, classify it, evaluate it, and perhaps even understand it.

Above all else, languages have made it possible for humans to enter into meaningful communication with each other. Over time, people have developed verbal devices and strategies to ensure that the flow of communication is effortless and smooth. These are learned in childhood, remaining largely unconscious throughout later stages of life. But even among speakers of the same language within a speech community, these devices cannot always avert misunderstandings and breakdowns in communication. Thus, it comes as no surprise to find that such breakdowns will occur, and even characterize, communication among speakers of different linguistic background. In today's "global village," as the Canadian cultural critic and communications theorist Marshall McLuhan (1911-1980) called a world where instant communication among people of different backgrounds is made possible through mass telecommunications technologies, the question of how language is used has clearly become a crucial one. Intercultural Communication (IC), as McLuhan maintained, would not only affect intersubjective modes of communication, but also radically alter the nature of traditional languages and cultures. No wonder, then, that studying the role of language in the global village is fast becoming an imperative. Although various linguists and communication theorists have started to look at the role of the Internet and other mass communications media on language, there still is no branch within linguistics aiming to do so systematically.

The goal of this book is to establish such a branch, which (as mentioned in the preface) can be called *global linguistics*. The main target of inquiry of global linguistics is the *koiné* that has crystallized in the many contexts that involve IC. This was the word used in Ancient Greece to describe the parlance based on the Attic language that became the common vernacular of the Hellenistic world, and from which later stages of Greek are descended. Also called a *lingua franca*, a koiné loses those indigenous features that have a community-specific communicative function, so that it can be used as a more generic medium of communication between peoples of different backgrounds.

Today, communication in the global village is largely koiné-based. And the global koiné is English, a language spoken in more parts of the world than any other language and by more people than any other tongue except Chinese.

Some of the most widespread languages function as regional koinés in certain areas of the world. Modern Standard Arabic (MSA), a modernized form of classical Arabic, has now become the koiné of the Arab world. Thanks also to the diffusion of Arabic language media, such as satellite television channels, newspapers and the Internet, MSA is now used as a common lingua franca by more than 200 million people, who speak the different dialects of Arabic as their native tongues. Russian is still an important lingua franca for the countries of the former USSR (Pavlenko 2006) and will likely continue to play an important role in the future, despite the encroachment of English and policies of "derussification" in some countries. Spanish, the third most spoken language after English and Chinese, is the official language of most Latin American countries and is widely spoken in the USA. None of these languages, however, can contend with English in its role as "global lingua franca" (Crystal 2003).

This chapter will touch upon basic concepts related to the study of koinés and the study intercultural communication generally. We also attempt to locate the position of global linguistics within the field of linguistics proper. Its specific aim is the study of how a koiné is used and how it develops in the global village.

2. Intercultural communication

For the present purposes, *intercultural communication* (henceforward IC) can be defined simply as the exchange of verbal messages (spoken or written) between individuals from different linguistic and cultural backgrounds by means of a *common language*.

The use of a koiné is the most common case, but it is not the only possibility. Various forms of *multilingual communication* (House & Rehbein 2004) where several languages are used – and mixed in different ways – by the participants in order to communicate are encountered in a variety of intercultural situations around the globe.

Looking more closely, we can see that the use of a koiné in IC is in itself a form of multilingual communication. The native languages of the participants deeply affect the interaction under the surface of the common lingua franca. Such exchanges can be problematic or awkward because the individuals participating in them tend to use the words and structures of the koiné either as carriers of their own culture-specific meanings or with inappropriate random meanings due to a lack of knowledge of the whole range of possible meanings they entail within the default language. Consider, as a simple initial example, the English word *affair*, which can mean a series of things, such as the following:

(1) something done or to be done (as in "Get your *affairs* in order")

(2) a professional or public transaction (as in "*affairs* of state")

(3) a social occurrence or event (as in "Their wedding was a big *affair*")

(4) a romantic or sexual relationship (as in "Theirs was a steamy *affair*")

Now, let's assume that two speakers, A and B, enter into a dialogue. A speaks a non-Indo-European language, having studied English as a subject in school; while B is a native speaker of English, and knows no other language. Having learned only meaning (1) above for *affair*, A makes the following statement during our hypothetical conversation:

(5) I am involved in an *affair* right now, and thus cannot help you out.

Upon hearing (5), speaker B will interpret *affair* in terms of meaning (4), rather than (1), since the way the sentence was put together suggests this meaning to a native speaker of English. So, B assumes that A is involved in a romantic relationship and, because of this strange reason, will not be able to help him out. The reason given by A will in effect seem bizarre to B, since in normal English parlance it is unlikely that a romantic affair would be given as an excuse for opting out of something; but it is nevertheless accepted by B as A's genuine excuse because of the form in which it was uttered. Needless to say, any dialogical follow-up to A's sentence will predictably be colored by this miscommunication of meaning.

This type of unwitting blunder and the interpersonal consequences it is bound to bring about is called, generally, a linguistic *calque*. In this case, the calquing process results from the fact that A is aware of only one meaning of the word *affair*. Actually, this is only one of several kinds of calques that characterize IC. Another common one is the use of a cognate in an erroneous fashion. Cognates are words in different languages that have the same origin. In some cases, they retain the same meaning in the different languages: for example, English *name* and Italian *nome* derive from Latin *nomen* (which itself comes from Indo-European *nó-men*) and have, by and large, the same set of meanings. On the other hand, *library* and *libreria* do not. In English, a *library* is a place in which books are kept for reading, reference, or lending; the corresponding Italian term is *biblioteca*. In Italian, the word *libreria* is a place where books are sold; the corresponding English term in this case is *bookstore*. The words *library* and *libreria* are known as deceptive cognates.

The following list of deceptive cognates shows how troublesome this source of calquing—known more specifically as *lexical interference*—can potentially be when native speakers of English and Italian enter into a conversation that unfolds in one or the other language as the common koiné:

Table 1. Italian-English deceptive cognates

English Word	Italian Cognate	Italian Meaning	Appropriate Italian
accident	accidente	*unexpected event*	incidente
argument	argomento	*topic*	discussione
assist	assistere	*to attend*	aiutare
brave	bravo	*good*	coraggioso
conductor (musical)	conduttore	*bus, train conductor*	direttore
confront	confrontare	*to compare*	affrontare
effective	effettivo	*actual*	efficace
factory	fattoria	*farm*	fabbrica
firm	firma	*signature*	ditta
library	libreria	*bookstore*	biblioteca
large	largo	*wide*	grande
lecture	lettura	*reading*	conferenza, lezione
magazine	magazzino	*department store*	rivista
sensible	sensibile	*sensitive*	sensato
stamp	stampa	*the press*	francobollo

2.1. Interference

The study of interference phenomena has, actually, a long tradition in linguistics, falling generally under the rubric of *contact linguistics* (Betz 1949, Haugen 1950, Weinreich 1953, Scotton, Myers, and Okeju 1973, Poplack, Sankoff, and Miller 1988). A primary focus of global linguistics will thus be to revamp and extend the study of such phenomena to intercultural contexts of all kinds at all levels of language use.

The extensive study of interference over the years has shown that linguistic borrowing, calquing, and other such "language mixing" phenomena have been significant factors in bringing about change and even in generating new forms of language. So, the phenomena surfacing in IC contexts are really not all that surprising. From time immemorial, people and communities have borrowed and adapted the forms and meanings of languages different from their own for various social reasons. The classic case is that of the so-called *pidgin* and *creole* tongues spoken in various parts of the world (Holm 1989). These emerged typically to make communication possible between two or more groups that speak different languages. Well-known examples include the Melanesian Pidgin English of the Solomon Islands and New Guinea, and Haitian Creole, based on French. Pidgins take shape when people of different language backgrounds have been brought together in specific situations (Bruce 1984). In such situations, people respond in a similar way—they construct a rudimentary language with a compact vocabulary and grammar that allows them to communicate effectively and efficiently for everyday social purposes. Some pidgins undergo standardization, developing into separate languages *creoles* (from the Spanish word *criollo* "native to the place"). This happens typically when people in pidgin-using communities marry. The children of such people are the first native speakers of the creoles. Such speakers develop their own culture and artistic traditions, some of which can even become renowned beyond the culture (such as the creole music of Louisiana). Creoles are testimony to the powerful instinct in humans to create language on the basis of need.

In a sense, the concept of pidginization can be used to explain what is taking place in IC contexts in the global village today. However, the pidginized forms that develop from such communication are hardly homogeneous. Real pidgins arise from a common linguistic substratum in a specific speech community. Given the different linguistic and cultural backgrounds of the speakers in the global village, the result is a pastiche of English forms that are often incomprehensible to all but their specific congeners. These are essentially ad hoc "global dialects" of English brought into being by adstratum forces. In effect, IC based on an English koiné is more accurately portrayable as "interdialectal" communication. Mutual intelligibility among intercultural speakers, as dialectologists call it (Chambers and Trudgill 1998: 3), occurs at a surface level through the common English code used. But, as we shall see in this book, at a deeper semantic and conceptual level, the intelligibility quotient can be very low indeed. In a nutshell, the variants of the English koiné that have developed, and continue to develop, in online and offline intercultural speech situations, are new dialectal forms of English that are springing up from multifarious modes of contact involving many acquired forms of English.

2.2. Communication (and miscommunication) in the global village

Interaction in the global village has made it saliently obvious that verbal communication rarely unfolds as a simple exchange of information, equivalent to a "replacement procedure", whereby information encoded in one language is recoded for speakers of another language directly without affecting the contents and the intent of the information. Ongoing research on IC is making it rather plain that a message can be interpreted correctly only if the sender and receiver possess the same kind of structural and conceptual knowledge built into the language used to transmit the message. In the global village, understanding how interpretation unfolds is becoming more and more of a necessity, since intercultural contacts and communicative exchanges have become the rule, not the exception. And these are starting to shape notions of identity, group membership, cooperation, competition, not to mention all forms of human interaction (verbal and nonverbal).

The scientific study of IC should, above all else, seek to provide insights into how such communication unfolds and how differences are really matters of "communication noise," as it can be called, rather than of anything else. Such insights can then be used to help foster greater understanding among diverse peoples and acceptance of culturally-based different worldviews. Thus, although the specific objective of global linguistics is to study the role of *verbal programming* (the construction of messages) in IC, it is obvious that in a broader scientific framework the non-verbal dimension (for example, body language and visual communication) would also have to be taken into account. Such study is, needless to say, beyond the scope of the present treatment, falling more appropriately in the domain of *global semiotics* (Sebeok 2001). For the present purposes, suffice it to say that the two most important dimensions of verbal programming are the *pragmatic* dimension and the *logico-semantic* one. They relate to different aspects of the meaningfulness of verbal messages. By *pragmatic* dimension we understand the fact that language is used as a means of *interaction* in a variety of social settings – or *interaction fields* (Rigotti & Rocci 2006). Speech is used to perform a variety of speech acts: such as to inform and to question, but also to make promises and requests, to complain, to apologize, to greet, to offer one's condolences and countless other social actions. As we will see in the following chapters, the felicitous performance and reception of these speech acts depend crucially on the participants' common understanding of the social situation and on the *inferences* they draw from a variety of subtle cues. The other key dimension is the *logico-semantic* one. It concerns how people use languages to *represent* the world conceptually, to *combine* simple concepts into more complex ideas, and use simple and complex concepts to *reason* about the world through valid inference schemes. Figure 1, below shows the main theoretical concepts associated with these two dimensions that will be gradually introduced in this book.

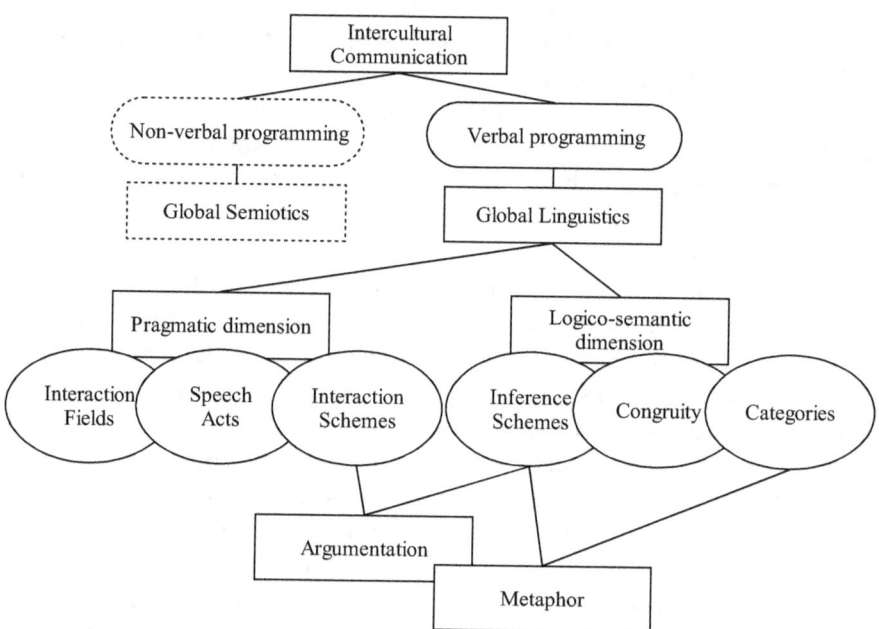

Figure 1. Aspects of verbal programming focused on by Global Linguistics.

Two phenomena relating to the semantic and the pragmatic dimension stand out as critical in view of IC: *metaphor* and *argumentation*. The semantic dimension crucially relies on a control of the *metaphorical strategies* that a language makes available to its native speakers to conceptualize the world in a certain light. This is particularly apparent when we need to make sense of complex and abstract conceptual domains. We do that metaphorically, in terms of our basic experience of the physical world. Consider, for instance, the highly complex social domain of economics and finance (Cf. Palmieri 2008 on discursive argumentative strategies in finance): both the layperson trying to come to terms with it and the professional grasp it figuratively using metaphors taken from the natural world. One important metaphor in this domain is the following: *Money is a liquid.* We understand the abstract consequences of a social convention such as *money* in terms of our basic understanding of the behavior of a familiar liquid like *water* – flowing, drying up, freezing, etc. It suffices to look at the headlines of the business newspapers to see how prominent this metaphor is.

(1) Europe's Central Banks <u>Inject</u> More Cash Into Financial System (*Wall Street Journal*, October 6, 2008)

(2) Iceland Missed Signs of <u>Liquidity Freeze</u> (*Wall Street Journal*, October 6, 2008)

(3) Deposits <u>Flow</u> to Healthier Banks (*Wall Street Journal*, October 16, 2008)

Argumentative strategies are an essential component of verbal communication in general, and are particularly critical for IC. An argument is an attempt at persuading the addressee by presenting *reasons* supporting a certain standpoint. In other words, when we present an argument we do not just try to influence other people (by any means) but we try to do that in a particular way: through reasoning. Arguments are "modes of gaining *warranted* assent, *reasoned* adherence, *voluntary* and *informed* acceptance" (Jacobs 2000: 264). Psychological studies have confirmed (Cf. Petty & Cacioppo 1986, O'Keefe 2002) that it is this kind of persuasion – dubbed the "central route of persuasion" in psychological parlance – that effects the deepest and most stable changes in the attitudes of people, as opposed to the more fickle and superficial changes operated by the "peripheral route" of persuasion, based exclusively on emotions, authority or on pure associations of ideas. It is quite natural, then, to think that healthy intercultural argumentation is necessary to IC in order to give a solid grounding to the cooperation of people from different cultures in a variety of social settings.

The problem is that very often intercultural argumentation does not work. Intercultural communication studies often report judgments of participants that evaluate the argumentations of people from other cultures as 'illogical', 'irrelevant' or as instances of 'muddled thinking' (cf. for instance Fitzgerald 2002: 87). Should we conclude that people from other cultures have *a different logic*? that they reason differently from us? A large share of Chapter 5 will be devoted to answering this important question.

As House, Kasper, and Ross (2003: 1-21) have cogently argued, like never before in the history of linguistics, the need to develop a framework for examining such dimensions is becoming critical. The authors go on to identify three sources of difficulty in IC taking the perspective of the speaker. We can gloss these three levels as follows:

1. The speakers are incapable of conceiving their message precisely in strictly conceptual terms: "I did not know what to say!"
2. The speakers are able to conceptualize the message, but cannot express it: "I did not know how to say it!"
3. The speakers are able to conceptualize the message and can program it appropriately, but do not do so for cultural reasons (for example, because native-culture rules of politeness prohibit them from doing so): "One cannot say that!"

Gumperz (1982) makes another important distinction between *non-communication* (when no meaning comes across to the hearer) and *miscommunication* (when an unintended message is communicated to the hearer). Finally, in a widely-quoted article, Thomas (1983) distinguishes two types of communicative failure that concern the pragmatic dimension:

1. Pragma-linguistic failure occurs when people misunderstand the pragmatic force of a linguistic expression. For instance, someone might think that the English sentence *Would you like an orange juice?* is an hypothetical *question* aimed at learning about the hearer's drinking preferences in general, rather than an *offer* (Wierzbicka 2003: 28).
2. Socio-pragmatic failure occurs when people perform a communicative action that the other culture considers inadmissible, or inappropriate to the social context. For instance, the French linguist Kerbrat-Orecchioni (2005) has observed that in Korean culture it is polite to ask new acquaintances detailed questions about work, family and children that a French person may well find embarrassingly personal.

As Klyukanov (2005) has aptly pointed out, these are the "hidden factors" that shape the outcome of IC. The study of IC is, in sum, gradually forcing linguistics to expand its field of inquiry into territories that would have been unimaginable before the advent of the global village.

3. Language

Throughout history people have sought to unravel the riddle of language. The ancient Greek philosophers defined it as a product of *lógos*, the power of reason residing in the human soul that, they claimed, had transformed humans from insentient brutes into sapient, rational creatures.

In other words, they understood that a language allows humans to converse in a logical fashion, that is, in a structured way that is considered to make sense among speakers of that language. The categories of thought mirror the categories of language, and when the latter are used by speakers in argumentation the assumption is made that hearers have access to the same categories. Problems arise when this is not the case.

In fact, the ancients also saw lógos as a potential barrier bringing about innumerable conflicts between individuals and nations. Not only because it manifests itself in different linguistic ways, but also because the categories and values embraced by different peoples can vary. When the ancient Greeks began to come into contact with the Persians and other Asian peoples, they experienced a deep cultural shock as they discovered that "a behavior which was despised at home was accepted and even commanded in another place" (Schulz 2001: 85). Herodotus (5th century BC), a Greek historian that can be considered also the first ethnographer, widely comments on the shockingly diverse habits of different peoples, offering a testimony of this discovery. As Schulz (2001) observes, the quest for reasonableness and universality that characterizes ancient Greek philosophy initially emerged also as an attempt to cope with this cultural shock.

So, the point of departure for global linguistics is the examination of language itself and its connection to logic and communication. Across the globe, the categories of language allow people to classify, remember, evoke, commemorate, and understand (in their own ways) the things and ideas that are relevant and meaningful to them. They constitute the realm of lógos. Without language, there would be no science, religion, commerce, government, literature, philosophy, nor any of the other expressive systems and institutions that characterize human lógos.

There are about 7,000 languages spoken in the world today. This number does not include dialects (local forms of a language). Many languages, however, are spoken only by small groups of a few hundred or a few thousand people. There are barely a little more than 200 languages with a million or more speakers. Of these, 23 have about 50 million or more speakers each. Of the current languages, more than half are expected to disappear in the next 100 years.

The use of languages, however, presents us with another striking fact: *multilingualism* is the norm in the world, *monolingualism* is an exception. In other words, in most countries of the world more than one language is spoken and many people regularly use two or more languages to carry out their daily affairs. Often the different languages spoken have different communicative and social functions. This specialization of functions is called *diglossia* (Ferguson 1959), or *multiglossia* when more than two languages are involved.

Patterns of triglossia are quite common: there are (1) several local or ethnic vernacular languages that are used for informal oral communication within the family, ethnic group or neighborhood, (2) a regional or national *koiné* used for daily business interactions, communication with people from other towns or regions, elementary education and mass media, and (3) an international language, which is used for higher education, official documents, technology, larger business transactions and international communication (Abdulaziz-Mkilifi 1972: 198). Quite often this third role is occupied by the English koiné. This pattern of triglossia can be found, for instance, in East and Central African countries such as Kenya and Tanzania, where Kiswahili acts at the regional koiné. In Tanzania, for instance, (1) there are 120 vernacular languages, (2) Kiswahili is spoken by 90% of the population and is used in primary education, (3) English is taught in schools and used as a medium for education from the secondary school onwards (Rubagumya 1991).

Multilingualism and the adoption of English as a global koiné are often seen as antithetic, to the point that the latter is seen as a threat to national languages and to multilingualism. Sometimes the term *linguistic imperialism* is used to describe the dominant position of English. Some recent research (House 2003), however, suggests that this view is simplistic as it overlooks the many ways in which people can "creatively"appropriate the English language and use it in conjunction with the local language.

Crystal (2003: xiii) goes as far as to argue that fostering multilingualism and a common lingua franca are really "two sides of the same coin" and are *both* desirable in view of IC. Multilingualism, as Crystal observes, "presents us with different perspectives and insights, and thus enables us to reach a more profound understanding of the nature of the human mind and spirit", while a common language is "an amazing world resource which presents us with unprecedented possibilities for mutual understanding, and thus enables us to find fresh opportunities for international cooperation". As Crystal observes, native speakers of English are "in a fortunate position", for they have fluent command of the global koiné.

In a sense, native speakers of English *can afford* monolingualism without apparent social disadvantages. If we look more closely at IC, however, English monolinguals pay a price too. Monolingual speakers are naturally less aware of the pitfalls of IC deriving from the use of a koiné. Every language casts its own net of categories and metaphors in order to grasp reality in its own way, drawing the distinctions that matter for a certain culture. Rigotti (2005a), citing the semioticians Lotman and Uspenskij, observes that knowing more than language allows people to distinguish more clearly the categories of a language from reality itself.

3.1. Universal principles

Languages throughout the world are built on the basis of the same principles. One of these can be called the "economizing principle." It asserts that with a small set of sounds they are able to produce an infinity of words, called *lexemes*, or bits of words known as *morphemes* (affixes, endings, etc.). The word *hands,* for instance, consists of the lexeme *hand* and the plural morpheme -*s*. Many linguists prefer to use the single term *morpheme*, designating a morpheme such as *hand* that has lexical or vocabulary meaning a *root morpheme* or *lexeme*; if it is purely grammatical (-*s, anti-, -ial*) it is called a *grammatical morpheme*. The economizing principle comes under various rubrics (duality of patterning, structural efficiency, the creativity principle). Essentially, it states that the sound system of every language, known as its *phonology*, consists of a limited number of sounds that, however, can be combined to form words ad infinitum. It is the same principle that undergirds the formation of numerals in the decimal system. More specifically, given the particular physiology and anatomy of the human vocal apparatus (consisting of the tongue, the teeth, the larynx, the vocal cords, the lungs, the palate, and other organs) the number of potential sounds that can be articulated by humans to make words varies from 20 to 60. However, the number of words that can be made with them is endless, since an infinitude of sound combinations can be constructed fitting the word-formation patterns available in any language.

A second universal construction principle can be called, simply, the "syntax principle." This asserts that all languages have rules for combining words to form phrases and sentences, again ad infinitum. These are not simple cumulative structures—that is, structures that are interpreted in terms of the sum of the individual meanings of their constituent morphemes. Rather, they are themselves meaning-bearing units. Syntax thus adds to the meaning-making capacity of language. Actually, this principle can really be seen as a sub-principle of the economizing principle.

A third principle can be called the "usage principle." This asserts that all languages have strategies of usage that are governed by culture-specific traditions. These guide how words, phrases, and sentences are used in conversations, dialogues and argumentation within specific social settings. Basically, the usage principle reminds us of the pragmatic dimension of language (§ 2.2). Essential to the pragmatic dimension is the communicator's knowledge of the *activity types* (Levinson 1979) or *interaction schemes* (Rigotti & Rocci 2006) in which language is used, of the cultural scripts (Goddard & Wierzbicka 1997) that guide people's communicative behavior, of the "speech genres" (Bakhtin 1986), of the culture-specific types of "speech acts" (Wierzbicka 2003) recognizable in different cultures and of the linguistic, stylistic and rhetorical forms that encode those schemes, scripts and speech-act types. Stubbs (2008) has presented a simple and quite effective example of what this kind of pragmatic knowledge is about:

Table 2. Social roles, discourse genres and settings (from Stubbs 2008)

Social role 1	Discourse genre	Social role 2	Setting
Scientists	*write research papers*	for their peers	in specialist journals
Professors	*give lectures*	to students	in universities
Preachers	*give sermons*	to congregations	in churches
Doctors	*give consultations*	to patients	in doctors' surgeries
Employers	*ask questions*	to potential employees	in job interviews
MPs	*give speeches*	to other MPs	in parliament
Journalists	*write editorials*	for readers	in newspapers
Judges	*pass sentences*	on the accused	in courtrooms

Stubbs (2008) observes that "there is an inherent and logical relation between social institutions, the professionals who work in them and their clients, and the language which is used there". The kind of language we use depends very much on the setting and the interdependent social roles of the people interacting. One cannot find, for instance, preachers giving *sermons* without a congregation hearing them, and, to make an obviously absurd example, you cannot have *journalists passing sentences on patients in universities*, or *judges giving lectures to potential employees in parliament*. Being able to communicate effectively in a language entails more than just knowing grammar and vocabulary as it is deeply intertwined with our cultural knowledge of appropriate situations and roles; what Scollon & Scollon (2001) call the fine "grammar of context". Culturally competent communicators use their tacit hypotheses about the social context and the ongoing activity to draw inferences that allow them to "read between the lines" of what is explicitly said. This essential activity of the hearer is called *pragmatic inference* (Moeschler 2004, Rocci 2006).

A fourth universal principle, which is of primary importance to Global Linguistics, can be called the "classificatory principle." This principle deals with the semantic dimension of verbal programming (§ 2.2).

The classificatory principle alludes to the fact that all languages serve a classificatory function and that the categories encoded by a language become intrinsic to the formation of people's worldviews. Although this principle was already well known in the ancient world, it really came to the forefront in the first part of the twentieth century through the seminal research conducted by Franz Boas (1858-1942) on American aboriginal languages. Boas (1940) discovered many things that suggested to him that languages provided people with the kinds of words and larger structures that relate to their particular environmental and social realities. For example, he noted that the Eskimo language (Inuit) had devised three basic lexemes for the animal that English speakers would call a *seal*:

(1) One is the general term for "seal" and, thus, equivalent to English *seal*.
(2) Another renders the idea of "seal basking in the sun." No similar lexeme exists in English.
(3) A third refers to a "seal floating on a piece of ice." Again, there is no counterpart to this lexeme in English.

The Eskimo language uses a larger "specialized vocabulary" to refer to this aquatic mammal, Boas suggested, because of the important role played by this mammal in Eskimo life. This does not mean, however, that the English language is therefore less capable of classifying reality. English speakers can refer to seal types if they desire by using accompanying descriptive terms: for example, *basking seal* and *floating seal*. However, these are not reflective of an obligatory lexicalization (the process of finding and using words to fit a situation). In Eskimo, on the other hand, the lexicalization of "seal" involves three distinct selections (as discussed above).

Specialized vocabularies serve specific classificatory functions across the world, encoding realities that are perceived to be critical by particular cultures. The ethnological record makes this saliently clear. For example, in its classification of plants, the Papago people of Arizona have devised four classes, that reflect their environment and economy accurately (Mathiot 1962):

(1) trees, which they have labeled "stick things" (*haiku uus*)
(2) cacti, which they call "stickers" (*hoi*)
(3) cultivated seasonals, which they designate as "things planted from seeds" (*haiku e es*)
(4) wild seasonals, to which they refer as something "growing by itself" (*hejal vuus^{h}nim*)

The Papago leave wild perennials that are neither cacti, trees, nor bushes unlabeled, because these play no direct role in their social reality. Similar naming strategies are used by cultures everywhere. However, specialized vocabularies are not permanently built into languages and often disappear when they are no longer needed. In contemporary technological culture, for example, specialized terms to name new devices (*iPod, BlackBerry*, etc.) are being devised on a regular basis. The proliferation of such terms bears witness to the growing importance of digital technologies in our culture. Not too long ago, we possessed a sophisticated terminology for referring to typewriters. Most of this specialized vocabulary has virtually disappeared, for the simple reason that we do not need it any longer, unless of course one is a collector of typewriters as antiques. In a phrase, changes in vocabulary mirror changes in society and culture. This topic, by the way, generally falls under the rubric of the *Whorfian Hypothesis* (WH), named after the American anthropological linguist Benjamin Lee Whorf (1897–1941), even though versions of the WH can be found before Whorf, especially in the writings of Romantic German scholars such as Johann Herder (1744-1803) and Wilhelm von Humboldt (1762-1835). And, of course, it was Boas who started the modern-day investigation of the classification principle, as pointed out. Whorf was, actually, the student of one of Boas's students at Columbia University, Edward Sapir (1884-1939). This is why, often, the WH is also called the Sapir-Whorf Hypothesis. Essentially, the hypothesis posits that language categories predispose native speakers to attend to certain concepts as being necessary. They do so because they are used to classifying the world in specific (specialized) ways. This does not imply, however, that people cannot understand each other. The paraphrases used above to convey the various meanings of the terms used by the Eskimo language to refer to seals show that there are always ways in which the resources of any language can be used for the purpose of cross-cultural communication.

Foley (1997) has shown that Whorf, contrary to what critics of the WH have suggested, did believe in universals and in the psychic unity of humanity, just as Sapir, and before him Boas did. Sapir (1924), in particular, observed that if we cannot translate a philosophical text such as Kant's *Critique of Pure Reason* into the Eskimo language it is due to the lack of appropriate abstract philosophical lexical terms and not to an inherent inferiority of the language or of the cognitive abilities of the Eskimo. Rather it has to do with their culture and way of life, which does not involve that particular kind of speculative activity. For instance, the Eskimo lack a word for *causation* – an abstract noun, which comes in handy only when you need to speculate on the concept as such! – but are clearly able to grasp causation intuitively as their grammar uses different forms for causatives (*The fire melted the ice*) and non causatives (*The ice melted*) (Cf. Sapir 1924, Foley 1997).

The WH is still a controversial notion within linguistics (see Lucy 1996 and 1997 for a review). However, as a framework for describing misunderstanding and miscommunication in IC, it is at the very least a useful one for Global Linguistics. Participants in a speech situation understand any information exchange in terms of the cultural categories expressed by their language. If referring to the *World Series*, a speaker will assume that the other understands that he or she is speaking about baseball. Such unstated knowledge colors all communication.

3.2. Language design

Each language is an equal among equals. No matter what sounds are used in word-design. The science of linguistics has always aimed to bring this out by developing a technical apparatus for describing and explaining the design principles used by all languages. One of the central characteristics of IC speech is the fact that speakers are often unaware of what design feature is breached and the effects this can have on understanding. To grasp what this implies, let's introduce errors into a specific subsystem of English on purpose. This allows us to focus on "what has gone wrong," by fleshing out what design principle has been contravened and what this might entail in communication terms.

Take, for example, the following English sentence into which a phonological error has been introduced:

(1) A *pfriend* of mine eats a lot of meat.

A native speaker of English, or indeed anyone who has studied the language even at an elementary level, can instantly point to the word *pfriend* as being decidedly "un-English." The other words, and the sentence itself, are otherwise well-formed in that language. Now, the question becomes: Why is the word *pfriend* un-English? What specific principle of English structure does it violate? Taken separately, each sound in that word is a legitimate one in English. The violated principle is thus not to be located in the nature of any one of the sounds in *pfriend*, but rather in a specific combination of two sounds /pf/. No English words exist, or can exist, with the cluster /pf/ at the beginning. The appropriate word in this case is probably *friend*.

This constraint on English word-construction is not a feature of all languages. In German, initial /pf/ occurs in all kinds of words: for example, *Pferd* ("horse"), *Pfennig* (a unit of currency, related to the English. *penny*), and so on. As the study of contact phenomena has shown over and over, when sound systems are in contact, interference occurs in a predictable fashion—non-native speakers unconsciously apply the phonological features of their phonological systems to speak the koiné. This produces sound calques that cumulatively lead to the formation of what is colloquially called an "accent." In IC, such calques are not as destructive of message interpretation as are other kinds, but they do enter into the picture in several ways that might in fact disrupt meaning exchanges. Above all else, phonological interferences identify an interlocutor as a non-native speaker of the koiné. Someone, who pronounces the /l/ sound of English words *kill, bill,* and *will* with the tongue touching the upper teeth, rather than arching it towards the back of the mouth, will be instantly recognized as a foreign speaker by native speakers of English.

Linguists refer to the sound units that languages make available for the creation of words as *phonemes*. In English, for example, the /p/ sound is a phoneme because it is the smallest unit of sound that can make a difference of meaning if, for example, it replaces the initial sound of *kill, bill,* or *will,* making the distinctive word *pill* (with each replacement). Phonemes are not letters; they are sound cues that signal points of meaning distinctions in an utterance. Phonemic interference is a constant source of misunderstanding in IC. For example, the English sounds /r/ and /l/ are phonemic in English: *lip* vs. *rip, link* vs. *rink*. But they are not distinctive in Japanese. So, in an IC setting where English is the koiné and speaker A is of Japanese origin and B a native speaker of English, the form *link* that may come up in a conversation will be interpreted in one of two ways (no matter who utters it). If B uses it, A might interpret it is either *link* or *rink*. If it is uttered by A, then B would only interpret it as *link*, even though A might have wanted to communicate the word *rink*.

It is relevant to note that phonological differences exist also among speakers in English speaking communities. Within any speech community, there is, actually, considerable variation in how words are pronounced. The way people speak will change not only according to where they live, but also according to their age, occupation, socioeconomic status, gender, etc.

Now, let's introduce another kind of error into the same sentence above, correcting *pfriend* to *aunt*:

(2) *A* aunt of mine eats a lot of meat.

Once again, a native speaker of English can easily spot the error. He or she would know that the correct form for the indefinite article should be *an*, not *a*. This is not a simple phonological error at the word level, however, because both are used:

a boy	*an* egg
a girl	*an* island
a man	*an* apple
a woman	*an* opinion

So, what aspect of English structure does the indefinite article form *a* contravene? The answer is *morphological* structure. The rule violated is, more precisely, *morpho-phonological*, regulating the choice of appropriate wordforms to use in a given phonological context: the indefinite article form *a* is used before nouns or adjectives beginning with a consonant, not a vowel. In the latter case, *a* is used. This principle probably has a basis in the nature of physical speech, being a kind of sub-principle of the economizing principle discussed above (§1.3.1). When the indefinite article occurs before a noun beginning with a consonant, the phonetic transition from *a* to the consonant is relatively effortless phonetically: *a boy, a girl, a man, a woman*, etc. However, if the noun begins with a vowel, then the use of *a* would require more effort to accomplish the transition—*a egg, a island, a apple, a opinion*, etc. As readers can confirm for themselves, a brief, but effortful, break between *a* and the subsequent vowel is unavoidable. This break is known technically as a *hiatus*. This analysis suggests two things: (1) that the phonological and morphological levels of language are interdependent systems; and (2) that the physical effort involved in speaking has an effect on language design.

Point (2) implies that an economizing tendency may be operative in determining the actual constitution of language forms, which manifests itself in many diverse ways in language and speech (Zipf 1935, 1949). The economizing principle suggests essentially that the ways in which human beings constitute their linguistic systems and exert themselves in speaking tend towards least effort.

The study of morphological systems includes determining not only how words are designed, but also what constitutes a word, and how units smaller than words, called morphemes (a we saw above), convey meaning. The particular features of a language's morphology have also been used by linguists as criteria for classifying it. For instance, languages have been classified according to the number of morphemes they use on average for constructing their words. In *analytic* or *isolating* languages, such as Chinese, words tend to be made up of single morphemes (one word = one morpheme); while in *synthetic* languages, such as Italian, words may contain several morphemes in combination (one word = combination of separate morphemes). In the case of some Native American languages, a single word may have so many component morphemes that it is the equivalent of an English sentence.

Needless to say, morphological interference is a potential source of misunderstanding in IC settings. For example, if speaker A (a non-native speaker of English) uses a word such as *informations* in a conversation, speaker B (a native speaker of English) might have difficulty understanding that this is speaker A's attempt to convey *pieces of information*. Speaker A assumes that the word *information* is a count noun that can be put into the plural (as it can in his or her native language), whereas in reality it is a mass noun in English denoting something that is indivisible into countable units.

Now, let's go back to our sentence, and introduce into it yet a third type of error:

(3) *Friend a* of mine eats a lot of meat.

In sentence (3) all words are well-formed phonologically and morphologically. Nevertheless, a native speaker of English will detect an error, instantly pointing out that the article is "out of place." The principle violated in this case is, thus, one of order or, more technically, phrase structure. It is a *syntactic* error—English articles must precede nouns and adjectives, not follow them. The "post-positioning" of the article, however, is an acceptable syntactic pattern in other languages, such as Rumanian: *casa* ("house") → *casele* ("the houses").

Syntactic interference is yet another source of miscommunication in intercultural conversations. In Italian, for example, some adjectives can come before or after the noun they modify. This dual syntax is used to signal differential nuances of meaning. This feature is absent in English. A speaker of Italian as a native language might however assume that the position of a the adjective *old* in English conveys the same sort of differential meanings that it does in Italian, where it is a dual-position form (Rocci 1996):

Old (in age)	*Old (known through long acquaintance)*
Lui è un amico vecchio.	Lui è un vecchio amico.
(*He is an old friend*).	(*He is an old friend*).

If the Italian speaker says "He is an old friend" while intending "He is a long-time acquaintance," the chances are that this meaning will not get across to a native speaker of English.

So far we have been concerned with infringements of some aspect of the "well-formedness" of words and word order. Now, let us consider the following version of our sentence, which is well-formed at all structural levels, but which still presents an anomaly:

(4) A friend of mine *drinks* a lot of meat.

Because the sentence is grammatically well-formed, native speakers are inclined to find a meaning for it. But real-world experience tells them that meat is eaten, not drunk. In effect, this sentence describes an impossible, incongruous situation. The sentence violates a *semantic* principle, namely the "principle of congruity" (Rigotti and Rocci 2001, Rocci 2005). In IC, semantic interferences tend to produce more deleterious effects on the interpretation of messages than do phonological, morphological or syntactic interferences, since speakers might not perceive them as semantically anomalous utterances, but rather as indicating something anomalous about the utterer and his/her communicative intentions, as is the case of deceptive cognates discussed above in § 2, Table 1.

The way in which we combine concepts obeys a law of logical congruity, which is arguably universal, but the lexicalization of concepts in different languages is largely the result of historical and cultural processes, needs, or traditions. In other words, the *incongruity* between the semantic feature [solid] implied by *meat* and the semantic feature [liquid] presupposed for the object of the English predicate *to drink* is strictly a *logical* one. The fact that English has two predicates *to eat* and *to drink* that differentiate the ingestion of solid and liquid nutriment is just a *cultural* fact about the English language, albeit one which is well motivated by human physiology. Languages may well differ in the categorical distinctions they draw. German, for instance, has two different predicates for "eating": *essen* and *fressen*. The first presupposes a [human] subject, while the second requires a [non-human] animal subject. So, in German it would be normal to say *Koalas fressen Eukalyptus* ("Koalas eat eucalyptus.") but one would not use *fressen* for people, except in sentences likening people to animals: *Hans frisst wie ein Pferd* ("John eats like an horse").

Consider the way in which an object that marks the passage of time is named in English and Italian. In the former language it is called a *watch* if it is a portable object and worn on the human body, usually on the wrist, but a *clock* if it is to be put somewhere else—for example, on a table or on a wall. In Italian no such semantic distinction has been encoded lexically.

The word *orologio* refers to any device for keeping track of time, regardless of its "portability:"

Italian	*orologio*	
English	*watch* (portable)	*clock* (non-portable)
Concept	"device for keeping track of time"	

Figure 2. Italian orologio compared with English watch and clock

This does not mean that Italian does not have the linguistic resources for making such a distinction, if needed. Indeed, the phrase *da + place* allows speakers to provide exactly this kind of information:

orologio da polso	=	wrist watch
orologio da tavolo	=	table clock
orologio da muro	=	wall clock

However, Italians apparently do not find it necessary to distinguish between watches and clocks as a necessary fact of life. They can refer to the portability of the device in other ways, if the situation requires them to do so. Speakers of English, on the other hand, refer to the portability distinction as necessary, attending to it on a regular basis, as witnessed by the two words in the English lexicon. Historically speaking, the word *watch* originated in the 1850s when people started strapping clocks around their wrists. As the psychologist Robert Levine (1997) argues, this introduced a fixation with watching time pass that has been imprinted into the English vocabulary. Clearly, the semantic system of a language reveals that language, thought, and culture are interdependent constituents of human life.

As mentioned above, this interdependence was formalized by the American anthropological linguist Benjamin Lee Whorf (1957) and, for this reason, generally falls under the rubric of the Whorfian Hypothesis (WH), which posits, to reiterate, that languages predispose speakers to attend to certain concepts as being necessary and others as not. But, as Whorf emphasized, this does not mean that understanding between speakers of different languages is blocked. On the contrary, through translation people attempt to understand each other. Moreover, Whorf claimed, the resources of any language allow its speakers to invent new forms, new categories, and new structures any time they want. For example, if for some reason we decided to refer to "men with earrings" as part of a new social typology of manhood, then by coining an appropriate word, such as *trings*, we would in effect etch this concept into our minds as a part of social lógos, as it can be called (see §3). When a man with an earring comes into view, we would immediately recognize him as a "tring," thinking of him as exemplifying a distinct class of individuals.

The WH has raised some interesting questions about social inequalities and the role of the language that encodes them. In English, terms like *chairman, spokesman,* etc. were often cited in the not-too-distant past as examples of how the English language predisposed its users to view certain social roles in gender terms. Feminist critics maintained (correctly) that English grammar was organized from the perspective of those at the center of the society—the men. This is why in the recent past (and even to some extent today) we would say that a woman married into a man's family, and why at wedding ceremonies expressions such as "I pronounce you man and wife," were used. Similarly damaging language was the kind that excluded women, such as "lady doctor," implying that doctors were not typically female. In matriarchal societies the reverse is true. Investigating grammatical gender in the Iroquois language, Alpher (1987) found that in that language the feminine gender was the primary one, with corresponding masculine nouns being marked by a special prefix. Alpher related this to the fact that Iroquois society is matrilineal. The women hold the land, pass it on to their heirs in the female line, are responsible for agricultural production, control the wealth, arrange marriages, and so on. Iroquois grammar is clearly organized from the viewpoint of those at the center of that particular society—the women.

4. Speech

Let's return one last time to our illustrative sentence, considering how it might be modified in response to different kinds of questions:

(1)
Question: What is it that a friend of yours eats a lot?
Answer: Meat.

(2)

Question:	Is it true that a friend of yours eats lots of meat?
Answer:	Yes, it is.

(3)

Question:	Who eats lots of meat?
Answer:	A friend of mine.

The use of the single word *meat* in (1) is sufficient to give the required information asked by the questioner. In this case, it is unnecessary to utter an entire sentence ("A friend of mine eats a lot of meat"). Incidentally, this is clearly another example of the economizing principle (§3.1) manifesting itself in a "sentence-abbreviating" tendency in the domain of conversation. The answer in (2) reveals a different type of response—a response intended to provide confirmation of what the questioner asks. And the answer in (3) provides the specific kind of information sought by the questioner. These answers show, above all else, that there is a difference, yet an inherent synergy, between the system of *language* itself (consisting of phonological, morphological, syntactic, and semantic sub-systems) and its use, or *speech*, to carry out communication. This synergy is a manifestation of what we called the usage principle (§3.1).

4.1. Language versus speech

Language is a mental code, governed by the principles discussed briefly above (§3.1). Speech, on the other hand, is the use of language to form and transmit messages. Speech can be vocal, involving the use of the vocal organs (tongue, teeth, lungs, etc.), or nonvocal, involving writing or gesture (for example). Language is acquired by exposure to speech samples in early childhood. Children quickly gain command of a language by simply being in regular contact with speakers of that language. They listen instinctively to speakers, gradually mastering the words to which they are exposed and associating them to objects, ideas, and actions. In a relatively short time, children then start making up sentences, using them as strategies for regulating interactions with others. By the age of 5 or 6, children have acquired the capacity to understand and control the main structures of their native language, communicating most of their needs, desires, and ideas through it.

As children grow and mature they start to realize that speech patterns reflect social values, routines, emphases, concepts, and the like. In a groundbreaking study, the American linguist William Labov (1966) showed, for instance, that even miniscule differences in pronunciation are governed by unconscious social perceptions. He did this by using the fact that some speakers in New York City pronounced the post-vocalic /r/ in words such as *car* and *floor*, while others did not. However, this was not due to some simple dialectal difference, but rather, to social mobility. The presence of /r/ was considered at the time to be a marker of good American English pronunciation; its absence was stigmatized as lower-class speech. Labov asked the employees of three New York city stores—Saks Fifth Avenue, Macy's, and S. Klein—the following question: "Excuse me, where are the women's shoes?" knowing that the answer was "the fourth floor," which contained the post-vocalic /r/ twice. He found that differences in pronunciation were linked to employment in stores of relative prestige. Rates of pronunciation of /r/ were highest in Saks, lower in Macy's, and lowest in S. Klein. He concluded that workers identified with the prestige of their employer and customers and that this identification was mirrored in language pronunciation and use generally. In subsequent studies, Labov (1967, 1972) found that pronunciation varies as well according to the formality of a speech event. The more formal the event, the more aware are speakers of the social value of pronunciation.

When the term *language* is used, what is meant is abstract mentally stored forms, patterns and meaning categories. In contrast, *speech* stands for concrete, unique utterances and contextualized communication events. Speech is individual and spatially, temporally and socially situated. An utterance is often seen as the expression of an individual speaker's attitudes, as an act corresponding to the speaker's goals and desires.

Given the uniqueness of each utterance, it is legitimate, then, to ask whether we should leave out the study of speech and be content with studying the regularities of language in the strictest sense (i.e. phonology, morphology, syntax and vocabulary). The latter option was adopted at the beginning of the XXth century by the influential Swiss linguist Ferdinand de Saussure and remained popular for a long time in linguistics. Saussure proposed that linguistics should focus on *langue* ("language"), the system of rules that members of a speech community recognize as their "language," rather than on *parole* ("speech"), or the actual use of these rules in unique conversations, writings, etc.

Not many years after Saussure, in the late 1920s, the Russian linguist and literary critic Mikhail Bakhtin and his disciple V. Voloshinov proposed an alternative view, where the dichotomy between language and speech is not an absolute one. They contend that Saussure is wrong in viewing "the individual utterance (*parole*)" as "an individual fact not susceptible to sociological analysis by virtue of its individuality" (Voloshinov 1973: 93). The error consists in seeing the utterance just as an expression of the speaker's inner world and ignoring its social nature. Utterances are not isolated but embedded in a continuous verbal interaction, as part of human activities within certain social settings. As soon as we look at these activities we see that all our utterances belong to definite *speech genres* Bakhtin (1986: 78-79), they have "definite and relatively stable typical forms" depending on the "sphere of human activity" to which the utterance belongs: *scientific papers, sermons, newspaper articles, political speeches and debates, news interviews, medical consultations, counseling, lectures, police interrogations, novels, poems, jokes, board meetings, blog posts, text messages, job interviews, term papers* and so on. It is within these culturally shared genres, oral or written, that individual speakers express their individuality and subjectivity. *Speech genres* occupy a middle ground between *language* and individual utterances.

In the early 1970s the American linguist Dell Hymes proposed that knowledge of language entailed more than *linguistic competence*, or language-specific knowledge—it also entailed the ability to use language forms appropriately in specific social and interactive settings. He called this kind of knowledge *communicative competence*, a term that has since become central in the study of speech. Hymes claimed that such competence was not autonomous from linguistic competence, but, rather, that it was interrelated with it. In other words, communicative competence represents the kind of knowledge that we display in dealing with the *pragmatic* dimension of verbal communication (§ 2.2). In fact, the words used in conversations are really cues of social meanings, not just carriers of semantic and grammatical information. To carry out a simple speech act such as saying hello requires, in actual fact, a detailed knowledge of the verbal and nonverbal cues that can bring about social contact successfully. An infringement or misuse of any of the cues will generally lead to a breakdown in communication.

Some of the cues used allude to social status, age, gender, and other social variables. Linguists use the term *register* to refer to the systematic use of socially-sensitive verbal cues. Take, for example, saying good-bye to someone in English. This will vary according to register as follows:

Formal:	Good-bye!
Mid-Formal:	Bye!
Informal:	See ya'!

The choice of one or the other cue is conditioned by a simple politeness rule: the formal register is used with social superiors or strangers and the informal register with close friends and intimates; otherwise the mid-formal register is appropriate. In other societies, such as in Java, politeness registers are tied much more strictly to a hierarchy of social distinctions. At the top of the social hierarchy are the aristocrats; in the middle the townsfolk; and at the bottom the farmers. The top register is used by aristocrats who do not know one another very well, but also by a member of the townsfolk if he or she happens to be addressing a high government official. The middle register is used by townsfolk who are not friends, and by peasants when addressing their social superiors. The low register is used by peasants, or by an aristocrat or town person talking to a peasant, and among friends at any level. The latter is also the form of language used to speak to children.

We all use registers unconsciously at different times of the day, as the linguist Martin Joos cleverly argued in his classic 1967 book titled *The Five Clocks of English*. To grasp what Joos contended, consider the different kinds of speech one would use during a typical day. How would one speak in the morning when one greets family members? How would one speak at one's place of work with co-workers? How would one speak at ones place of work with superiors? How would one converse with friends after hours? How would one communicate late at night with a romantic partner? Answers to such question would provide a repertoire of speech cues that are socially-coded and thus have great import in communicative settings. Needless to say, having no access to the system of cues can potentially lead to conflictual situations in IC settings. If speaker A (a non-native speaker of English) were to use a highly formal register or a style that when talking to a friend, then he or she might be misconstrued by B (a native speaker) as attempting to be ironic or emotionally distant. On the other hand, if A uses a highly intimate form of speech to a superior, miscommunication based on various modes of interpretation would tend to surface. If the speech act does not match the clock, to extend the figures of speech used by linguists, then miscommunication between speakers is a distinct possibility. Using the *tu* (familiar) forms to a stranger in Italy, rather than the *Lei* (polite) forms, will be considered to constitute an act of impoliteness or downright rudeness, unless the speaker reveals that he or she is a foreigner either directly or indirectly through an accent. Saying *ciao* ("hi"), rather than *scusi* ("excuse me") to a policeman in order to get his attention will tend, initially at least, prompt a negative response (if any). Breaking this rule of discourse is perceived as a break in social manners, not as a lack of linguistic knowledge.

Linguistic forms that encode aspects of the social relationship between the participants include the use of first names (and/or last names), of various titles either accompanying names (like *Mr.*, *Ms.*, *Miss* in English) or used in isolation (like *Sir* or *Madam* in English), but also, in languages like French, Italian or German, the choice of the personal pronouns used to refer to the interlocutor and/or the corresponding person morphemes of the verb. In fact, in the languages of the world similar functions are associated with a great variety of lexical and grammatical morphemes. In order to refer to this broad class of linguistic devices the term *honorifics* is often employed.

The Korean language is well known for its complex system of *honorification* (Yoon 2004). Korean honorifics combine the lexical choice between plain and honorific nouns (e.g. "meal" *pap* vs. *cinci*) and verbs ("eat" *mek-* vs. *tusi-*) and different grammatical morphemes for marking the same grammatical function according to the honorific status of the person being referred to. The subject of a sentence, for instance, can be marked either by the *plain* nominative case *–ka* or by its honorific version *–kkeyse*. Compare the following two Korean sentences (the lexemes and morphemes marked for *honorific* status are in **bold**):

(1) *Minho-ka pap-ul mek-ess-ta*

"Minho had a meal"

(2) *Minho halapeci-**kkeyse** **cinci**-lul **tusi**-ess-ta*

"Minho's grandfather had a meal"

As Yoon (2004: 194) reminds, "the Korean conceptualization of social interpersonal relationships is hierarchical and vertical": speakers are lead to class interlocutors as "people above me" (superiors), "people like me" (peers) and "people below me" (inferiors). Interestingly, the key factor in determining who is to be treated as superior is the relative *age* of the participants. The social power of the participants is also taken into account but only as a secondary factor. In their use of the honorific system in speech, Koreans continuously attend to age differences between the speakers, even very small ones: "An age difference of even one year is meaningful in Korea. Indeed, when they are at the same age people sometimes count months and even days, especially among cousins" (Yoon 2004: 201). It is not surprising, therefore, that Korean speakers will try to learn the age of a new acquaintance as soon as possible or at least to estimate it as accurately as possible: this is necessary in order to be able to choose the proper speech register and honorifics to address the interlocutor.

4.2. Argumentation

Communication always involves different minds. If people's minds were not different, if they were exact copies, there would be no point in communicating. Communication is always to some extent intercultural. As we will see in the following chapters, communication also involves a starting common ground on which communication can grow and that is going to provide the foundations for bridging the gap: a common language, common experiences, a common human nature, perhaps. We have seen that the ancient Greeks believed that lógos, the faculty of reason, was universally shared by humans, and thus part of this common ground.

Argumentation is a mode of communication where *differences* and *reason* play a special role. Over the last twenty years the scholars of the Amsterdam School (Cf. van Eemeren, Grootendorst and Snoeck Henkemans 2002) have developed a pragmatic approach to argumentation that proved fruitful in understanding and evaluating arguments in a variety of social settings. This approach treats argumentation as a means for resolving a difference of opinion. More specifically, argumentation is an attempt to resolve a difference of opinion in a reasonable way, by putting forth arguments (reasons) supporting a standpoint in a way that would be acceptable to a reasonable critic. The scholars of the Amsterdam School stress the double nature of argumentation as a social and as a rational activity. It is also a verbal activity: something that is done through speech.

Being a means for resolving differences, argumentation is potentially a critical resource for IC. In fact, as we have already observed, in many intercultural situations argumentation turns out to be problematic. This has led some people to dismiss argumentation as inherently confrontational and unsuitable for a fruitful intercultural dialogue.

In the experience of one of the authors of this book and of other non-Anglophone argumentation scholars (van Eemeren, personal communication) this negative attitude towards the concept of argumentation – seen as conflictual – is more frequently encountered among native English speakers. In fact, the conflictual aspect of argumentation is made very prominent in the English language itself. The notion of argumentation is presented in a particular cultural light that is encoded in the language. Consider the English word *argument*. It basically has two main meanings:

- *argument 1:* a fact or assertion offered as evidence that something is true; a course of reasoning aimed at demonstrating a truth or falsehood.
- *argument 2:* a verbal dispute; a quarrel.

The first meaning is the original one, the meaning of the Latin word *argumentum* from which the English word derives. The second meaning, however, is certainly more common in everyday speech and more productive linguistically: when I say that someone is *very argumentative* I don't mean that she is a very logical person, but rather that she is prone to dispute. The development of this second meaning is something specific to the English language. Interestingly, if we look at other languages such as French, Italian or Dutch that have similar words derived from the Latin *argumentum*, we find that they do not have the second meaning. Only the first, logical, meaning is present. In these languages there is no suggested association of argument with aggressiveness or quarrel.

The etymology of the Latin word *argumentum* is not related to conflict, but rather, as observed by Rigotti and Greco Morasso (2009), to the idea of an *instrument for showing*, for leading another to notice or acknowledge something.

$$\underbrace{\text{A r g u}}_{} \text{-} \underbrace{\text{m e n t u m}}_{}$$

arguere: "to show, to bring someone to acknowledge something"

- *mentum* is a suffix which means "instrument". For instance, *monu-mentum* is the "instrument for reminding," *docu-mentum* is the "instrument for informing," etc.

In contrast, in English the connection between argumentation and conflict is bolstered by a rich system of figurative expressions based on the arch-metaphor *Argument is war*, which was famously illustrated by Lakoff and Johnson (1980):

(1) Your assertions are *indefensible*

(2) He *attacked* each of my arguments

(3) His argument *misses the mark*

(4) The author in his thorough unobjective fashion has *marshaled up* all the good, indifferent and bad arguments.

In view of IC it is important to be aware that the English language chooses to focus mainly on the fact that arguments are presented when there is a difference of opinion between people, and highlights the potential for conflict that is inherent in such a situation. This should not blind us, however, to the consideration of other aspects of argumentation, and first of all to the fact that this verbal activity is meant to resolve differences of opinion rather than to exacerbate them and turn them into conflicts.

Other more constructive, or at least neutral, metaphors can be applied to argument. Consider, for example, the following utterances in English:

(1) I don't get the *point* of your theory.

(2) You theory is *diametrically opposite* to mine.

(3) Your theory is *circular*; it simply does not make sense.

(4) Your theory is *parallel* to hers.

The hidden logic in such utterances is that theories can be envisioned as having geometrical form. This probably crystallized from the fact that geometry has always played a critical role in the development of mathematics, science, and other theoretical enterprises.

In this book we will devote particular attention to argumentation as a mode of communication critical to IC by examining its problem solving potential and its intercultural pitfalls in Chapter 5.

5. Linguistics

The first attempt in history to describe a language scientifically can actually be traced to the fifth century BC, when the Indian scholar Panini compiled a grammar of the Sanskrit language of India. His sophisticated analysis is the first ever to show how words are governed by design principles, being constructed from smaller structures or units. For several centuries thereafter, virtually nothing was written on language, until the Greek scholar Dionysius Thorax, who lived between 170 and 90 BC, wrote a comprehensive grammar of Greek that has remained a basic model to this day, showing how the parts of speech relate to each other in the formation of sentences.

It is useful here to take a rapid historical look here at the origin and development of linguistics, determining where and how global linguistics would fit in the historical paradigm of this science.

5.1. An historical sketch

Modern linguistics started in the sixteenth and seventeenth centuries, when the first language surveys were conducted in order to determine which grammatical facts were universal and which were specific to different languages. In the eighteenth century, the surveys became increasingly more accurate culminating in Sir William Jones' (1746–1794) assertion in 1786 that Sanskrit, Greek, and Latin developed from a common source. Shortly thereafter, the German philologist Jacob Grimm (1785-1863) and the Danish philologist Erasmus Christian Rask (1787-1832) started comparing languages systematically, noticing that in some the sounds in related words corresponded in regular ways. For example, they noticed that the initial /p/ sound of Latin *pater* ("father") and *pedem* ("foot") corresponded consistently to the initial /f/ sound in the English cognates *father* and *foot*. They concluded that this linked Latin and English historically. The method of making such linkages came to be called *comparative grammar*—a term coined initially in 1808 by the German scholar Friedrich Schlegel (1772-1829).

The study of sound correspondences led the early comparative grammarians to conclude that some languages must have descended from the same undocumented language. One of these was Proto-Indo-European (PIE). The prefix *proto-* was introduced to indicate a hypothetical language that had left no documentation, but which could be reconstructed by the method of comparison. The /p/-/f/ difference noted by Grimm and Rask, for instance, was explained as a sound shift in English, whereby the PIE consonant /p/ developed to /f/, or /p/ > /f/ for short (> = "develops to"). It was logical to assume that the Latin /p/ was closer to the original PIE consonant, given that Latin was older than English and thus closer in time to PIE. Likewise, the English word *thaw*, which begins with *th* (= /θ/), probably developed from PIE /t/, since /t/ is found in Greek and Latin versions of the same word—*tekein* and *tabes*.

By the latter part of the nineteenth century extensive research had been conducted on PIE. Differences among the languages descended from PIE were explained as sound shifts of various kinds. In this way, the early comparative grammarians were able to construct the first-ever model of the Indo-European language family, dividing the languages into main branches (the languages closer in time to PIE) and lower branches (the modern day descendants of Celtic, Germanic, Latin, and others):

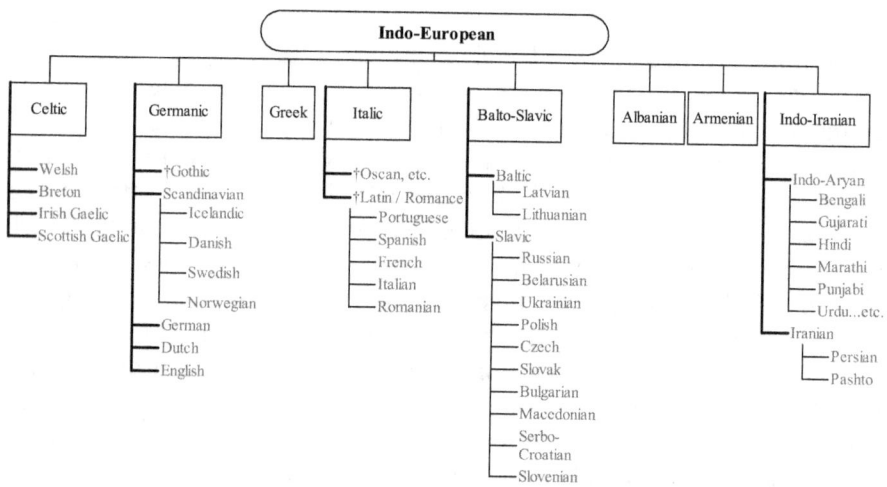

Figure 3. A simplified representation of the Indo-European language family

From this line of research, a school emerged, based mainly in Germany, called the *neogrammarian school*, which formally introduced the notion of "sound law" to explain sound shifts. To explain exceptions to sounds laws, the neogrammarians introduced the notion of borrowing. For example, according to one sound law, Latin initial /d/ should correspond to English /t/, as it does in *dentem* vs. *tooth*. The English word *dental*, however, has a /d/ sound instead. The conclusion drawn by the neogrammarians was that English borrowed it directly from Latin without modifying the pronunciation of the initial /d/, whereas *tooth* (which has the expected /t/) was a native English version of the PIE word, manifesting that it underwent the /d/ > /t/ sound shift.

Towards the end of the nineteenth century, the Swiss philologist Ferdinand de Saussure (1857-1913) put the finishing touches on the blueprint for the emerging new science of language study by making a distinction between the comparative study of sounds, which he called *diachronic*, and the systematic study of a language at a specific point in time, which he called *synchronic*. As noted above, he also proposed that the new science should focus on *langue* ("language"), the system of rules that members of a speech community recognize as their "language," rather than on *parole* ("speech"), or the use of the rules in actual conversations, writing, etc. Saussure used an analogy to chess to illustrate the difference between the two. Only people who know the rules of the game can play chess. This constitutes knowledge of the *langue* of chess, allowing people to play the game no matter what size the board might be, what substance the pieces are made of, and so on. The actual use of this knowledge to play a specific game of chess is *parole*. This involves knowing, essentially, how to apply the rules in response to certain moves of the opponent. The goal of *linguistique* ("linguistics"), as he called it, was to understand the nature of *langue* (Saussure 1916).

Basic to Saussure's plan for the study of *langue* was the notion of *différence* ("difference, opposition"), which claims that the structures of a language do not take on meaning and function in isolation, but rather in relation to each other. For example, the linguist can determine the meaning and grammatical function of the word *cat* in English by opposing it to the word *rat*. This opposition will show, among other things, that the initial consonants /k/ and /r/ are important in English for establishing the meaning of both words. From such oppositions we can see, one or two features at a time, what makes the word *cat* unique in English, allowing us to pinpoint what *cat* means by virtue of how it is different from other words.

Saussure's approach came to be known as *structuralism*. In America, it was adopted in the early twentieth century by the anthropologist Franz Boas, and a little later by his student Edward Sapir (§ 3, 3.1). However, unlike Saussure, Boas did not see the goal of linguistics as a study of *langue* in itself, but rather as the description of how *langue* reflected the cultural emphases of the speech community that used it. Linguists would thus have to explain why, for example, in the Indonesian language the social status of the person addressed is mirrored directly in the vocabulary used; and why in the language spoken by the Nuer, a herding people of eastern Africa, there are so many words for the colors and markings of cattle. In both cases, the structure of the two languages reflects, respectively, the cultural importance of social rank and livestock. In English, on the other hand, there are fewer words for describing livestock, but many for describing music (*classical, jazz, folk, rock*, etc.), revealing the importance of music in the daily lives of those who live in an English-speaking culture. The study of the relation between language and culture is such an obvious one, Boas claimed, that it requires little or no justification. In a certain way, Boas can be considered to be the founder of global linguistics, since his objective was to show that people living in different cultures, and using different languages, had all developed parallel systems for understanding their worlds—none of which was superior to any other.

By the early 1930s, as American structuralists applied and expanded the basic Saussurean-Boasian paradigm, it became obvious that a standard repertoire of notions and techniques was required. This was provided by Leonard Bloomfield (1887-1949) in his influential 1933 textbook titled *Language*. For two decades after, linguists went about the painstaking work of documenting the structures of different languages and of relating them to different cultural emphases, using a basic Bloomfieldian manual of techniques.

The first major break from this tradition came in 1957, when the American linguist Noam Chomsky (1928-) argued that an understanding of language as a universal faculty could never be developed from a piecemeal analysis of the disparate sounds, word forms, etc. of widely-divergent languages. Chomsky argued that a true theory of language would have to explain why all languages seem to reveal a similar unconscious plan for constructing their sentences. He proposed to do exactly that by shifting the focus in structuralism away from making inventories of isolated facts of language to a study of the "rule-making principles" that went into the construction of sentence types. The basis of Chomsky's approach can be seen in the analysis he put forward of the following two sentences:

(1) John is eager to please.
(2) John is easy to please.

Both these sentences, Chomsky observed, would seem to be built from the same structural plan on the "surface," with each consisting of a proper noun followed by a copula verb and predicate complement:

Proper Noun	Copula Verb	Predicate Complement	
↓	↓	↓	↓
John	is	eager	to please
John	is	easy	to please

Figure 4. Surface syntactic structure

However, despite the same plan, they mean very different things: the meaning of the first one can be paraphrased as "John is eager to please someone" and that of the second one as "It is easy for someone to please John." Chomsky thus concluded that the two sentences had become merged into the same surface structure as the result of the operation of a *transformational rule*. In fact, transformations are a powerful tool for the analysis of meaning because they enable us to find deep semantic similarities between linguistic constructions that appear superficially different, as well as to draw semantic distinctions between apparently similar constructions. English adjectives offer a good illustration. We can observe that not all attributive adjectives accept the transformation "Adjective + Noun ⇒ Noun *that is* Adjective", which works passably well for *red* (1) and *square* (2) below.

(1) a *red* apple = an apple that is red
(2) a *square* table = a table that is square
(3) an *alleged* murderer = *not* a murderer who is alleged, *but* someone who is alleged to be a murderer
(4) a *former* president = *not* a president who is former *but* someone who once was a president
(5) a *hard* worker = *not* a worker who is hard *but* someone who works hard.
(6) a *good* teacher = *not* a teacher who is good *but* someone who teaches well.
(7) a *strong* supporter = *not* a supporter who is strong *but* someone who supports strongly. (Examples adapted from Seuren 1985: 68)

Those adjectives that do not conform to the *that is* transformation are called *non predicative* and can be divided in several semantic classes according to the transformations they admit. One such grouping is illustrated by (5), (6) and (7) above. Zeno Vendler, a philosophically minded linguist, perfected this method and used it for analyzing philosophically important words such as *good*. For instance, Vendler discovered that the adjective *good* differs from an adjective denoting a physical quality, such as *red*, because it implies the reference to a goal or purpose, which is often tacitly understood:

(1) This is a good knife > This knife is good for cutting > This knife cuts well.
(2) This is a red knife > *This knife is red for... ?? > *This knife ...?? redly.

Many misunderstandings in IC concern precisely this sort of tacit parameters such as the *purpose* with respect to which the *goodness* of a thing or action has to be evaluated. Vendler's (1963) classic transformational analysis of the meaning of *good* is still worth reading.

While Chomsky contributed to inspire important work on semantic analysis during the 1960s, his goal was, in fact, rather different. For him transformations were not a means for analyzing meanings. He suggested something truly radical for linguistics: he claimed that as linguists studied the nature of the syntactic rules of different languages they would eventually come to the conclusion that they could be conflated into one universal set of rule-making principles (Chomsky 1957, 1965, 1975, 1982, 1986, 1995, 2000, 2002). Chomsky's proposal became immediately attractive for obvious reasons. Above all else, it gave substance to the age-old belief in western philosophy that the rules of grammar can connect the apparently messy and idiosyncratic variety of superficial linguistic forms to arguably universal logico-semantic forms. These deep universal forms would be behind the human ability to translate from one language into another (Seuren 1985: 68).

However, since the late 1960s, various schools of linguistics have come forward to challenge the Chomskyan paradigm. It has been pointed out, for instance, that abstract syntactic rule-making principles do not explain the semantic richness of languages. Successive versions of Chomskyan *generative grammar* – as the approach came to be known – posited a very small inventory of syntactic principles. Much to the dismay of those, like Seuren (1985), who identified the universal level with meaning, Chomsky insisted that these universal principles had no relation with the need of expressing meanings in communication. This view, known as the hypothesis of the *autonomy of syntax*, represented a huge stumbling block for those who were primarily interested in meaning and thought that what is universal in language is not arbitrary but corresponds to universal communication needs.

Moreover, according to Chomskyan generative grammar, syntactic rules do not add meanings of their own, but simply act as an invisible glue assembling words (and their meanings) into sentences. Recently, alternative approaches to syntax, called *construction grammars* contended that the Chomskyan view leaves out most of what is interesting in the grammar of languages. Construction grammarians have discovered a host of language-specific grammatical patterns conveying culture-specific meanings, expressing speakers' attitude or performing certain moves (speech acts) in social interaction. Consider, for instance, the English patterns exemplified below: (1) expresses the incredulity of the speaker, while (2) is used to notice an incongruity and request an explanation for it (Kay & Michaelis, in press).

(1)   Him get the first prize?
(2)   What are you doing smoking?

As a result of these debates, contemporary linguistic theory and methodology have now become more eclectic and less partisan to one school of thought or the other than they ever have been at any time in recent history.

Another reason for the slow downfall of Chomskyan linguistics as mainstream theory is the fact that it is based on the presupposition that syntax is the only "engine" of language and that the structures it creates determine meaning. Jackendoff (1997: 15) refers critically to this assumption as "syntactocentrism". In fact, in languages syntactic structures are not the only way of mediating between sounds and meanings. In Russian, for instance, word order does not affect syntactic case relations (Bonvillain 2008: 28). The English sentence "The cat is chasing the dog" is rendered in Russian in any one of six orders (ʃ = palatal sound similar to English *sh* in *shoe*):

(1)   Koʃka sobaku presleduet.
(2)   Koʃka presleduet sobaku.
(3)   Sobaku presleduet koʃka.
(4)   Sobaku koʃka presleduet.
(5)   Presleduet koʃka sobaku.
(6)   Presleduet sobaku koʃka.

The reason is that each word is marked for case and, thus, its position in the sentence is syntactically irrelevant:

koʃka = *cat* (in the nominative case marked by final -*a*)
sobaku = *dog* (accusative marked by -*u*)
presleduet = *is chasing*

Does this mean that in Russian word order is meaningless? Quite the contrary. The fact that morphemes carry much of the burden of expressing syntactic relations in Russian frees word order so that it can be shaped to reflect the communicative purpose and the context of utterance. As suggested by Rigotti (2000), syntax can be regarded as but one tool in a composite "toolbox" of structures that different languages employ in different ways in constructing meanings.

Today, linguistics is divided into theoretical and applied subfields. The former is concerned with building language models or theories to describe languages and to explain the similarities and differences among them; the latter is concerned with applying the findings of linguistic research to language teaching, dictionary preparation, speech therapy, computerized machine translation, and automatic speech recognition. There are now also a number of branches that are concerned with the relation between language and the subject matter of cognate academic disciplines. These include sociolinguistics (sociology and language), psycholinguistics (psychology and language), and neurolinguistics (neuropsychology and language). As is our hope, global linguistics, too, could easily be envisioned as a branch, rather than a separate approach to language. In all approaches, versions, fields, and subfields of linguistics, however, there are certain notions and techniques that have withstood the test of time and that now constitute a standard repertoire of procedures for the scientific study of all languages. These notions will be used throughout this book.

5.2. Global Linguistics

The late American semiotician and linguist Thomas A. Sebeok (1920-2001) sought to establish a "global semiotic movement" starting in the late 1990s with the aim of bringing together scholars working in cognate fields to focus their efforts on studying how signs are used across the globe (Sebeok 2001). In a similar fashion, and with a similar intent, the goal of global linguistics (GL) is fundamentally to bring together scholars to study how speakers of different languages interact in intercultural settings. Its main research orientation will be ethnographic and thus involve participant observation. The central idea behind this approach is that the linguist can reach a better understanding of languages used in intercultural settings by documenting the kinds of interference phenomena that characterize such settings.

Chomsky encouraged linguists to break away from the previous ethnographic tradition by claiming that the task of the linguist was to describe the "ideal knowledge" of a language, which he called linguistic competence. And this, he suggested, was known only to the native speakers of a language and, thus, could never be distilled from the data collected by a non-native observer. So, ideally, linguists themselves should be native speakers of the languages they aim to investigate, since they can analyze their own intuitions better than anyone else can. Given the importance that Chomskyan generative grammar had attained in the 1960s and most of the 1970s, many mainstream linguists abandoned the ethnographic method. By the 1980s, however, the utility of the ethnographic method was reestablished by a surge of interest in investigating how language varies according to social situation. Ironically, this revival of interest may have been brought about by the fact that generative grammar research had produced an overload of theories, making it virtually impracticable as a research enterprise in search of a universal set of rule-making principles.

The foregoing comments in no way are meant to suggest that GL should be devoid of theory. Boas collected volumes of data on the Kwakiutl, a native society on the northwestern coast of North America, from which he was able to glean overarching principles of grammatical design. Boas showed, in effect, how many of the forms of Kwakiutl and other indigenous languages were reflexes of broader tendencies within the language faculty of humanity. Boas thus provided a paradigm for investigating language both as a faculty of mind and as a strategy for social living. GL research should unfold, in a similar fashion, as a comparative and cross-cultural form of inquiry, studying the languages of groups of people in order to determine how their similarities and their differences shape IC.

The focus in GL should be more specifically on how native-language competence influences IC. In a way, Boas, Sapir, and Whorf were the precursors of GL. Through their in-depth studies of the indigenous languages of North America, they showed that the categories of one's particular language are much more than simple mediators of thought in communication. They saw them as the "shapers" of the very thought patterns they embodied. Languages provide us with the categories to organize our experience of the world. Without categories, there would not be any experience but only "a kaleidoscopic flux of impressions", as Whorf (1956: 153) put it. The main objective of GL is, in fact, to study the "linguistic systems in the mind," as Whorf so eloquently said, to grasp how these shape the course of dialogue and conversation among peoples reared in "different systems."

To conclude this opening chapter, it behoves us to elaborate upon what we mean by the term *global*, given its various ambiguous uses and the many different perceptions that it evokes today in an ever-expanding context of *globalization*. Many people see globalization as a positive step in human civilization that will enhance worldwide cooperation. Supporters believe that the development of a global economy, for instance, will make the world more prosperous and ecologically sensitive. In addition, these people feel that globalization can promote peace, by reducing tensions between governments. Opponents of globalization argue, on the other hand, that the process simply makes it easier for powerful nations to take advantage of weaker ones, giving excessive privilege to corporate interests, weakening labor protections and interfering with the cultural traditions of individual countries.

GL is not a social or a political science. It is a branch of linguistics and thus has no direct interest in resolving the globalization debate. Its aim is not the evaluation of trends in globalization, but rather an examination of the role of language in global communicative contexts. We are firmly convinced that this is an urgent area of study because language is what defines human interaction. Any changes in language imply changes in interaction and, ultimately, in human life. In a fundamental way, GL is a response to McLuhan's challenge to study the role of human communication in the global village. McLuhan is perhaps best known for coining the phrase "the medium is the message," which became popular in the 1960s. He argued that in each major cultural era the medium in which information is recorded and transmitted is decisive in determining the character of the era. For example, he called the period from 1700 to the mid-1900s *the age of print*, because the print medium was the chief means by which people gained and shared knowledge and spread it throughout the globe. Print encouraged individualism, nationalism, democracy, the desire for privacy, specialization in work, and the separation of work and leisure. Since the 1950s, this situation has changed radically. We now live in an age of mass electronic communications, which makes it possible for people in all parts of the world to interact on a daily basis and, thus, to become deeply involved in the lives of everyone (no matter where they live)—hence the term "global village." As McLuhan also predicted, the spread of electronic communications technologies would lead to the growth of new international communities and new forms of communication. Studying these forms is a primary objective of GL.

Chapter 2
Speech

> *There is no pleasure to me without communication: there is not so much as a sprightly thought comes into my mind that it does not grieve me to have produced alone, and that I have no one to tell it to.*
>
> Michel de Montaigne (1533–1592)

1. Introductory remarks

In the history of linguistics as a science, the focus has been put mainly on the internal mechanics of languages—that is, linguists have traditionally been interested in understanding how the bits and pieces of language in general (and in different languages in particular) cohere together to produce forms and structures that bear meanings, allowing people to use them for various psychological and social purposes. In a word, the emphasis has been on *langue*, or linguistic competence, rather than on *parole*, or speaking in a meaningful or purposeful way. However, the scientific analysis of language would not be complete if linguists stopped at *langue*—a gap that linguistics started to bridge a few decades ago. Research on *parole*, or *speech*, since the early 1970s has shown that language is a highly adaptive and context-sensitive communicative instrument. Linguistic structures are not only linked to each other in the internal system of *langue*, but are also susceptible to the subtle influences that talking has on them. In a phrase, the internal structures of language are pliable entities that are responsive to verbal interaction. *Langue* and *parole* are really two sides of the same coin, rather than separate dimensions.

The focus in this chapter is on how this intrinsic dualism affects meaning exchanges in intercultural discourse. In this area of analysis, GL will clearly need to borrow selectively from those contemporary branches of linguistics that deal with speaking directly, in order to be able to carry out its own mode of inquiry more effectively. Thus, notions from pragmatic linguistics and sociolinguistics, for example, will be interspersed throughout the chapter. In terms of the universal principles discussed in the previous chapter (§1.2.1), this chapter will deal primarily with the usage principle.

2. Dialogue

In a series of pivotal studies, written from the 1920s to the 1940s partly in collaboration with his colleague Valentin Voloshinov (1895-1936), the Russian literary scholar and linguist Mikhail Bakhtin (1895-1975) suggested that the most effective way of understanding how verbal *parole* works and how it differs from *langue* is to look at the role of *dialogue* in human social life. Bakhtin saw dialogue as the primary means through which people communicate meaningfully with each other. So, even though verbal artifacts such as the novel are not, strictly speaking, dialogical, they are nevertheless best understood as having an implicit dialogical form and function (Bakhtin 1981). In a phrase, the Bakhtinian concept of dialogue provides linguistics with a template for documenting and assessing how language is used for various social functions. Needless to say, it constitutes a topic of fundamental interest for GL.

2.1. Didactic and philosophical functions

The use of dialogue, or purposeful conversation between people, has been part of didactic and philosophical traditions across time and across cultures. Its validity as a "knowledge-gaining" strategy is evidenced by the fact that it is still part of education and most forms of philosophical inquiry today. Studying what dialogue is, therefore, no trivial pursuit for linguists. It was used by Socrates, after all, in the form of a question-and-answer exchange as a means for achieving self-knowledge. Socrates believed in the superiority of oral dialogic argumentation over writing, spending hours in the public places of Athens, so as to engage in dialogue with anyone who would be interested in doing so. In fact, in Chapter 5, we will argue that argumentation – be it oral or written – is best understood in terms of a critical discussion where a difference of opinion is resolved by testing the participants' standpoints against what is accepted as evidence by both parties.

Dialogue goes on all the time in human life. It is so instinctive that we hardly ever realize consciously what it entails. It may even define internal thought processes. As the Russian psychologist Lev Vygotsky (1962, 1978) showed in his pioneering work on childhood development, internal dialogue, as he called it, surfaces in early life as a means for the child to come to grips with the reality-making nature of language and its various socializing functions. In effect, when children speak to themselves as they play, they are engaging in investigative dialogue, testing out meanings and concepts imprinted in the phonic substance of words.

It was Plato who introduced the use of the dialogue into philosophical inquiry. Except for the *Apology*, all of Plato's writings are constructed in dialogical form (to greater or lesser degrees). After Plato, the dialogue was seen as belonging primarily to the literary and theatrical domains, being revived as an investigative tool by early Christian philosophers, especially St. Augustine, Boethius, and later by Peter Abelard. The use of dialogue for inquiry continued in Medieval universities in the golden age of Scholasticism (1100-1300) under the guise of the *quaestio disputata* ("debated question"), a practice where two scholars took the opposed roles of "respondent" and "opponent" and discussed the solution to a problem of philosophy, medicine or science (Lawn 1993). This kind of discussion was at the heart of the Scholastic method of inquiry and teaching. While this particular form was later abandoned, dialogue continued to be used by various European thinkers in philosophical and scientific inquiry. For example, in 1688, the French philosopher Nicolas Malebranche published his *Dialogues on Metaphysics and Religion*, contributing to the genre's didactic and philosophical revival. The Irish prelate George Berkeley employed it as well in his influential 1713 work, *Three Dialogues between Hylas and Philonous*. But perhaps the most important reintroduction of the investigative dialogue, and certainly the most famous one, was by Galileo in his *Dialogue Concerning the Two Chief World Systems* of 1632.

It is worth noting in the context of Global Linguistics, that the philosophical use of dialogue is by no means exclusive to the Western tradition. The rich tradition of Buddhist argumentation and dialectics is an example. Contrary to an unfortunately popular misconception vehemently denounced by Tillemans (2008), Buddhists are not "engaged in another, more non-conceptual approach to understanding in which argumentation has no place", a form of thought that is "somehow essentially meditative, irenic and beyond the fray of argument". They do place a great emphasis on the role of logical inference (*anumāna*) both "for oneself" and "for others", that is manifested in argumentation – which is communicated inference (Rocci 2006). Buddhist argumentation is deployed in the form of debate (*vāda*), and debate skills and practice have been an important pillar of the education of the Buddhist monk for centuries.

In many ways we still live in the shadow of the *age of print* (Chapter 1, § 5.2), a period where the production and transmission of knowledge was inevitably associated with the technology of the book. It is therefore easy to fail to appreciate the importance of dialogue for the construction and the transmission of knowledge in earlier periods of history, and, potentially, in today's and tomorrow's Global Village.

2.2. Social and interactional function

Bakhtin became interested in the dialogue, not just as a philosophical or literary form, but as the prototype of language use in social context. What stands out from his writings is the view that dialogue legitimizes the importance and social value of interlocutors, revealing the relations that hold among them. It is not, therefore, a simple vehicle for the passive exchange of information. As Bakhtin (1986: 68) put it: "a passive understanding of the meaning of perceived speech is only an abstract aspect of the actual whole of actively responsive understanding." Simply put, the needs, desires, and social agendas of the interlocutors in a dialogical interaction influence the ongoing choice of linguistic forms and constrain their meanings. At the same time, the listener in a dialogical exchange is constantly in an "active responsive attitude" towards what he perceives and understands: "from the speaker's first word" showing agreement or disagreement by "augmenting the topic, applying it, preparing for its execution, and so on" (Bakhtin and Voloshinov 1986: 102). As Bakhtin and Voloshinov (1986: 102) go on to explain:

> For each word of the utterance that we are in process of understanding, we, as it were, lay down a set of our own answering words. The greater their number and weight, the deeper and more substantial our understanding will be. Any true understanding is dialogic in nature. Understanding is to utterance as one line of dialogue is to the next.

During dialogue, the interlocutors enter "osmotically" into each other's psyche, so to speak. This is evidenced in face-to-face dialogue by the many nonverbal signals (nodding, smiling, etc.) emitted during the exchange, which indicate an unconscious process of assimilation or rejection of the message. However, as Bakhtin observed, osmotic responses may be "silent" and delayed in time. This happens when the dialogue form does not occur in a face-to-face interactional setting as, for example, when people read a novel. In every situation, however, the function of dialogue is to evoke purposeful reactions (Bakhtin 1981: 279-281).

3. Conversation and discourse

The social-interactional form of dialogue is commonly called a *conversation*. The functions of conversation cover the whole range of human activities, from greeting to arguing. These reveal that grammatical and lexical forms are not "passive structures," as Bakhtin pointed out, but rather pliable forms that are sensitive to situational variables, including the social status of the speakers, their ages, the intent of each one, the goal of the conversation, and so on and so forth. Think of the kind of grammar and words that people use to carry out the following functions and, more importantly, how these vary according to language and culture:

Table 3. A first foray into the functions of speech

approving	explicating social relations	reacting to statements
arguing		remembering
asking for opinions	expressing notions of entity	renouncing
begging	expressing notions of quantity	reporting
comparing		self portrayal
congratulating	expressing spatial relations	showing satisfaction
demanding		showing surprise
disapproving	forgetting	suggesting
ending contact	getting angry	thanking
exchanging facts	initiating contact	understanding
explicating family relations	keeping track of time	warning
	narrating	etc.
	offering to do something	
	ordering	

Although there is some leeway in the linguistic choices that can be made to carry out any one of the above functions in specific social situations, these are not subject to personal whims. Indeed, the choices are governed largely by conventional and stylistic conventions. In other words, there is a culturally determined *discourse system* (Scollon & Scollon 2001) that supports our daily interactions and assists in bridging between the linguistic system proper and its use in a variety of social situations for a variety of purposes.

3.1. Conversations

Conversations of all kinds exhibit several main characteristics. For example, they all have an initiation strategy—a set of verbal cues that inform interlocutors that a conversation is about to start—and an exit strategy—a corresponding set of verbal cues that inform interlocutors that a conversation is about to end. Consider the following snippets of conversation, each of which shows how a hypothetical high school student in the United States would say "good-bye" to various people (see also Chapter 1, § 4.1). These constitute, in effect, different exit strategies from conversations that are sensitive to the social relation the student has with each of the persons:

Good-bye to a teacher:	Good-bye, sir/madam!
Good-bye to the mother:	See ya' later, ma!
Good-bye to a peer:	I gotta' split!/I gotta' chill!

Notice, first and foremost, that the formulas used in each case are not interchangeable—the adolescent would not normally say "I gotta' split" to a teacher, and vice versa, he or she would not say, "Good-bye, sir/madam," to a peer. The reason is that each formula involves an unconscious reference to a system of social roles, which is mapped onto linguistic forms by the discourse system. The adolescent thus articulates an instinctive acknowledgment of the relevant social role through the words selected.

This type of social and cultural knowledge imbues all conversations. As observed in Chapter 1, the use of titles (and honorifics generally) usually indicates the conveyance of respect required when addressing a social superior or someone in a position of authority. This is the function of the terms *sir* and *madam* in English. On the other hand, abbreviated words—*ya'*, *ma'*, *gotta'*— convey a different, more informal, perception of social relations. In saying *see ya' later*, the adolescent is reassuring the mother that he or she will return to the household in short time; in saying *I gotta' split*, he or she is confirming to a peer that there is a close bond between them that he or she must temporarily and unwillingly undo. Such snippets of conversation signal differences in relations among speakers. Similar examples can be used to show how language mirrors all kinds of social phenomena, from age differences to group-based identities. People are extremely sensitive to socially-coded language cues, using them typically to evaluate speakers and to place themselves effectively in social realities all the time. This kind of practical knowledge is clearly different from the knowledge of word formation or sentence structure in themselves. As mentioned in the previous chapter, it constitutes a pragmatic form of knowledge known as communicative competence (Chapter 1, § 4.1).

In intercultural situation the lack of knowledge of the proper mapping between social roles and situations and linguistic forms leads to *pragmalinguistic failure* (Chapter 1, § 2.2). Moeschler (2004) offers an interesting example concerning conversational exit strategies: an American girl studying at the university of Geneva – in the French-speaking part of Switzerland – had taken the habit of exiting conversation with her classmates by saying – in French:

Bon, je me casse. Literally : "Well, I'm splitting"

This behavior caused puzzled reactions in her Swiss French peers. The case is a rather subtle instance of calquing. The construction used by the American student actually exists in colloquial French and indeed can be used as an exit strategy in conversation. It was therefore all too natural for her to assume a perfect pragmatic equivalence between the French construction and American English constructions such as *I gotta' split!*, etc. As Moeschler (2004: 68) observes:

> The problem is that the verb *se casser* strongly implicates that the person who is leaving is unhappy, angry, furious, etc. *Se casser* is a special way of leaving social groups, especially those including friends. This implicature was perfectly understood by the French native speakers who were sitting at the table with her, but she clearly did not intend to leave in an angry way. What she meant to strongly implicate, through a familiar way of speaking, was her very friendly relationship with her friends. But she failed, not because she did not know the context or the meaning of the word, but because she did not know what it implicated.

It is worth pausing a moment on Moeschler's analysis of this intercultural misunderstanding: the communicative failure does not involve a strictly linguistic error (see the examples in Chapter 1, § 3.2), nor does it involve a lack of knowledge of the context or social situation, that is a sociopragmatic failure (Chapter 1, § 2.2). The problem can be categorized as a pragma-linguistic failure, due to the lack of knowledge of what is conventionally implicated by the use of a given linguistic form in a particular social situation.

3.2. Communicative competence

We have seen that communicative competence bridges linguistic knowledge and knowledge of social contexts. One of the most important bricks of this bridge – if not its keystone – is represented by the conventions of the *discourse genres* (cf. Bakhtin 1986) appropriate to the situation. Many genres are known to every member of a cultural speech community (albeit with different degrees of skill): greetings, farewells, congratulations, whishes. Other genres are not shared by the entire speech community: they are the purview of specialists of certain spheres of human activity. As Bakhtin (1986: 80) observed, "many people who have an excellent command of a language often feel quite helpless in certain spheres of communication because they do not have a practical command of the generic forms used in the given spheres." A native speaker of English, who is perfectly fluent in the language, might still not be able to write an academic paper according to the proper conventions of that speech genre. Conversely, someone may well be able to write such a paper, but be strikingly awkward when it comes to face-to-face conversation in certain social settings.

It is not easy to describe communicative competence. Above all else it is part of a general social-strategic competence, as it may be called. As noted above, the efficacy of *See ya' later, ma!* as an exit strategy, for example, depends on the personal knowledge that the adolescent has of his or her mother's expectations—namely, that she expects him or her to come back home. The successful outcome of a conversation depends largely on how interlocutors are able to anticipate and satisfy the needs and expectations of people in specific interactive situations.

Needless to say, lack of communicative competence is a major factor in IC breakdowns. Consider a hypothetical case-in-point. Let's assume that a non-native speaker of English (A) wants to exit a conversation with a native speaker (B). The language of interaction is English. A and B are colleagues at work, having recently become close friends. To show her friendliness, A uses the expression *I'm takin' off*, which she had learned as part of her study of English at school as a kind of informal exit strategy, believing that it allows her to convey a sense of friendliness toward B. B, however, will probably perceive it as an abrupt or brusque statement, since that is what the expression generally conveys to a native speaker. Whatever the consequences of this infelicitous choice of words, the fact remains that A is unaware of the potential damage that her words may wreak to her relationship with B.

The study of conversations has shown, over the last few decades, that statements (such as the one used by A) are not constructed in the mind as autonomous language units conveying their own bits of information, but rather as components of a larger *discourse strategies* (Gumperz 1982), whose knowledge is part of communicative competence. In other words, conversing successfully involves, among other things, the ability to use language strategically. Some forms, for example, have a *gambit* strategic function, that is, they allow speakers to open a conversation, to keep it going, to make it smooth, to repair any anomaly within it. The following are common English gambits:

(1) Uh huh…yeah…hmm…aha…
(2) You agree, don't you?
(3) May I ask you a question?
(4) He arrived Monday; sorry, I meant Tuesday.

The grunt-like expressions uttered in (1) are used by interlocutors to signal to speakers that they are paying attention to what is being said. In English, total silence is not an appropriate gambit in this case, although it may be so in other languages. The gambit in (2) is called a *tag question*—a questioning strategy that is designed to seek approval, agreement, or consent, not an answer. Utterance (3) is an opening gambit for initiating, taking a turn, or entering into a conversation. In English, expressions such as *May I? Sorry, but could you tell me…? Excuse me?* are all opening gambits. Utterance (4) is a gambit known as a *repair*. When there is a minor breakdown in a conversation, or something is not explained properly, repairs allow the speaker to solve the problem.

Table 4. Typical speech strategies in English

Function	Protocols
initiating contact	"Hello!"
	"How are you?"
ending contact	"Good-bye!"
	"I've got to go!"
thanking	"Thank you!"
	"How nice of you!"
congratulating	"Good work!"
	"Congratulations!"
showing satisfaction	"I'm really pleased with you!"
	"That's delightful!"
approving	"I agree with you."
	"I commend you on what you've done."
disapproving	"I disagree with you."
	"What you've done is wrong."
showing surprise	"Why did you say that?"
	"I'm surprised at what you said."
offering to help	"May I help?"
	"Is there anything I can do?"
renouncing	"I'll never accept that!"
	"Just give it up!"
suggesting	"Wouldn't it be better if you called her?"
	"Let me suggest that you do it right away."
warning	"I'm concerned about what you said."
	"Be careful!"
begging	"Please, don't do it!
	"I beg you not to do it!"
reporting	"She said that she was coming too."
	"I heard that he had become rather rich."
comparing	"He's as smart as she is, don't you agree?"
	"But she is much more clever."
remembering	"I recall that she had already graduated."
	"I remember those times very well."
forgetting	"I forgot that."
	"I didn't remember that event."
self portrayal	"I know I could have done it better."
	"I can do this, if pushed hard enough."
getting angry	"I'm beginning to lose my patience with you!"
	"This is annoying!"
understanding	"I completely empathize with you."
	"I realize it now."
ordering	"Do it right now!"
	"Stop talking, please!"
gossiping	"Did you hear what he did?"
	"They say that she is not that rich!"

Gambits constitute a fraction of the many speech strategies available to speakers of a language. Table 4 lists a few expressions that allow interlocutors to make appropriate or strategic commentaries about someone or something in English. These provide only a miniscule sampling of the vast array of social functions that speech serves.

3.3. Discourse

The word *discourse* has two meanings. In its basic meaning discourse refers to a *speech* or to a *text*, that is to an instance of language use spoken or written. In this basic sense, the entirety of this chapter is about discourse. There is however a second meaning of the word discourse that is of paramount importance for GL.

According to this second acceptation of the word, *discourse* refers to the *particular way* in which language is used in a certain social group, community, institution, social class, ethnic group, sub-culture, ideology, generation, etc.: so that one can say "the discourse of economists", "the discourse of the liberals/conservatives", "corporate discourse", or the "discourse of baby-boomers" versus "the discourse of generation X", etc. We can surmise that here discourse refers to what is typical, recurrent, characteristic (both at the level of content and at the level of form) in the speech or texts exchanged within these communities. In turn, typicality and recurrence in linguistic usage reveal the values, practices and social rules which account for these particular ways of using language to produce texts or speech. This second meaning of discourse has become popular in the social sciences, in particular, through the work of French historian and philosopher Michel Foucault (1971), but already played an important part in Bakhtin's own conception of discourse, in particular through the notion of *discourse genres*, which we introduced above (Cf. Bakhtin 1986). Following Scollon and Scollon (2001) we have used the term *discourse system* to refer to this broadened notion of discourse. The Scollons characterize the discourse system as follows:

> Now we have come to the broadest concept of discourse, which is the study of whole systems of communication. For example, we might study the language of dealers in foreign exchange, of public school teachers, or of members of the North American "Baby Boom" generation. Such broad systems of discourse form a kind of self contained system of communication with a shared language or jargon, with particular ways in which people learn what they need to know to become members, with a particular ideological position, and with quite specific forms of interpersonal relationships among members of these groups. (Scollon and Scollon 2001: 107)

The discourse system bridges between language as a code and its uses in a variety of fields of social interaction. One aspect of discourse systems is the extension or specialization of the linguistic code to cater for the needs of people engaged in a particular interaction field. For example, the type of vocabulary and syntactic style adopted by specific occupational groups, known as *jargon*, constitutes a discourse style that distinguishes members of that group from others, tying them together socially. This kind of style bonds certain people together, identifying them as belonging to a particular social category, such as a profession, a social class, etc.

It should be mentioned that jargon is not all there is to discourse style, nor is it always restricted to professionals. From childhood on, we are all expected to acquire the jargon of mathematicians, including terms such as *equation, coordinate, factoring,* and *prime number*. Only terms with a lower frequency in educational contexts are perceived to be part of true "math jargon:" for example, *matrix, fractal, parameter,* or *imaginary number*. The line between professional jargon and common jargon is obviously a thin one, given the fact that most people have had some degree of formal education and given the technological nature of modern societies. A term like *iPod* is hardly viewed as jargon today, even though it comes from a specific domain of technology. It is obviously crucial to distinguish between the kind of specialized discourse used by professionals and specific groups and common social discourses, as they can be called. The latter are of primary interest to GL, since they are unconscious shapers of worldview, revealing cultural emphases, biases, and the like. In English, for example, there are several hundred words for describing a promiscuous female, but only a handful for a promiscuous male. The discourse system in this area reveals, therefore, that English-speaking society sees female sexual behavior as less appropriate than similar male behavior.

The ability to recognize and use different styles of language according to situation is an essential component of communicative competence, enabling people in a speech community to recognize discourse genres and what their role is in a society. For instance, when someone receives a card sent by a friend, rather than one sent by a dentist, in the mail, one immediately can formulate specific hypotheses as to the nature of the card's content even before reading it. The friend might have sent it to wish the receiver a happy birthday, to congratulate him or her for having achieved something, and so on. A card from a dentist would hardly have a similar function. Its purpose is to remind a patient about an appointment or to request payment for some service. Similarly, one can generally tell an article apart from an advertisement in a newspaper because of structural and content differences—from page layout and typography to the use of images—that identify each one distinctively (Pateman 1980: 609).

Discourse also has many socio-political functions. In communist Poland, for example, the *podanie* form of discourse flourished for a specific reason—it allowed common people to write their requests to the authorities in a strategic fashion (Wierzbicka 2003). In a *podanie*, petitioners were expected to ask the authorities for "favors" and to portray themselves as highly dependent on their "good will." The word *podanie* and the discourse genre it designates have no equivalent in English, because the practice of asking favors from authorities has never had the same significance in English-speaking societies that it had in communist Poland, where people's lives "were dominated, to a considerable degree, by their dependence on the arbitrary decisions of bureaucratic despots" (Wierzbicka 2003: 193). The socially-strategic significance of this discourse practice was corroborated by the term used in Polish to designate the A4 paper format, *papier podaniowy*, which means "paper for writing *podanie*." If we compare the *podanie* genre to an English bureaucratic genre, such as an application form, we can easily flesh out socially-significant differences from them. As Wierzbicka (2003: 195) puts it: "a person who is writing an *application* is *applying*, not *asking for* or *requesting*" and thus an application in an English-speaking country can be *unsuccessful*, but not *refused* or *rejected*. This was never the case with *podanie*.

4. Speech functions

The study of communicative competence involves, generally, the documentation and analysis of the speech functions that allow people to interact meaningfully. The objective of this section is to take an overall look at some of the relevant work and theories on functions (albeit rather selectively) in order to glean the implications that such work has for the study of IC. Of these, the two most relevant ones for GL (in our opinion at least) are Roman Jakobson's communication model and John Searle's speech act theory. Both posit that successful conversations involve the ability to utilize the repertoire of grammatical and lexical structures in a language in socially-strategic ways. Since many structures are markers of social status, age, gender, and so on, they are bound to affect the outcome of any interaction in IC, where different cultural backgrounds and worldviews imprinted in native-language structures come constantly into play.

4.1. Jakobson's model

Consider the two utterances below, both of which are intended to convey the same kind of function (the expression of anger), but in different ways:

(1)   Don't do that, stupid!
(2)   It is best that you not do that!

Clearly, (1) would be uttered only by someone who is on close or intimate terms with an interlocutor; whereas (2) would be uttered by someone who is only on formal terms (unless there is an ironic subtext to the utterance). The differential formality register built into the two utterances can be deduced by the presence or absence of the emotional qualities in the sentences themselves—(1) is abrasive and emotionally-charged; (2) is evasive and emotionally-neutral. Note also that the choice of verb tense is synchronized with the register—the verb in (1) is in the imperative (which, in English, is a tense commonly used to command intimates), but the verb *do* in (2) is in the subjunctive (which is a tense that reflects formal style). In a word, the two sentences differ as to their "emotive" function, as the linguist Roman Jakobson (1896-1982) argued in the late 1950s.

Jakobson saw the study of such functions as critical to understanding the overall nature of human interaction. He saw the functions as connected to structural constituents of verbal communication. He identified the following six as the basic ones (Jakobson 1960):

Context
Addresser ——— Message ——— Addressee
Contact
Code

Figure 5. Jakobson's constituents of verbal communication.

The *addresser* is the one who initiates a dialogue or conversation and the *message* is what he or she wishes to communicate. The *addressee* is the intended receiver of the message, and the *context* is what permits interlocutors to decipher the intent of the message and thus to extract an appropriate meaning from it. The mode of *contact* between the addresser and addressee is the set of personal and social relations between interlocutors that shapes the overall register and meaning of the interaction (as formal, friendly, etc.). The *code* provides the linguistic (and nonverbal) resources and cues for constructing or deciphering the message.

Jakobson matched these constituents to six speech functions:

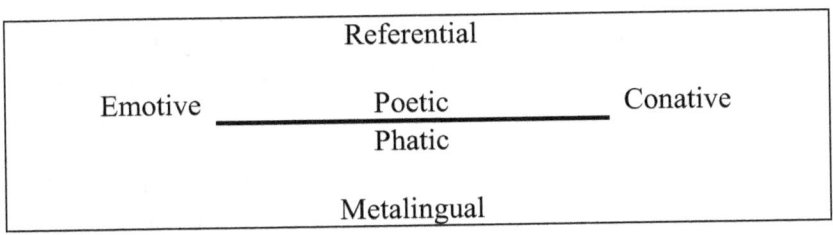

Figure 6. Jakobson's functions.

As we saw above, the *emotive* function correlates with the addresser's goal behind his or her message. Its structure and contents, thus, convey the addresser's intentions, emotions, attitudes, social status, etc. The *conative* function is the effect the message is intended to produce on the addressee. The *referential* function corresponds to the context in which an utterance is delivered, indicating that the message is constructed to convey specific information about the world. The *poetic* function is intended to draw attention to the form of the message itself, forcing interlocutors to focus on its particular design. The *phatic* function undergirds a message designed to establish social contact. Finally, the *metalingual* function underlies messages designed to refer to the code used. Below, in Table 5, are speech samples that show – in a highly simplified fashion – the connection between Jakobsonian constituents of verbal communication and functions.

Jakobson's use of the term *phatic* comes, likely, from the work of anthropologist Bronislaw Malinowski (1922). Malinowski defined it as the exchange of words and phrases that are important less for their dictionary meanings than for their social contact function. When we greet someone with *How are you?* we hardly expect a medical report, as would a doctor. The function of that statement is simply to allow people to make contact (with a health-wish subtext). Malinowski also argued that the study of phatic communication would allow linguists to understand how its varying forms reveal differing cultural emphases and evaluations of what constitutes norm-based behavior

Table 5. Communicative constituents, functions and sample utterances.

Constituent	5. Function	6. Speech Sample
addresser	emotive	"I didn't realize that!"
addressee	conative	"You should believe me."
context	referential	"As I said, that puzzle has only one solution."
message	poetic	"I like to hike with my bike."
contact	phatic	"Hi! How's it going?"
code	metalingual	"The word noun is a noun."

.Violation of phatic speech rules is a major source of misunderstanding in intercultural dialogue. Below is a conversation that took place in Toronto in 2005 between a non-native speaker of English (A) and a native speaker (B) before the start of a lecture that was being delivered at a scholarly conference at the University of Toronto. It was recorded by one of the authors of this book as part of a general recording of all aspects of the conference. A and B were participants who had met at previous conferences:

> A: Hey, hello. Nice to meet you here.
> B: Indeed. How's it going?
> A: It is not going well. Among other things, I have had various personal problems; my job is now insecure. Would you like to know anything else?
> B: That's OK. Sorry to hear about all that.

The "wrong turn" in the dialogue took place when A provided unrequested personal information because A interpreted B's protocol *How's it going?* as a literal request for such information, not as a simple phatic strategy. B's exit from what he perceived to be A's unfolding personal narrative was a simple one ("Sorry to hear about all that"), but the rest of the dialogue suggests that A did not perceive it as such:

A: Why did you ask, then?
B: Just a way to say hello.
A: Oh, I didn't realize.
B: No problem.

A comparable incident occurred when a student of Chinese background, who had been living in Switzerland for two years, reported to one of the authors of this book that when he first settled in Geneva, in the French speaking part of Switzerland, he was puzzled by the behavior of his neighbor the first time they made contact. The neighbor greeted him with a smile and *Bonjour* ("Good-day") which, the student declared, made him blush, since he perceived it as a strategy for engaging in an extended conversation. The student tried, subsequently, to start such a conversation, but when he had managed to put together something meaningful to say the smiling neighbor was already gone on his way. "In China," the student explained to one of the authors, "we don't usually greet strangers, and when we greet someone it is in order to start a conversation." The student had failed to recognize the greeting as a simple phatic strategy, misinterpreting it instead as a gambit for starting a conversation. In fact, as explained by Ye (2004) the Chinese discourse system draws a sharp distinction between strangers (*shēngrén*, literally "uncooked person") and old acquaintances (*shúrén*, literally "cooked person") activating different cultural conversational scripts for the two kinds of people. Children are taught from an early age to greet *shúrén*, but this behavior is not expected in children nor in adults when they interact with *shēngrén*. Ye (2004: 221) presents an interesting example from the Chinese film *The Story of Qiuju* to explain how the Chinese *dǎ zhāohu* differs from English "greetings":

> Throughout this film, *dǎ zhāohu* never takes place between strangers, not even in the situations where "greetings" are expected by Anglo cultural norms. A telling example is at the beginning of the film when the protagonist Qiuju takes her injured husband to see a physician at a country clinic. There was no exchange such as "hello" or "how are you" between doctor and patients when they come into each other's field of vision. The doctor simply asked "*Zěnmele?*", which means "What happened (to you)?".

Moreover the traditional Chinese greeting is never purely formulaic – e.g. just saying *Hello* – but involves a gambit to start a short conversation, which may well be purely *phatic* as regards its function. Typically, this takes the form of a question whose answer is obvious in the context of the speech event. Here is another example from the same film (Ye 2004: 221):

A: Are you eating noodles, aren't you?
B: Yes. I'll give you some.
A: I've eaten. You eat.

Another Jakobsonian function that is also a common source of misunderstanding in IC settings is the emotive one (Wierzbicka 1999, 2003). Wierzbicka (2003: 64-65) offers a particularly telling example of this, based on her experience with IC training in Australian hospitals:

> Anglo-Saxon doctors and nurses are accustomed to thinking that pain should be borne stoically and that one should only cry in real extremity. Therefore they are unsympathetic to people who complain, cry and scream at pains which can be considered minor, a behavior acceptable to Italians and Greeks. This can lead to very unsympathetic treatment by doctor and nurses, and to the general idea that Mediterranean people are cowardly because they complain about things that only hysterically cowardly Anglo-Saxons would mention.

Many similar examples can be easily added to Wierzbicka's. In a phrase, it is obvious that Jakobson's model is extremely useful in providing a broad framework for discussing a large array of the communication interferences in intercultural dialogues. We would like, however, to add a seventh function to Jakobson's list—namely the *ritual* function. Religious rites, sermons, prep rallies, political debates, and other ceremonial gatherings are anchored in a discourse genre that makes it possible for participants to feel a common emotional bond. The use of ritualistic language is not to create new meanings, but to assert communal sense-making and, thus, to ensure cultural cohesion. People typically love to hear the same speeches, songs, and stories at specific times during the year (at Christmas, at Passover, etc.) in order to feel united with the other members of their group.

The importance of this function cannot be emphasized enough. In many ancient societies, certain words were perceived as sacred forms. Those who possessed their knowledge were thought to have supernatural or magical powers. In many cultures, just knowing the name of a deity was purported to give the knower great power—a fact encoded in early myths. For example, in Egyptian mythology, the sorceress Isis tricked the sun god Ra into revealing his name in order to gain power over him and all other gods. In some traditional Inuit tribes, an individual will not pronounce certain words, such as his or her ancestral name, fearing that this senseless act could break the magical spell of protection that such words bring with them. Belief in the magical powers of language is not limited to oral tribal cultures. It abounds even in modern societies. "Speak of the devil," we say in common parlance, and "he will appear." When someone sneezes, uttering "Bless you" is meant to ward off sickness. Lack of familiarity of such rituals in intercultural dialogue is a potentially damaging source of misunderstanding.

6.1. Speech Act Theory

One of the primary functions of speech is to bring about some action. The utterance "Be careful," for instance, has the same kind of effect as the action of putting a hand in front of someone in order to block him or her from crossing the road carelessly. The statement "I sentence you to life imprisonment" uttered by a judge has the same effect as marching the accused person directly to prison and locking him or her up.

The theory of speech acts, as such utterances are called, starts with the book *How to do things with words*, written by philosopher John L. Austin in 1962, and expanded a few years later by John R. Searle in his 1969 book, *Speech acts*. There are three main levels of the speech act identified by the two scholars:

(1) *locutionary* = the act itself of saying something: "He said to me, 'You can't do that'."
illocutionary = the act of uttering something with a purpose or rationale in mind (asking and answering questions, giving information, assurance, identifying, etc.): "He protested against my doing that."

(2) *perlocutionary* = the act of uttering something and thereby producing sequential effects on the feelings, thoughts, or actions of interlocutors: "He stopped me, bringing me to my senses."

According to Searle, there are five basic types of illocutionary acts:

(1) *assertives,* which are acts designed to get an interlocutor to form a belief about the world or to think about it: *stating, concluding, representing, deducing, reminding.*

(2) *directives,* which are acts intended to get an interlocutor to do something: *commanding, inviting, asking, requesting, begging, permitting.*

commissives, which are acts committing the speaker to some future course of action: *offering, promising, pledging, threatening*.

(3) *expressives*, which are acts allowing the speaker to express a psychological state, or an attitude towards the interlocutor: *thanking, congratulating, apologizing, condoling, deploring, welcoming*.

(4) *declaratives*, which are acts allowing the speaker to bring about a change in an institution (a school, a business, a church, a club, a game, the government of a country) thanks to the social role that the speaker has within said institution (chairperson, principal, teacher, CEO, priest, referee): *appointing, resigning, nominating, pronouncing*.

These five basic kinds of illocutions are illustrated schematically in Table 6.

There are, clearly, many points of similarity between speech act theory and Jakobson's communication model: assertives cover roughly the same ground as referential speech; while directives correspond, for the most part, to the conative function.

Two important categories introduced by Searle, which are not present in Jakobson's model are the commissives and the declaratives; both are essential to understand how discourse shapes social reality, by covering the creation and activation of interpersonal commitments and obligations and the workings of institutions like schools, businesses, governments, etc. In other words, these two kinds of speech acts are important for GL because they allow us to understand how language is used to create the conventions that make up social reality. For instance, being fired or fined 5,000 dollars are not physical events. They are entirely the conventional product of a culture. Nevertheless, they are quite real in affecting the lives of the members of a society that accepts these conventions. In a "primitive" society of hunters-gatherers, these declarative speech acts would be meaningless.

Table 6. Illocutionary acts

Type	Illocutionary point	Varieties	Examples
Assertives	to get the addressee to form or attend to a belief	to inform, to remind, to explain, to gossip, to argue, to hypothesize, etc.	"There's someone at the door." "It must have rained. Because the ground is damp."
Directives	to get the addressee to do (or say) something	to request, to order, to ask, to question, to forbid, to warn, to advise, to advertise, to invite, to encourage, to implore, etc.	"Can you pass me the salt, please?" "Come here!" "Great idea. You should write a book about it."
Commissives	to commit the speaker to doing (or not doing) something	to promise, to offer, to pledge, to threaten, etc.	"I'll never do it again." "I'll bring something to eat and drink."
Expressives	to express feelings towards the addressee	to compliment, to congratulate, to sympathize, to apologize, to greet, etc	"Hi!" "I'd like to offer my heartfelt condolences." "Kudos! Well done."
Declaratives	to change an institutional state of affairs	to condemn, to appoint, to initiate a ceremony, etc.	"You are fined 5,000 dollars for driving way too fast." "You're fired!" "Time out!"

Commissives, representing the social obligations we take up, are equally important to understand the functioning of a social interaction field (Rigotti and Rocci 2006b). When I see a building bearing the sign Restaurant, I interpret it as a promise and I expect that the people there would serve me a meal for a sum of money. This is more than a simple expectation. I would be quite puzzled, maybe even outraged, if the patron said: "Sorry, we don't serve meals to strangers". At the same time, by performing the speech act of ordering a meal I take up an obligation to pay the bill. As observed by Stubbs (2008: 15), "different kinds of promises and contract formation are the most basic trait which pervades social behavior".

Searle's expressive category correlates somewhat with Jakobson's emotive and phatic functions. But the overlap is not total. In various European cultures a serious apology, as opposed to a purely polite apology, entails the use of a number of linguistic elements beyond the display of the appropriate feelings ("I'm sorry"). The admission of responsibility ("It was I who broke your vase"), the confession of wrongdoing ("I've been really careless"), the commitment not to repeat something incorrectly ("I'll pay more attention in the future"), and, the request for forgiveness ("I hope you will forgive me") cannot easily be included in the expressive category identified by Searle (Tolmach Lakoff 2001). Apologies typically have an assertive dimension (admitting the wrongdoing), a commissive one (the disavowal of bad behavior), and a directive one (the request for forgiveness). In certain formal settings (such as religious ones) apologies can have also institutional or ritualistic consequences. In this respect, Clark (1996: 136) observed that a general problem with Searle's scheme is that speech acts are presented as belonging to one and just one category, rather than allowing for overlapping, criss crossing, and interweaving.

It is also not at all clear that the speech acts identified by Searle have equal importance in languages across the world (Rosaldo 1982). One could legitimately ask, for instance, if *promising* is a significant speech act in all cultures. Egner (2006) considers the relevance of the notion of *promise* for West African cultures. Promises are frequently the cause of intercultural misunderstanding between West Africans (e.g. Ivorians) and Westerners – like Americans or Europeans. For instance, an Ivorian speaker can "promise" to her European friend that she will attend her party and then go on to mention casually that the day of the party she will be six hundred miles away from the place (Egner 2006: 444). Such a behavior on the part of the Ivorian would seem a "false promise" to the Westerner and would lead to a very frustrating interaction. The Westerner may even think that her interlocutor reasons with a "different logic", one which easily admits contradiction. The reality is less exotic. In fact, from the viewpoint of the Ivorian speaker, the speech act is to be intended as a "polite promise", expressing the *wish* of the speaker to be there. This is something that the Westerner could understand but failed to recognize. Egner (2006) shows that West African language encode with different expression the "polite promise" and the "binding promise" and that the latter is always the result of some "negotiation" carried out in conversation. These subtle signals are however lost in an intercultural exchange carried out in a *koiné* language.

It is worth noting that some sort of polite promises exist also in European and American cultures. For instance, in order to end a business conversation on a friendly note, one of the participants may say:

We should really get together to have lunch sometime.

Interestingly, Scollon and Scollon (2001: 6) point out that this closing gambit can be a source of misunderstanding when communicating with Chinese interlocutors. For a Western businessperson it is clear that this vague promise is not an actual invitation but "just a conventional way of parting with good feelings toward the other." A Chinese participant, however, might interpret the move rather differently. Chinese conversational style favors the collocation of important information towards the end of the exchange. As a consequence, a Chinese interlocutor will be particularly attentive to what is said toward the end, and will take the speech act as a serious invitation. After a few weeks, the hypothetical Chinese businessperson would begin to feel that his western counterpart "has been rather insincere because he has not followed up his invitation to lunch with a specific time and place" (Scollon and Scollon 2001: 6). Again the example shows that the problem lies in a failure to recognize the proper cues signaling the actual nature of the speech act.

In conclusion, the above examples have shown that, for the basic tasks of GL, a combination of Jakobson's and Searle's models of speech will suffice to initiate research and inquiry into the ways in which the lack of appropriate discourse competence shapes IC negatively.

7. Meaning

The word *meaning* has been used constantly in this book, even though we have not given it a specific definition or explication. The branch of linguistics that studies meaning is (as mentioned) called semantics (Chapter 1 § 3.2). Semantics traces its theoretical roots to the work of the French linguist Michel Bréal (1832-1915), who was among the first to develop a framework for analyzing the evolution of word meanings in different languages in *psychological* terms, with a particular focus on the role of figurative processes in evolutionary tendencies.

During the twentieth century, though, semantics has developed mainly in close connection with *philosophy* and *logic*. This is not by chance, because since the times of Plato and Aristotle many fundamental hypotheses on what meaning is have been put forth by philosophers reflecting on the relationship between language, thought and reality. This orientation of linguistic semantics led to privilege mainly universal questions with a certain disregard for the semantic peculiarities of the different languages. Even though this attitude is legitimate in a philosophical perspective, for the practical purposes of GL what is particular and variable matters as much as what is general and invariant.

Recently, however, the linguistic field has witnessed a growing interest in *contrastive semantics* and in the application of the analytical tools of logico-philosophical semantics to the task of comparing the semantic organization of different languages (see the studies collected in Jaszczolt and Turner 1996 and 2003) and cultures (Wierzbicka 1997). At the same time, a new *cognitive semantics* school has also flourished, which places an emphasis on figurative meaning processes in discourse (Allwood and Gärdenfors 1998, Danesi 2004a, Dirven and Verspoor 2004, Geeraerts 2006). In many ways this school took up the original goals of linguistic semantics as it was understood by Bréal and other early researchers.

The logico-philosophical and the cognitive-linguistic traditions have been often seen as opposed. In the perspective of GL, we see them as largely complementary for understanding how meaning construction processes affect IC, as the following presentation will show. The basic picture of semantics outlined in the following pages draws both from an approach called "Congruity Theory" (Rigotti and Rocci 2001, Rocci 2005, Rigotti 2005, Rigotti, Rocci and Greco 2006), which has logico-philosophical roots, and from current cognitive theories of figurative language (Danesi 2004a).

To illustrate how semantic interference can influence IC, consider the following two examples of recorded conversation, which show understanding problems involving homonymy and hyponymy. Homonyms are words with the same pronunciation and/or spelling, but with different meanings. If the homonymy is purely phonetic then the items are known as homophones (for example, *aunt* vs. *ant* and *bore* vs. *boar*). If the homonymy is orthographic, then the words are known as homographs (*play* as in *Shakespeare's play* vs. *play* as in *He likes to play*). It is not the case that all homographs are homophones: for example, the form *learned* has two pronunciations in *He learned to play the violin* vs. *He is a learned man*. Homonyms force speakers in a dialogue to focus on what each item means by comparison and contrast and, thus, what makes each one unique. Homonymy is a frequent source of speech gaffes in intercultural settings, as the following conversation fragment of two students at the University of Toronto shows: A is a non-native speaker of English, and B a native speaker. The conversation was observed (and then recorded in a notebook) by one of the authors of this book as he overheard the students before a class:

A: Do we have to study that?
B: Yes, it's an important play.
A: No, I mean the drama.
B: Same thing.

A obviously did not process the word *play* as a homonym. He interpreted it as standing for "action in a game," not for "dramatic work."

The second example of interference involves hyponymy. A hyponym is a word that includes (implicates) the meaning of a more generic one, called a hyperonym: for example, the meaning of *scarlet* includes the meaning of *red*, and the meaning of *tulip* includes (implicates) *flower*, etc. English distinguishes *orange* (or *lemon*) *jam* from other kinds of *jam* with a specific word (*marmalade*), while the Italian *marmellata*, on the contrary, indicates any kind of jam. That is the source of the misunderstanding in the following conversation excerpt between a student of Italian background (A) and a native-speaking English student (B), which, again, took place before a class at the University of Toronto:

A: Do you always eat marmalade?
B: No, but I eat jam regularly.
A: How can you eat traffic?
B: No, not a traffic jam—jam!

Clearly, A did not know that *marmalade* was just one type of *jam*. He had obviously learned to use the word *jam* idiomatically, in the sense of "a crush or crowded mass, as in *She was delayed by a huge traffic jam*.

7.1. Conceptual structure: predicates and arguments

Semantics is about the relationship between language and the world, or, more precisely, about the way people use language to speak about the world as they "grasp" it. Not only the world as it exists, but all possible worlds that we can imagine, desire, fear, etc. – as we will see in Chapter 3 – the ability of conceiving possible worlds is essential to explain human action, interaction, and communication. In a phrase, semantics is about language and *concepts*.

One fundamental distinction in the way language enables us to grasp the world is that between *predicates* and *arguments*. This distinction has a venerable philosophical tradition – harking back to Plato – and is cognitively grounded in the neurophysiology of visual perception (Hurford 2003). Arguments are entities, things, beings that may exist in a world, to which we can refer and about which we can say something. Think of words like *it*, *this*, *something* etc. These words are used to manifest arguments in different communicative situations. Our picture of the world, however, would be rather bleak if it was populated only by naked entities. There would not be much to say *about* things apart from pointing to them.

Entities, in fact, are beings characterized by *predicates*, that is particular modes of being, properties, features, characteristics, like *to be red, to be round, to run, to be taller than something else, to move,* etc. When one or more entities (arguments) are characterized by a mode of being (predicate) we have a situation, a possible state of affairs, like *This is red*. Congruity theory represents conceptual structure– that is the meaning – of verbal utterances in terms of *predicate-argument structures*. We can consider a simple example:

The cat meows

This is a sentence formed by a predicate (*meows*) and only one argument (*the cat*). The predicate is a mode of being, the argument is an entity that can be in that way of being. Predicates vary with respect to the number of arguments they qualify. We say that predicates have a certain number of *argument places*, or *slots*, that have to be filled appropriately in order to obtain a complete situation.

Table 7. Predicate-argument structures

Predicate	Structure	Arguments	Examples
meow	*meow* is a singular (monadic) predicate; it suggests a filler for a specific slot or place in the sentence	x_1 = the cat	"The cat (x_1) *meows*."
black	*black* is also a monadic predicate	x_1 = the cat	"The cat (x_1) is *black*."
drink	*drink* is a dyadic (two-place) predicate	x_1 = the cat x_2 = the milk	"The cat (x_1) *drinks* the milk (x_2)."
think	*think* is a dyadic predicate	x_1 = John x_2 = that the cat is sleeping	"John (x_1) *thinks* that the cat is sleeping (x_2)."
under	*under* is a dyadic predicate	x_1 = the cat's bowl x_2 = the table	"The cat's bowl (x_1) is *under* the table (x_2)."
because	*because* is a dyadic predicate	x_1 = the cat meows x_2 = the cat is hungry	"The cat meows (x_1) *because* it is hungry (x_2)."
give	*give* is a triadic (three-place) predicate	x_1 = John x_2 = a bowl of milk x_3 = the cat	"John (x_1) *gives* a bowl of milk (x_2) to the cat (x_3)."

A caveat is in order here: the word *argument* in the terminology of semantics does not mean the same as *argument* in argumentation theory (see Chapter 5). In fact, the two uses are not related: they are homonyms, like the *bank* of a river and the *bank* that lends money. In argumentation, an *argument* is a discourse aimed at providing reasons supporting a standpoint. In semantics, *arguments* are entities, participants in a proposition. Semantic arguments have been also called the *actants* of the predicate (Mel'chuk 2004), because they are akin to the participants in a narrative scenario. Since the two meanings of *argument* are well entrenched in the respective disciplines, we decided to keep them despite the ambiguity. After all, these are the terms that the students will find in other books.

The structures formed by predicates and arguments have a unitary and new sense resulting from the congruous combination of conceptual elements that are made one for the other: this is called *compositionality*. The meaningful combination of predicates and arguments represents a fragment of a conceivable world, that is, a conceivable situation or state of affairs. This shows how deeply language and human reason are connected. We can say that by means of the articulation of language, human experience is structured and becomes readable, since language provides the categorical network by means of which it is possible to recognize the different aspects of reality we can experience. We introduced this property of language in Chapter 1, as the "classificatory principle".

It is a fact that the categorical grids that different languages provide to people to read the world are different: some languages provide us with predicates that are not available in other languages. Some, however, appear to have universal validity. For instance, it seems that distinguishing between *living* and *nonliving* things, between *people* and *animals*, between *males* and *females*, among other things, constitutes categories that serve basic practical functions for people cross-culturally. But many other categorical distinctions are culture-specific. Although people across the world may see the same rainbow, the number and range of the rainbow's hues they can name will depend on how many color terms are made available to them by the languages they speak. Some languages have everyday words for a dozen colors; others can get by with only a couple (or none at all). As mentioned in the previous chapter (Chapter 1, § 3.1), according to the classificatory principle, cultures encode only those aspects of reality that they consider important to them.

The same type of comparison could be made for virtually any phenomenon. American words like *jock* and *nerd* do not have any equivalents in many languages, probably because they refer to concepts that are relevant to American youth culture. In Italian, the word *jock* has no equivalent for the likely reason that sports do not play the same role in Italian high schools as they do in America.

Lexical richness in a given semantic field is an indicator of cultural relevance. Curiously, the English language has many words at its disposal to refer to ghosts in general such as *ghost, haunt, phantom, phantasm, spectre, spirit, spook, wight, wraith*, or to specific types of ghosts, like *banshee* (a borrowing from Irish) and *poltergeist* (a borrowing from German), while Italian relies on fewer words: *fantasma, spettro* and the generic *spirito*. This is less surprising if we consider the importance of the *ghost story* as a genre in English literature, compared to its virtual absence the Italian literary tradition.

It is important to observe, in view of IC, that even if each language provides a unique set of linguistically manifested categories to read the world, the predicates manifested by the lexicon of the different languages are usually not simple or 'atomic' meanings. Usually they are semantic composites, bundles of simpler predicates by means of which they can be explained. An internally complex predicate can be translated, or better *explicated*, in terms of simpler predicates.

Jakobson (1963: 79) observed that "for the linguist like for the ordinary language user, the meaning of a word is nothing but its *translation* by another sign which can be substituted for this word, especially by 'another sign in which it is more fully developed'". This relationship between meaning and translation has an important consequence for IC: culture-specific meanings can be translated and explained. For instance, the predicate *jock* may not be lexicalized in Italian, but I can very well use the Italian language to explain its meaning in American English and its significance in American youth culture.

How is it possible to determine if a predicate includes another predicate as one of its component parts? As far as meaning is concerned, *inclusion* corresponds to logical implication (or entailment): a predicate includes another predicate as a meaning component if it implicates (entails) that predicate. Consider the following sentences (* = anomalous):

(1) *We have been walking for three hours in a forest with no trees.
(2) *He killed many people, but they didn't die.

We perceive these as being nonsensical, despite the fact that they are grammatically well-formed. In order to discover if a predicate is indeed implicated by another predicate one can set up a simple, but quite clever, *semantic test* where one tries to conjunct the predicate with the negation of the expected implication: the nonsense that hence arises shows that the negated feature is indeed included to the proper content of the predicate. Example (1) shows that having *trees* is part of the meaning of forest; while (2) shows that the sad fact that the victim *dies* is part of the content of the predicate *kill*. By looking at the implications of predicates we can try to resolve complex predicates into their components, so that we can account for semantic relationships between predicates within the semantic system of a language, or compare the meanings of predicates belonging to different languages. A very simple example of this kind of *componential* analysis is shown below in (1-5), where the meanings of the English words *man, woman, boy, girl* and *child* are analyzed using three semantic traits and the logical connectives of conjunction (&) and negation ($\sim$) (cf. Lyons 1995: 110).

(1)   *man* (x_1) = HUMAN (x_1) & MALE (x_1) & ADULT (x_1)
(2)   *woman* (x_1) = HUMAN (x_1) & FEMALE (x_1) & ADULT (x_1)
(3)   *boy* (x_1) = HUMAN (x_1) & MALE (x_1) & $\sim$ ADULT (x_1)
(4)   *girl* (x_1) = HUMAN (x_1) & FEMALE (x_1) & $\sim$ ADULT (x_1)
(5)   *child* (x_1) = HUMAN (x_1) & $\sim$ ADULT (x_1)

Componential analysis can cover a lot of ground in unraveling the surprisingly rich internal structure of predicates. Consider the following three predicates, which show levels of incremental semantic complexity:

(1)   *father* (x_1, x_2) = HUMAN (x_1) & MALE (x_1) & ADULT (x_1) & PARENT (x_1, x_2)
(2)   *to kill* (x_1, x_2) = ALIVE (x_2) & (CAUSE $(x_1,$ BECOME $(x_2, \sim$ ALIVE $(x_2))$
(3)   *to hope* (x_1, x_2) = HUMAN (x_1) & EVENT (x_2) & GOOD (x_2, x_1) & THINK $(x_1,$ FUTURE (BECOME $(x_2,$ TRUE $(x_2)))))$ & WAIT (x_1, x_2)

The explication of the predicate *to hope* in (3) deserves a short commentary. It shows that only human beings can possess *hope* (since it is unlikely that other animal possess this concept, at least in human terms), and it makes explicit the fact that *hope* implies an event or an action, not a thing. We cannot say **Mary hoped the steak*, but only *Mary hoped to eat the steak*. It also specifies that the event must be good: someone cannot hope to break a leg, unless there is a specific reason for it (to avoid military conscription, for instance). Finally, *hope* implies *thinking* that a good event will unfold in the future (if one waits for it).

As mentioned, the basic format of analysis presented above is a subset of the full analytical apparatus of Congruity Theory (Rigotti and Rocci 2001, Rigotti, Rocci, and Greco 2006). This theory is one among several current semantic theories providing sophisticated tools for explicating linguistic meanings in terms of their components (Mel'chuk 1981, 2004, Jackendoff 1983, Pustejovsky 1995, Wierzbicka 1996, Van Valin 2005). A particularly interesting paradigm for GL is the one put forward by Anna Wierzbicka (Wierzbicka 1996, 1997), since she has attempted to enumerate, through extensive research, the minimal set of universal semantic features or *primes* that provide the basic universal building blocks for complex predicates across languages. As she puts it (Wierzbicka 2003:

xvii): "In a nutshell, this theory postulates that semantic analysis should be based on empirically established universal human concepts, that is by simple concepts realized in all languages as words or word-like elements, such as GOOD and BAD, KNOW, THINK, WANT and SAY, DO and HAPPEN and fifty or so others."

7.2. Compositionality

Compositionality is a critical feature in how we link language to real-world states and objects. Structurally, it explains why we do not put together predicates and arguments randomly or mechanically, but rather implicatively (Rigotti and Cigada 2004: 87): every predicate selects particular classes of arguments fitting – or congruent – with its argument slots. Sentences such as *The cat drinks* or *He gives* make sense only insofar as they suggest implicit arguments in the context of a specific utterance. The former makes sense if the act of drinking is connected to substances such as *milk* or *water*; the latter will not be perceived as an incomplete thought only insofar as it is used in an utterance to suggest generosity: *Yes, it's true. John is very generous. He gives (always)*. The meaning of utterance is, thus, compositional. Syntax in Congruity Theory is seen, therefore, as a mirror of underlying compositional structure.

Let's look at a number of anomalous utterances, designed to bring out the importance of compositionality in ensuring congruity between language and reality. Consider, first, the following dialogue:

(1) A: John rented his flat.
(2) B: To whom?
(3) A: To nobody in particular; he just rented it.
(4) B: How much did he ask for it?
(5) A: He did not rent it for money.
(6) B: What?

A's statements in (3) and (5) are interpreted as nonsensical because they negate two of the arguments presupposed by the predicate *rent*. This has, in fact, a five-place (pentadic) argument frame:

someone (x_1) *rents* something (x_2) to someone else (x_3) for a certain price (x_4) and for a certain period of time (x_5).

So, one can only conclude that A is either joking or that he or she does not know the meaning of the predicate *to rent*. Now, consider the following anomalous sentences, which have been marked with argument symbolism for the sake of convenience:

(1) *The tablecloth (x_1) hopes that the economic situation will improve.
(2) *Luigi reads a closet (x_2).
(3) John (x_1) reads the political situation (x_2) insightfully.
(4) This program (x_1) cannot read this type of file (x_2).

As we have seen, the predicate *hope* requires that the first of its two argument slots (x_1) be filled by a lexical item referring to a human being, since only human beings can experience hope. In example (1) above, the argument *tablecloth* violates this semantic criterion. Similarly, (2) is perceived as meaningless because the predicate *read* requires that a readable written text fill its second argument slot (x_2). *Closet* does not meet this criterion. Now, we do not perceive either of the last two sentences as anomalous, despite the fact that in (3) the argument *political situation* (x_2) does not satisfy the logical requirement of being a written text and in (4) the x_1 and the x_2 slots are filled inappropriately because the verb *read* requires an animate argument. The reason why we do not perceive either sentence as anomalous is because of figurative meaning (Chapter 1, § 4.2).

Let's pursue this aspect of compositionality further. Consider the animal designated by the word *cat*. The dictionary defines a *cat* as a small carnivorous mammal domesticated since early times as a catcher of rats and mice and as a pet, existing in several distinctive breeds and varieties. This is its literal meaning and can be shown componentially as: MAMMAL (x_1) & RETRACTILE CLAWS (x_1) & WHISKERS (x_1) & LONG TAIL (x_1), etc. However, that is not all there is to its uses. Consider the use of *cat* in sentences such as the following two:

(1) He's a real cool cat.
(2) He let the cat out of the bag.

The meaning of (1) can be summed up as "an attractive and suave person, such as a player or devotee of jazz music." The meaning of (2) is that of "a secret." In both cases, however, the figure of a cat is implied. In (1), the individual is perceived to move slowly, sleekly, and rhythmically like a real *cat*. Example (2) reveals that cats are considered to be secretive animals (in human ways of course). This extensional process is known as *trope*.

7.3. Denotation versus connotation

Apart from the distinction between *literal* and *figurative* meanings, there is a different key distinction to be made in the realm of word meanings, namely that between *denotation* and *connotation* (cf. Rigotti and Rocci 2006a).

Denotation is essentially the set of meanings built into language forms at a descriptive or classificatory level. But language forms are used in speech not only to describe things, events, etc., but also to evaluate them in specific ways. These evaluations are made possible by the connotative uses associated with language forms. For instance, the Italian words *ubriaco* and *sbronzo* both denote a person in a state of drunkenness. However, they convey a vastly different assessment of that very same state. The word *sbronzo*, which is perceived as colloquial and inappropriate in a formal situation, conveys negative nuances of scorn or ridicule. The word is thus never used in a higher register, such as in a serious conversation about alcoholism, since it would convey an uncaring and judgmental attitude towards the problem on the part of a speaker. The word *ubriaco*, on the other hand, does not have such connotations built into it.

This kind of connotative implicature is operative in various speech styles. It is used, for instance, to counteract unpleasant thoughts or ideas associated with something. The English words *prostitute* and *whore* have roughly the same denotative content, but the latter is laden with negative connotations; *die* and *pass away* also have the same denotative content, but the latter has a more euphemistic ring to it, allowing the speaker to distance himself or herself emotionally from the reality of death. Interestingly, connotative strategies are often connected with ritualistic uses of language (§2.3.2). An expression such as *speak of the devil and he appears* implies an unconscious fear of bringing about bad things by speaking about them (Allan 2005). The word *undertaker* ("one who undertakes a job") was once a euphemism for the more explicit *mortician*. Now, *funeral director* is a euphemism for *undertaker*. Such replacements are designed to attenuate the possibility of calling forth death by uttering a certain word. In some languages the names of fearsome predatory animals are also forged through such connotative euphemism: for instance, the Russian *medved* "bear," literally means "the honey eater" and the English word *bear* itself comes from a Proto-Germanic word *beron*, which probably meant "the brown one" (Allan 2004).

Connotation extends into all domains of speech and manifests itself through various lexical and grammatical devices. Consider the following two sentences (Allan 2005):

(1) Tom's dog killed Jane's rabbit.
(2) Tom's doggie killed Jane's bunny.

The words *doggie* and *bunny* suggest that the speaker is talking to a child, unless he or she is using an ironic style. We can also glean the emotive intent of speakers from this particular style—a parent scolding a child would not use it, since it is normally used as part of a strategy of endearment. The word *doggie* achieves its intended connotative effects by means of a morphological modification—a diminutive suffix. Such suffixes are common in Italian for conveying a playful, friendly, good-humored, or even mischievous attitude (Dressler and Merlini Barbaresi 1994):

(3) *Non toccare l'acquetta!* ("Do not touch the [little] water!")
(4) *Posso avere un caffeuccio?* ("May I have a [little] coffee?")

In both (3) and (4) the connotative intent of the suffixes (*acqua → acquetta, caffè → caffeuccio*) is to impart friendliness or to inject a little joviality into a speech situation, so as to minimize the force of a command or a request. This acknowledges implicitly how important the action or desirable the requested item is to the speaker.

Clearly, the study of connotation is crucial for GL, since it has rather important implications for the analysis of miscommunication in intercultural settings. Using words unwittingly to refer to the nationality one's interlocutor tend to have very negative consequences. Massive Italian emigration during the first part of the twentieth century, for instance, gave rise to a number of derogatory terms used commonly to refer to Italian immigrants (or Italians in general): the American *dago*, the Australian *wog*, the French *rital,* the Swiss-German *cinkali*, among others, would fall into this category. Needless to say, if any one of these were used in an IC setting unwittingly, there would be a strong possibility for conflict to ensue.

7.4. Conceptual interference

The foregoing discussion brings us to a further consideration of one of the most destructive sources of intercultural misunderstanding, namely the unconscious tendency of interlocutors to put together messages on the basis of native-language word meanings (§1.3.2). This phenomenon can be called *conceptual interference* (Danesi 2000, 2003). This topic will be discussed in greater detail in a subsequent chapter. Suffice it to say here that it suggests a general principle governing IC:

> When speakers create a message in their non-native language they tend to conceptualize the message in terms of their native logico-semantic system. That is to say, they use the words and structures of the non-native language as carriers of native-language concepts. The result is a message that is structurally correct, but conceptually anomalous.

Such interference can be denotative or connotative. By and large, the former is less damaging than is the latter. In line with the classificatory principle, denotative interference involves misunderstandings of a literal nature—for example, replacing *clock* for *watch* in an expression such as "The clock I am wearing is not working" might produce a quizzical reaction, but certainly not one that might evoke conflict. Connotative interference is more damaging because, as discussed above, it often involves meanings steeped in culture-specific traditions or else evaluative discourse. It is unlikely that non-native speakers of English will have had access to the connotative meanings of *cat* discussed above, and if they have, it is unlikely that they will have had opportunities to use them correctly.

A large portion of connotative meaning-making is based on metaphor. It is thus instructive to take an initial quick look at this phenomenon here. In the metaphor "The professor is a snake," there are two referents, not one, that are related to each other as follows:

- There is the primary referent, *the professor*, which is known as the *topic* of the metaphor. It is the argument of the utterance.
- There is a secondary referent, *the snake*, which is known as the *vehicle* of the metaphor. This is the predicate of the utterance.
- Their predicate-argument linkage VEHICLE (*topic*) creates a new meaning, called the *ground*, which is not the simple sum of the meanings of the two referents, but involves a type of semantic

chemistry or admixture of the two, guided by the need of preserving congruity. This is an implicature resulting from the reciprocal adaptation of the predicate and the argument.

It is not the denotative meaning of the predicate that is transferred to the argument, but rather the culture-specific characteristics perceived in snakes, and the evaluative connotations associated with them—"slyness," "danger," "slipperiness," etc. This set of connotations produces the ground.

The discovery of the crucial role played by metaphor in semantic systems was brought out by a groundbreaking 1980 book, *Metaphors We Live By*, written by George Lakoff and Mark Johnson. The basic tenet of the book was that a specific linguistic metaphor was not a simple isolated example of poetic fancy, but rather a token of an unconscious thought formula. Lakoff and Johnson termed this formula a *conceptual metaphor*. For example, a specific metaphorical utterance such as "The professor is a snake" is considered to be one of the specific manifestations of a thought formula that links human personality with animal types, or [people are animals]—"John is a serpentine person;" "Mary is a sweet little butterfly;" "My friend is a friendly gorilla;" "Your cousin is a big cuddly bear;" etc. Each use of the formula produces, as can be seen, a different connotative portrait of personality, depending on which animal predicate is chosen.

Each of the two parts of the conceptual metaphor is called a *domain*: [people] is the *target domain*, because human personality is the "target" of the conceptualization process; and [animals] is the *source domain*, because it encompasses the class of vehicle-predicates that deliver the intended connotative meanings (the "source" of the meaning in the conceptual metaphor). Similarly, when talking of *ideas* in terms of geometrical figures and relations—"Those ideas are diametrically opposite to mine;" "Our ideas are parallel;" etc.—the target domain is that of [ideas] and the source domain [geometrical figures/relations]. The sentences are, thus, specific utilizations of the conceptual metaphor [ideas are geometrical figures/relations]. Lakoff and Johnson trace the psychological source of conceptual metaphors to what they call *image schemas* (Lakoff 1987, Johnson 1987, 1989, 2007, Lakoff and Johnson 1999). These are the mental images that guide the choice of source domains in the construction of concepts. One type of schema, for example, involves orientational thinking—up vs. down, back vs. front, near vs. far, etc. This is embedded in conceptual metaphors such as [happiness is up] ("Today my spirits are up;" "My joy reaches the sky"). Another type involves thinking of abstractions as substances. This undergirds conceptual metaphors in which activities, emotions, ideas, etc. are portrayed as being "contained" in something, such as the "mind." This produces conceptual metaphors such as [the mind is a container]—"My mind is empty;" "My mind is full of wonderful memories;" etc. The extensive work on conceptual metaphor theory (CMT) since the early 1980s has shown how extensive connotative-metaphorical thinking is and how it imbues all kinds of discourses (see, for instance, Honeck and Hoffman 1980, Casad 1986, Kövecses 1986, 1988, 1990, 2002, Langacker 1987, 1990, 1999, Gibbs 1994, Janssen and Redeker 2000, Fauconnier and Turner 2002, Wolf and Dirven 2006, Radden and Dirven 2007, Goatly 2007).

It is obvious that CMT is of central importance to GL, given that in IC conceptual metaphors are potential sources of misunderstanding and miscommunication. Misunderstanding could emerge when, for example, English speakers might want to portray someone as having a treacherous personality by using the snake concept as they talk to someone who speaks a language in which this animal has a different array of connotative meanings. Miscommunication could occur when, for instance, English speakers might want to portray an idea in terms of a geometrical concept as they talk to someone who speaks a language from which the relevant conceptual metaphor is absent. The following dialogue, which occurred between one of the authors of this book (A) and one of his students of oriental background (B) during a class discussion, bears the latter case out:

A: Your idea is actually parallel to mine.
B: Excuse me professor, I do not understand. Why geometry?
A: It's just a way of speaking.
B: Oh, I understand. Ideas are like lines. Thanks.

Clearly, the student had no initial access to the conceptual metaphor [ideas are geometrical figures], which is a widespread one in English conversation when the topic is about ideas. However, he was able to quickly understand the analogy between the two domains (as his last statement reveals). The following two utterances were recorded as well by one of the authors of this book during an interaction with a non-native speaking student. In them, the student used *near* as a synonym for *close*:

(1) *I haven't been *near* emotionally with my family for years. (*Correct version*: I haven't been *close* emotionally with my family for years).

(2) *But I want to get *near* to them. (*Correct version:* But I want to get *close* to them).

The anomaly is due to the fact that *closeness* is used in English as a metaphorical vehicle to deliver the abstract argument of "emotional bonding." Consider, finally, the following Italian sentence, which was uttered by a student of English-speaking background in Lugano during a class taught in Italian:

(3) *Io *sono caduta* in amore un anno fa (Intended meaning: "I *fell* in love a year ago").

The student who uttered this sentence assumed that the English conceptual metaphor [love is a trap] manifests itself in exactly the same way in the vocabulary choices of Italian—but it does not. Italian uses the [love is a container] metaphorical formula, which manifests itself in sentences such as *Mi sono innamorata* (*approximately:* "I went into love").

8. Utterances

As discussed above (Chapter 1, § 3.1), a crucial aspect in how interlocutors determine the meaning of an utterance is *context*. This is the real-world situation that constrains what an utterance means. Consider a sentence such as "The pig is ready to eat" (Danesi 2004b). In this utterance the word *pig* has at least three meanings according to the social context in which it is used:

(1) If uttered by a farmer during the feeding time of a pig, then the utterance means literally: "The animal called a pig is ready to eat."
(2) If uttered by a cook who is announcing the fact that he or she has finished cooking pork meat, then the utterance has a different meaning: "The cooked pig is ready for people to eat."
(3) If uttered critically by a person to describe someone who appears to be gluttonous and to have a ravenous appetite, then the utterance has metaphorical meaning: "The person who appears to have the manners and appetite of a pig is ready to eat."

As work on communicative competence has shown since the 1970s, it is virtually impossible to separate purely linguistic competence (knowledge of phonology, morphology, syntax, and semantics) from knowledge of how to make words and sentences bear meanings in specific utterances. In effect, linguistic word meanings and the meanings of the utterances that we construct with words are governed by contextual factors, which dictate what meanings are relevant, how ambiguities can be resolved, how the general backdrop of activities and objectives in communication make words hang together cohesively, and how implicit meanings can be inserted or extracted from a speech event.

In his classic study of utterances (See Chapter 1, § 4.1), Dell Hymes (1971) identified eight basic contextual variables that shape a speech event. He cleverly named each variable so that its initial letter would be a letter in the word *speaking*:

S	= *setting and scene*: the time, place, and psychological setting
P	= *participants*: the speaker, listener, audience involved in a speech act
E	= *ends*: the desired or expected outcome
A	= *act sequence*: how form and content are delivered.
K	= *key*: the mood or spirit (serious, ironic, jocular, etc.) of the speech act
I	= *instrumentalities*: the dialect or linguistic variety used by the speech community
N	= *norms*: conventions or expectations about volume, tone, rate of delivery, etc.
G	= *genres*: different types of performance (joke, formal speech, sermon, etc.)

Figure 7. Hymes' contextual variables

These specify rather accurately what context is all about. As can be seen, it constrains linguistic meaning by linking it with psychological, cultural, and social factors. For instance, we have already seen how knowledge of (G) genre conventions helps identify the general purpose and the ends (E) of an utterance in various examples above and in the previous chapter. In turn, the knowledge of the general ends (E) of the utterance will act as a powerful means for restricting the addressee's interpretation of the message.

8.1. Common Ground

To grasp how context affects the outcome of an utterance, it is relevant to use the notion of *common ground* as developed in pragmatics (Stalnaker 1973, 2002, Clark 1996, Greco 2003). This refers to the fact that a successful conversation involves implicit knowledge of the relevant values and beliefs that are shared, or assumed to be shared, by the participants. No conversation can start from scratch, so to speak, as it would, hypothetically, between an extraterrestrial alien and a human. Each speech event revolves around a set of premises and assumptions that speakers take for granted. This set forms the *common ground* of the conversation. Hymes' model above covers most of the common ground features that guide utterance construction and interpretation.

For instance, when the conversation is face-to-face, the physical environment, the setting, and scene (S) is part of the common ground:

(1)   Could you open the window, please?

This utterance can only be understood as literal (denotative) by an addressee, only if there really is a window in the physical context that is recognizable as such to both interlocutors. Opening a window presupposes that some event in the interaction field (humidity and heat) is the stimulus for the utterance. The social context of the interaction, called the *interaction field* (Rigotti and Rocci 2006b), is also assumed to be part of the common ground. For instance, someone in a movie theatre line-up might ask someone else in the same line-up the following question:

(2)   At what time does it start?

The interlocutor would easily understand that the *it* referred to the movie because the interaction field—the line-up—is part of the common ground. Although interaction fields may appear to be self-evident, this is not necessarily so in IC. Someone who is accustomed to buying consumer goods in a supermarket may hesitate in interpreting the discourse strategies of merchants in a North-African *souk* because of his or her lack of familiarity with that commercial interaction field.

Often interaction fields are associated with relevant *interaction schemes* (Rigotti and Rocci 2006b) that provide a ready-made recipe for interaction. Simple interaction schemes that we use in routine situations may take the form of a *script*. Scripts are part of the cultural common ground of human communities and enable people within these communities to interact smoothly in a variety of social situations. They are a bit like the "autopilot" of human interaction. A classic example of scripted social event is dining at a restaurant:

Table 8. The restaurant script

(1) Enter	(7) Wait for the meal
(2) Greet waiter	(8) Eat the meal
(3) Follow waiter to table	(9) Ask for the bill
(4) Sit down	(10) Wait for the bill
(5) Read menu	(11) Pay the bill
(6) Order meal	(12) Leave.

There is an inverse relationship between routines and intercultural communication. Shared knowledge of routine procedures like the *restaurant script* is an important part of the cultural common ground. What typically happens in intercultural settings, is that routine communication becomes de-routinized. Tasting the typical dishes of a foreign culture is a basic form of intercultural encounter and at the same time an important tourist attraction. It does not come however without its share of risks of cognitive and social stress and its possibilities for misunderstanding. Important elements in the restaurant script may vary dramatically in different cultures and this may cause confusion and stress in the tourist. Cohen and Avieli (2004: 764) consider the case of Western tourists in East Asian countries:

> It is a common practice in China, Hong Kong, Taiwan, Vietnam, and other countries to display in restaurants live animals intended for cooking. Fish, shrimps, and eels are kept in water tanks, while several kinds of birds, reptiles and mammals (such as chicken, quails, snakes, rabbits, bamboo-rats, and even cats and dogs) are kept in cages at the entrance of restaurants. The display is intended to demonstrate variety, quality, and freshness. The local clients point to the creature of choice, which is promptly killed, cleaned, and cooked to order (indeed, game restaurants in the West might display the catch for similar reasons, yet the killing is never done in front of the diners).

Differences in the non-linguistic aspects of the script, combined with the lack of knowledge of the language may prevent the tourists from identifying the local dishes and ordering them, even in cases where the tourists have already had contact with some version of the local cuisine in "ethnic" restaurants in their home countries. Many travelers are familiar with the saddening experience of giving up – out of frustration and ignorance – the search for a typical restaurant to end up in a fast-food restaurant belonging to some globalized franchise which beaconed reassuringly with its glaring colors in the midst of the foreign city. Interestingly, as in intercultural encounters the reliance on routines is put into question, both the argumentative aspects of communication (Cf. Chapter 5) and the relational dimension (Cf. Chapter 3, § 6) come to the fore.

As a conversation unfolds, each new utterance within it makes sense only if it "updates" the common ground, so to speak, with new information. At the same time, each utterance *presupposes* that certain kinds of information are already present in the common ground. The hearer thus needs to know what the information is about, and more generally how it relates to previous information. Now, consider the following utterance:

(3)   The man with the red tie has gone away.

In order to make sense of (3), an interlocutor must be able to relate *the man with the red tie* with a person who had been present in the common ground. Otherwise, the new bit of information (*has gone away*) would not make any sense in terms of updating the common ground.

The common ground also makes it possible to decipher the function of various devices in utterance construction that are designed to keep the conversation flowing smoothly with minimal effort and time—in line with the economizing principle (Chapter 1, § 3.1). Consider the following two utterances, which relate the same information, but in different ways:

(4)   Debbie went to the mall yesterday. Debbie ran into a friend at the mall. Debbie and the friend greeted each other. Debbie hadn't seen the friend in a while.
(5)   Debbie went to the mall yesterday. She ran into a friend there. They greeted each other. She hadn't seen her friend in a while.

Version (4) appears stilted and odd to a native-speaker of English, even though each sentence in it is well-formed. Version (5) reads more like ordinary conversation because in English, as in other languages, the repetition of elements already in the common ground is discouraged in normal conversational style. For this reason, the language makes available several devices that allow for the same information to be conveyed without the repetition. Devices that refer back to some word or syntactic category are called anaphoric. In the second utterance above, *she* refers back to *Debbie*, *there* to *the mall*, and *they* to *Debbie* and the *friend*. Anaphora can thus be seen to be a "repetition-eliminating" strategy, at the same time that it preserves utterance meaning. Cataphora is the opposite of anaphora. It is the strategy of anticipating some word or syntactic category in an utterance. The pronoun *she* below has a cataphoric function, anticipating the argument *Debbie*.

(6)   While she was at the mall yesterday, Debbie ran into a friend.

Dialogue between interlocutors of different languages is often characterized by a lack of such devices. Although this is not as injurious to intercultural comprehension as is, for example, an infelicitous exit strategy or an unintentionally insulting connotative statement, it can lead potentially to a negative perception of the non-native interlocutor as someone who is tedious and tiresome, even if this is not the case.

When interlocutors cannot be sure of what the common ground is, they sometimes employ *grounding strategies*, as they can be called, to elicit appropriate information (Clark 1996: 221-252). Consider a variant of the conversation above. In this case, more than one movie is being shown at the theater:

A: At what time does it start?
B: Which one?
A: The one about pirates.
B: I think at 7:30.
A: Thanks.

B's response is designed to narrow the field of meaning so as to be able to respond appropriately. Although this example appears to be a rather trivial one, it is not. If there were no other movie, B's response would lead to a vastly different set of interpretations, ranging from the ironic to the nonsensical.

Clark (1996: 100) distinguishes between two main types of common ground—the personal and the communal. The former is the common ground that interlocutors who know each other share; the latter is the background information that is assumed to be possessed by those living in the same community. Family members, for example, possess a large array of shared recollections, in-jokes, and the like. An outsider participating in a family conversation will often be struck by the ability of certain words or phrases to evoke laughter or some other reaction, given that such an item would fail to evoke such reactions in other non-personal contexts. Medical doctors, on the other hand, belong to a specific community in which a common medical jargon makes up a large part of their communal common ground in speech interactions. This can be called "inside information." In a conversation between a patient and a medical doctor, the patient assumes that the doctor knows a lot about diseases, about cures, and so on. However, since the patient does not share the same common ground, he or she stands "outside" the common ground shared by doctors. Thus, it is unlikely that their conversation will unfold in the same way as it would among doctors. This distinction is important in IC settings where a large share of the assumed common ground is composed of outside information. For instance, an American student (A) might assume, rightly or wrongly, that a fellow student from Kenya (B) knows the name of the current president of Kenya, knows how to speak Swahili, and maybe also that B knows a good deal about Kenyan animals such as the lion or the giraffe. All these presuppositions constitute bits of outside information for A, who assumes that they are instead part of the inside information known by a Kenyan such as B.

8.2. Contextualization

The process of constraining the meanings inherent in the common ground can be called, simply, *contextualization* (Rigotti and Rocci 2006c). Contextualization can occur within the language or outside of it. This former is known as *collocation*—it is what allows speakers to recognize idioms as idioms, rather than nonsensical utterances. For instance in deciphering the meaning of "He let the cat out of the bag," (See above § 4.2), a native speaker of English would not interpret the noun *cat* as an autonomous predicate to be combined compositionally with the rest of the sentence, but rather as part of an idiomatic formula. This is because connotative uses of words, as we have seen, are specific to a semantic system and are forged within it. However, in the disambiguation of homonyms, the external context is what allows us to decipher utterance meaning. If someone were to use the phrase *pig* during a conversation in the context of a farm, then the meaning of the word as a farm animal would come into focus. However, in the context of a conversation about rude people, this meaning would be suppressed and the metaphorical-connotative one presupposed by the conceptual metaphor [people are animals] would materialize instead.

As a salient example of how contextualization works, consider the following utterance (from Sperber and Wilson 1986: 190):

(1)　Peter's bat is too gray

As we have seen, homonyms such as *bat*, which can refer to either a piece of baseball equipment or a particular type of mammal, are disambiguated in context. If we are speaking about baseball, and we have previously identified *Peter* in our common ground, the utterance becomes constrained as to its meaning, but it nevertheless contains two underdefined constituents that need to be related to each other in context—the genitive ending *'s* and the adverb *too*. The former does not provide information about the relation of the bat to Peter—Does Peter own the bat? Did he choose it? Similarly, with respect to the adverb *too*, one can ask: Why is it too gray? Too gray *for what*? The utterance must thus be contextualized further. This is done by providing further information about Peter, the bat, and so on.

Sometimes the context intervenes not to provide the missing elements but to enrich the results of compositionality, by subtly reciprocally adapting the predicate and the argument involved. Consider for instance a basically compositional combination like *red car*. In order to fully understand it is necessary to enrich the results of compositionality (something is a car and is red) with our knowledge of the world: a red car is not red everywhere: the tires, the steering wheel are probably of another color. Sometimes this reciprocal adaptation of predicate and argument becomes more evident, as in the following examples taken from Langacker (1990):

(2)　She heard the piano.
(3)　I'm in the phone book.

In order to make the argument *piano* fit the argument slot (x_2) of the predicate *to hear* in (2), one must know that the utterance refers to the *sound* that a piano makes when played and not to the *piano* itself as a solid body. Similarly, in (3) one must know that a phone book contains not the actual body of a person but a person's name, phone number, and address.

Examples (2) and (3) are metonymic utterances, whereby a part of something is used to represent something else or a whole. In fact, we have already encountered a similar process of reciprocal adaptation between predicate and argument when we have presented the relation between topic and vehicle in the interpretation of metaphorical utterances (§ 5.4).

8.3. Conversational inferences and non-verbal cues

The role of context is not limited to enriching the meaning of utterances. Contextual information available in the common ground is also combined with the meaning of the utterance – what is said – in order to work out the meanings that speakers convey implicitly in a verbal interaction – what is implicated. This form of reasoning is called *conversational inference* and plays a critical role in IC (Rocci 2006, Moeschler 2004). This reading between the lines is also of fundamental importance to understand how utterances hang together in a discourse to form broader units of meaning.

The distinction between *saying* and *implicating* was introduced by Herbert Grice, in his famous 1967 Williams James Lecture on "Logic an Conversation" at Harvard University. Grice called this reasoning *conversational implicature*. He illustrated it as follows (Grice 1991: 306):

A: How is John getting on his new job at the bank?
B: Oh, quite well I think; he likes his colleagues, and he hasn't been in prison yet.

B's answer appears to contain an irrelevant remark about John having not been in prison yet. Speaker A, however, likely infers that B was implying something more, such as, for instance, that John "is the sort of person likely to yield to the temptation provided by his occupation" (Grice 1991: 306). How does A arrive at this (tentative) conclusion implied by B's utterance? How, more specifically, does the conversational implicature occur? Grice proposes that it occurs through a cooperation on the part of the interlocutors reflecting a "common purpose, or set of purposes" upholding the raison d'être of the conversation—that is, the conversational participants want to be cooperative, contributing meaningfully to the purpose of the exchange. So, A extracts from B's utterance that B wanted to communicate more than what he actually said. It is this pattern if inferential reasoning that characterizes utterance meaning and which, obviously, can be a source of misunderstanding in intercultural conversations.

Now, consider the following exchange:

A: I wonder if she will help him?
B: She's his mother.

In order to understand what B's answer implies, A needs to infer that it is based on the principle that "A mother will always help her children." From this, A can draw the conclusion that the mother alluded to in the conversation will help the *him* spoken about.

The common ground plays a fundamental role as the source of the premises of our conversational inferences. The more the common ground between the interlocutors is restricted or dubious, the more their conversational inferences will be likely to go wrong. This is a fundamental point to bear in mind when addressing intercultural misunderstanding. In Chapter 5, we will consider the importance of this aspect of the common ground in argumentative interactions.

Conversational inference is clearly dependent on knowledge of the *activity type* underlying the conversation (Levinson 1979; Rigotti and Rocci 2006b). Without a notion of the kind of activity in which the conversation takes place, and, in particular, of its purpose – the E variable in Hymes' SPEAKING model of context – the very notion of conversational cooperation becomes rather hollow. Being cooperative in a relaxed chat among friends is not the same as being cooperative in a focused problem-solving discussion in a corporate meeting. Scollon and Scollon (2001: 28-32) provide an insightful example of the role of the activity type in conversational inference. During a board meeting in a company, a member refers to a decision that had been taken at the previous board meeting. The chairwoman turns to the secretary of the meeting, and the following dialogue ensues:

Chairwoman: Do you have the minutes?
Secretary: Yes, here they are. I think 2.4.3 is what you will need.

The secretary interprets the question of the chairwoman as a request to consult the minutes of the previous meeting and to locate the relevant text. In her effort to cooperate, the secretary goes well beyond what the chairwoman said in her utterance. The secretary does this because she knows her role in the context of the board meeting activity, which she associates with the member's previous utterance. The goals of the meeting and the secretary's role in the meeting activity are components of the activity type. These provide guidance to the cooperative efforts of the interpreter of the utterance. As Scollon and Scollon (2001: 32) emphasize: "One major aspect of becoming educated as a professional communicator is learning the very specialized contexts of business and other professional work environments."

The meaning of a conversation can also be inferred from contextualized non-verbal cues. Take, for instance, the gestures used during speech. Some can have quite specific meanings, such as those for saying good-bye or for asking someone to approach (Morris 1979). Others unconsciously reinforce the meanings in utterances. The latter have been designated *gesticulants* by David McNeill (1992). After videotaping a large sample of people as they spoke, McNeill found that the gesticulants that accompany speech exhibit imagery that portrays what the speaker is thinking about. He classified these into five main categories. First, there are iconic gesticulants, which, as their name suggests, bear a close resemblance to the referent or referential domain of an utterance: for example, when describing a scene from a story in which a character bends a tree back to the ground, a speaker observed by McNeill appeared to grip something and pull it back. His gesture was, in effect, a manual depiction of the action talked about, revealing both his memory image and his point of view (he could have taken the part of the tree instead). Second, there are metaphorical gesticulants. These are also pictorial, but their content is abstract, rather than purely iconic. For example, McNeill observed a male speaker announcing that what he had just seen was a cartoon, simultaneously raising up his hands as if offering his listener a kind of object. He was obviously not referring to the cartoon itself, but to the genre of the cartoon. His gesture represented this genre as if it were an object, placing it into an act of offering to the listener. This type of gesticulant typically accompanies utterances that contain metaphorical expressions such as *presenting an idea, putting forth an idea, offering advice*, and so on. Third, there are *beat* gesticulants. These resemble the beating of musical tempo. The speaker's hand moves along with the rhythmic pulsation of speech, in the form of a simple flick of the hand or fingers up and down, or back and forth. Beats basically mark the introduction of new characters and themes in an utterance. Fourth, there are *cohesive* gesticulants. These serve to show how separate parts of an utterance are supposed to hold together. Beats emphasize sequentiality, cohesives globality. Cohesives can take iconic, metaphorical, or beat form. They unfold through a repetition of the same gesticulant. It is the repetition itself that is meant to convey cohesiveness. Fifth, there are *deictic* gesticulants. Deixis is the term used in linguistics to designate signs referring to some form of indication, location, etc. *(here, there, up, right,* etc.). Deictic gesticulants are aimed not at an existing physical place, but at an abstract concept that had occurred earlier in the conversation. These reveal that we perceive concepts as having a physical location in space.

McNeill's work gives us a good idea of how the gestural mode of representation intersects with the vocal one in normal conversations. Gestural cues are also used in utterance to relay emotional meaning (for example, the typical hand movements and facial expressions that accompany happiness, surprise, fear, anger, sadness, contempt, disgust, etc.); to help monitor, maintain, or control the speech of someone else (as, for example, the hand movements indicating *Keep going, Slow down, What else happened?* etc.); and to convey some need or mental state (for instance, scratching one's head when puzzled, rubbing one's forehead when worried, etc.).

It is interesting to note that linguists have discovered languages where the two modalities—gesture and vocal speech—are complementary codes. One of the best-known examples is the gesture language developed by the Plains peoples of North America as a means of communication between tribes with different vocal languages. For example, the sign for a white person is made by drawing the fingers across the forehead, indicating a hat. The sensation of cold is indicated by a shivering motion of the hands in front of the body; and the same sign is used for winter and for year, because the Plains peoples count years in terms of winters. Slowly turning the hand, relaxed at the wrist, means vacillation, doubt, or possibility; a modification of this sign, with quicker movement, is the question sign. This sign language is so elaborate that a detailed conversation is possible using the gestures alone (Mallery 1972).

Chapter 3
Communication

> *The great enemy of clear language is insincerity. When there is a gap between one's real and one's declared aims, one turns as it were instinctively to long words and exhausted idioms, like a cutlefish squirting out ink.*
>
> George Orwell (1903–1955)

1. Introductory remarks

In the previous two chapters, we introduced and dealt specifically with those areas of general linguistics and pragmatics that, we believe, are of direct relevance to the study of IC and, thus, to be included as part of the overall purview and scope of GL. Now, since the study of IC also involves the study of communication in both its verbal and nonverbal dimensions, it is necessary to look somewhat beyond linguistics proper, so as to bring into the domain of GL the kinds of notions and research paradigms found in the broader domain of communication sciences that are relevant to the investigation of IC.

In general terms, communication is the process of exchanging messages. As such it is not unique to the human species. Research has shown how remarkably rich and varied animal communication systems are. Scientists have recorded and identified, for instance, birdcalls for courting, mating, hunger, food bearing, territoriality, warning, and distress. Whales and dolphins have been found to have the ability to communicate over long distances underwater and to have a vast array of signals at their disposal. However, human communication is unique in the fact that it is based on and shaped by the human *language faculty*, a species-specific ability which does not have equivalents in the animal realm, except perhaps, in a very limited fashion, in the great apes such as the gorilla and the chimpanzee (Foley 1997). There are several properties that set human language apart from animal communication. Needless to say, we cannot possibly go into any depth or detail here. We will just mention two of them, which are particularly important. The first feature is the *symbolic* nature of words (Deacon 1997). Words refer to aspects of the world on the basis of an arbitrary social convention holding within a cultural group. In an English speaking community, for instance, the convention holds that uttered tokens of the symbol *cat* refer to instances of a particular class of experiences involving a small feline animal. It has been argued that the emergence of conventions marks at the same time the beginnings of language and "social reality" (Searle 1995). The second property is twofold and is represented by the "syntax principle" – allowing us to combine signs recursively within hierarchical structures of potentially indefinite complexity – coupled with its semantic correlate, the "compositionality principle" – allowing us to combine predicates (modes of being) and arguments (entities) to represent possible states of affairs, fragments of a conceivable world.

Jointly with symbolism, compositionality creates a powerful means of representation that frees human communication from specific stimulus-situations. Human communication is not limited to providing signals conveying a definite pragmatic message within a specific stimulus-situation (e.g. the mating call of a bird or mammal). It allows us to represent compositionally all sorts of possible states of affairs that are not bound to the here and now of the utterance situation: information about the world, narratives of what happened in the past, detailed action plans, hypotheses and forecasts on what might happen.

The investigation of animal communication falls under the rubric of *ethology*. The study of human communication falls instead under the rubric of *communication sciences*. The goal of this chapter is to provide a schematic overview of the main features of human communication, highlighting primarily those aspects that are particularly relevant to GL.

2. Human communication

At a purely biological level, a message can be received successfully (that is, recognized as a message) by another species only if it possesses the same kind of sensory modality used by the transmitting species. Of these, the tactile modality is the one that seems to cut across human and many animal sensory systems. There is no doubt that a household cat or dog and a human enter into a rudimentary form of tactile communication on a daily basis. Sharing the same living space, and being codependent on each other for affective exchanges, they do indeed transmit their feeling-states to each other through an exchange of body signals and especially by means of touch. However, there is no way for humans to be sure that cats or dogs have the ability to understand the broader range of feeling-states implied by tactile words such as *embrace, guide, hold, tickle*, etc. Clearly, interspecies communication is realizable, but only in a restricted sense. It can occur in some modalities, partially or totally, according to species. If the sensory systems of the two species are vastly different, however, then any message exchange is likely to be impossible.

As we have said, the main distinguishing features of human communication are associated with language. Although the voice is the main medium through which linguistic messages are transmitted, humans have devised other media to extend the range of the voice and the ear. Early societies developed simple tools, such as drums, fire and smoke signals, and lantern beacons, so that they could be seen or heard over longer distances. Messages were also attached to the legs of carrier pigeons trained to navigate their way to a destination and back home. In later societies, so-called "semaphore" systems of flags or flashing lights were employed to send messages over relatively short but difficult-to-cross distances, such as from hilltop to hilltop, or from one ship to another at sea. Marshall McLuhan (1951, 1962, 1964) claimed that the type of technology developed to record and transmit messages determined how people processed and remembered them. Therefore, any major change in how information is transmitted brings about a concomitant paradigm shift in cultural systems. Ancient cuneiform writing, impressed indelibly into clay tablets, allowed the Sumerians to develop a great civilization; papyrus and hieroglyphics transformed Egyptian society into an advanced culture; the alphabet spurred the ancient Greeks on to extraordinary advances in science, technology, and the arts; the alphabet also made it possible for the Romans to develop an effective system of government; the printing press facilitated the dissemination of knowledge broadly and widely, paving the way for the European Renaissance, the Protestant Reformation, and the Enlightenment; radio, movies, and television brought about the rise of a global village in the twentieth century; and the Internet and the World Wide Web ensconced this village solidly into human life as the twentieth century came to a close.

The term *information* invariably comes up in any discussion of communication, and thus requires some commentary here. It is defined as the flow of data that, in human communication, becomes meaningful when it is related to some context and code. Computers also process data, but without any understanding of what the data represents. Information is sometimes measured in terms of the probability structure of the signals used to communicate it. A ringing alarm signal carries more information than one that is silent, because the latter is the "expected state" of the alarm system and the former its "alerting state." The one who developed the mathematical aspects of information theory was the American telecommunications engineer Claude Shannon (1916-2001). He showed, essentially, that the information contained in a signal is inversely proportional to its probability. The more probable a signal, the less information "load" it carries with it; the less likely, the more informative (Shannon 1948).

Shannon devised his model in order to improve the efficiency of telecommunications systems. It essentially depicts information transfer as a unidirectional process, from a source to a receiver, that is dependent on probability factors—that is, on the degree to which a message is to be expected or not in a given situation. It is called the *bull's-eye model* because a sender is defined as someone or something aiming a message at a receiver as if he, she, or it were in a bull's-eye target range:

Figure 8. The bull's-eye model of communication.

Shannon also introduced several key terms into the general study of communication: channel, noise, redundancy, and feedback. *Channel* is the physical system carrying the transmitted signal. Vocally-produced sound waves, for instance, can be transmitted through the air or through an electronic channel (for example, the radio or the Internet). The term *noise* refers to some interfering element (physical or psychological) in the channel that distorts or partially effaces the information contained in a message. In radio and telephone transmissions, noise is equivalent to static; in vocal speech transmissions, it can vary from any interfering exterior sound (physical noise) to the speaker's lapses of memory (psychological noise). Noise is why communication systems have *redundancy* features built into them. These enhance the prospect of decoding a message even if noise is present. For instance, in verbal communication the high predictability of certain words in many utterances (*Roses are red, violets are...*) and the patterned repetition of elements (*Yes, yes, I'll do it; yes, I will*) are redundant features that greatly increase the likelihood that a verbal message will get decoded successfully. Finally, Shannon used the term *feedback* to refer to the fact that senders have the capacity to monitor the messages they transmit and thus to modify them to enhance their decodability. Feedback in human verbal communication includes, for instance, the physical reactions observable in receivers (facial expressions, bodily movements, etc.) that indicate the effect that a message is having as it is being communicated.

It is obvious that speakers of different languages will perceive noise and feedback differently, since each language has different devices for counteracting noise. Certainly, lack of familiarity with redundancy features and how to use them in counteracting noise is something that affects the course of communicative exchanges in intercultural contexts. Non-verbal feedback conventional forms (Kirch 1979) also vary subtly across cultures: according to culture and social context nodding with one's head can be interpreted as "Go on, I'm listening" or alternatively as "Yes, I agree with you". In certain cultures the same function is realized through a different movement of the head: in Bulgaria and in parts of India people shake their head sideways to say "Yes", a gesture that would rather convey "No, I disagree" to a North American observer. According to different cultures and social settings, smiling to the interlocutor may signal benevolence, amusement, mockery, embarrassment or just mere default politeness. Shannon's model is thus useful in providing GL with a basic terminology for describing some general aspects of IC, but it tells us little about how culture-specific meanings shape and ultimately determine the outcome of human communication events. Nevertheless, key concepts such as noise and redundancy will inform some of the discussion in this and subsequent chapters, especially when they surface as relevant to the analysis of breakdowns in IC.

2.1. Communication and interaction

In addition to *information*, there are two other terms that require some attention here—*communication* itself and *interaction*.

The word *communication* derives originally from two Latin morphemes the noun *munus* and the prefix *con-*, which means "together, jointly". *Munus* had an interesting double meaning: it could mean a "free gift" as well as a "a task to be accomplished" (Rigotti and Cigada 2004: 1-3). The underlying idea seems to be that with every gift or honor comes a responsibility, an obligation or commitment. *Communicatio* originally referred to an exchange of *munera*, that is, of things that were perceived to be both gifts and tasks. Just as a *gift* implies a *task* to be accomplished, so too each communicative event implies a set of tasks or commitments on the part of the interlocutors. Searle (2001: 147) explains the pivotal role of commitments in speech acts as follows:

> Just about every speech act involves a commitment of some kind or other. The famous examples are speech acts like promising, where the speaker is committed to carrying out a future course of action, but asserting commits the speaker to the truth of the proposition asserted, and orders commit the speaker to the belief that the person to whom he or she gives the order is able to do it, to the desire that he or she should do it, and to permitting the hearer to do it. In short, what people have thought of as the distinctive element of promising, actually pervades just about all speech acts.

Thus, it would seem that the term communication was forged, originally, as a concept attempting to capture the fact that human verbal interaction involves an exchange of values and a commitment to that exchange. This etymological analysis would explain why conduit metaphors (Reddy 1976) exist virtually across languages in discourse related to communication. In English, for example, the following expressions with the words *give* and *get* bear this out:

(1) The lecturer *gave* his audience many interesting ideas to think about.
(2) I didn't *get* anything from our conversation.
(3) He *gave* me his word.
(4) Do you *get* what I am saying?

In effect, such statements are linguistic instantiations of the conceptual metaphor [communicating is giving and receiving] or, more simply, [communication is exchange]. The very fact that communication and exchange are linked conceptually indicates that they implicate each other unconsciously. Communication itself may, in fact, have come about in the human species to ensure that exchanges took place on a regular basis in early cultures—exchanges designed to guarantee survival, continuity, cooperation, friendship, and so on. If all this is indeed true, then the most problematic aspect of any IC interaction inheres in the risk of getting an unconscious impression from the interaction that the "gifts offered" by an interlocutor are the wrong ones at best, or dangerous ones at worst. In a phrase, communication seems, psychologically, to involve a sense of giving in return for something received and, vice versa, of receiving in return for something given (even if the whole exchange is an imaginary or hypothetical one). When this sense is lacking, the communicative event is fraught with difficulties that may lead to disagreement or even conflict.

As we will see, we take *interaction* to mean quite literally an exchange of actions that unfolds between people. The commercial transaction, the exchange of goods represents perhaps the clearest prototype of an interaction. On the other hand, interaction is also used in a slightly different way almost as a synonym for communication. We would rather say that interaction is a form of behavior that is dependent primarily on a successful communicative exchange – intended both as an exchange of information and as an exchange of commitments. Any further exchange of material or symbolic goods among humans is impossible if there is no such a baseline communicative exchange.

This fundamental principle has, actually, been recorded in different forms from the beginning of time. For example, it is found in the Biblical story of the Tower of Babel, which is worthwhile repeating here, since it shows how crucial ancient peoples thought this principle was for understanding the basis of human difference and of the human diasporas:

> Now the whole Earth used the same language and the same words. And it came about as they journeyed east, that they found a plain in the land of Shinar and settled there. And they said to one another, "Come, let us make bricks and burn them thoroughly." And they used brick for stone, and they used tar for mortar. And they said, "Come, let us build for ourselves a city, and a tower whose top will reach into heaven, and let us make for ourselves a name; lest we be scattered abroad over the face of the whole earth." And the Lord came down to see the city and the tower which the sons of men had built. And the Lord said, "Behold, they are one people, and they all have the same language." And this is what they began to do, and now nothing which they propose to do will be impossible for them. "Come, let Us go down and there confuse their language, that they may not understand one another's speech". So the Lord scattered them abroad from there over the face of the whole earth; and they stopped building the city. Therefore its name was called Babel, because there the Lord confused the language of the whole earth; and from there the Lord scattered them abroad over the face of the whole earth. (*Genesis*, 11: 1-9)

This story enfolds two important philosophical subtexts. First, it shows that no human interaction or cooperation is possible without communication. Where communication is clogged, the common human enterprise is blocked. Thus, we are reminded of the essential relation between communication and human interaction: no interaction can succeed if its participants do not communicate. Second, the story tells us that differences among people are mirrored in linguistic differences. This is humanity's plight (for better or for worse). As a corollary, therefore, it is obvious that interactions between individuals of different languages and different cultural backgrounds will, by their very nature, be problematic ones.

In a sense, the global village is a modern-day Babel. Diversity in linguistic background is the norm, not the exception, in this village. The study of communication and interaction in the global village must thus start by identifying not the sources of the diversity, but the common platform on which human interaction unfolds. The sources of diversity are best understood by comparing them to the commonalities shared by people in communicative behavior. One part of the shared platform is made up of the various sensory modes people have at their disposal for exchanging messages. Human communication is, needless to say, multimodal, that is it can unfold through different sensory modes, each of which can reinforce the flow of communication, or replace some other mode within it. Below is a basic typology of the communicative modes:

Table 9. Communicative modes

Sensory Mode	Features
Auditory-vocal	This mode characterizes speech, vocal signaling, some symptoms (for example, coughing and snoring), musical effects (for example, whistling), and voice modulation (to communicate identity and feeling-states).
Visual	This mode characterizes sign languages, writing, and of course visual representation (drawing, sculpting, etc.).
Tactile	This mode characterizes communication by means of touch (handshaking, hugging, etc.).
Olfactory	This mode characterizes communication by means of smell (using perfumes, colognes, etc.)
Gustatory	This mode characterizes communication by means of taste (food, drinks, etc.).

Humans across the world have the instinctive ability to use all sensory modes to communicate, in part, jointly, or in exclusivity: the auditory-vocal mode is used in speech, the visual one in writing, the tactile one in such interactions as handshaking, the olfactory one in the use of perfumes, the gustatory one in food tastes, and so on. Communication between people of different cultural backgrounds will thus probably occur in some modes, but not in all, because each mode plays a different role in different cultures. Humans also use different media to communicate and interact. There are three main kinds of media:

Table 10. Communication media

Medium	Examples
Natural	the voice (speech), the face (expressions), and the body (gesture, posture, etc.)
Artifactual	books, paintings, sculptures, letters, etc.;
Mechanical	telephones, radios, television sets, computers, videos, etc.

A verbal message can be delivered through a natural (body) medium, involving articulation of the vocal organs, gesture, etc. Or else it can be transmitted by means of markings on a piece of paper or on a computer screen—that is, through the artifactual medium of writing. Finally, it can be converted into radio or television signals for mechanical (electromagnetic) transmission.

Of all the mechanical media, the digital one has become dominant today, given the instantaneity and reach that such a medium allows. Through websites, e-mails, text messages, and the like, communication in the "Digital Galaxy" is fast becoming the main form of intercultural interaction. And because it involves the transmission of messages in as rapid a fashion as possible, the risk of such messages being misunderstood by receivers of different backgrounds is increasing. In a face-to-face interaction, the body's accompanying modes often allow for successful message flow by supporting the content of the exchange through a series of complementary signals, such as gestures. In digital communications this option is often lacking.

2.2. Communication as joint action

If human interaction depends on communication, then communication itself involves actions of various sorts. In order to understand the notion of *communicative action*, it is necessary to consider the structure of human actions and their relationship to the world. The notion of *world* and of its relation to language constitutes a question that intrigued the Austrian-British philosopher Ludwig Wittgenstein (1889-1951) throughout the evolution of his philosophical reflection, and which he studied in an in-depth way for the first time in his *Tractatus Logico-philosophicus* (1921). Wittgenstein argued in the *Tractatus* that language is composed of complex propositions that can be analyzed into less complex propositions until one arrives at simple or elementary propositions. Correspondingly, the world is composed of complex facts that can be analyzed into less complex facts until one arrives at simple, or atomic, facts.

Wittgenstein's notion of world, as it is defined in the first proposition of his *Tractatus* ("The world is everything that is the case."), as a matter of fact, is not sufficient to fully account for human actions: human beings act in order to bring about a state of affairs that does not exist – is not the case – at the moment of the performance of an action. For instance, if Mary decides to prepare a cup of coffee, it's precisely because that cup of coffee is not there. If she had a cup of steaming coffee in front of her, emanating its inviting aroma, there would be no need of performing that action. Thus, interestingly, the cognitive representation of human action entails the reference to a plurality of worlds, relating to desires, requirements, future possible developments, opportunities and risks, and so on.

Therefore discourses refer to the world in which the discourse participants live as well as to a host of other "worlds", which can relate in a number of ways with the participants' world. This phenomenon relies on the very basic human cognitive ability of thinking that *things might be otherwise*, that is thinking of *alternatives*: states of affairs other than what is the case. The logico-philosophical tradition developed the theoretical notion of *possible worlds* to deal with reasoning about alternatives (Rocci 2009). Worlds are populated by *states of affairs*. These subsume *events* which, in turn, subsume *actions*. The latter, on their part, subsume *communicative actions* (See Figure 9).

States of affairs include both static states (such as *the table is black*) and dynamic ones (such as *this table has been moved*). Dynamic states are divided into *events* (states that happen) and *actions* (things that are done), although it is often difficult to determine if something is an event or action. For instance, is *letting the roast burn in the oven* an action or an event? In one way, it is an event since it is not intentionally performed; on the other hand, it might be construed as an action, because whoever let the roast burn did not invest enough activity into monitoring the roasting event.

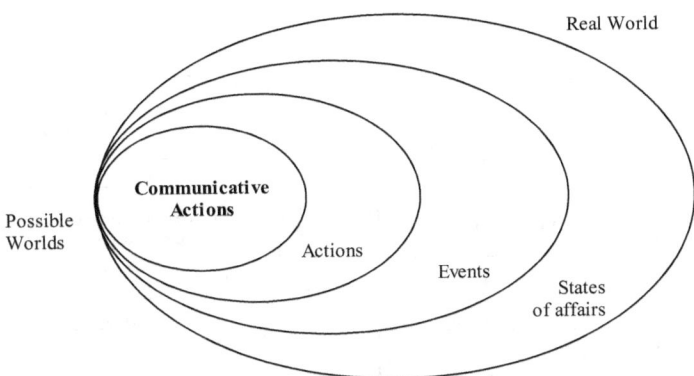

Figure 9. Communicative actions, actions, events and states of affairs

Actions constitute a category of events whereby an individual or group pursues a goal to bring about a desired state of affairs. Communication is a type of action, which might be called simply *joint action* (Cf. Clark 1996). Thus in order to approach intercultural communication as a type of joint action, it is necessary to take an overall look at the structure of actions themselves.

3. Action and its representation in language

The foregoing discussion implies that communicative exchanges involve joint actions performed by two (or more) agents (A, B, etc.). So, in the study of IC it is useful, first and foremost, to have a rudimentary model of what an agent aims to accomplish by carrying out an action. Figure 10 below is a synthetic representation of one such model (Cf. Rigotti 2005b, Greco Morasso 2008).

The model in Figure 10 shows that agent A acts in order to modify the actual world so as to achieve a new state of affairs in line with his or her desires. A possesses a specific form of understanding of the world, intended here in the widest sense of the word. He or she has a desire and thus imagines a world in which this desire can be realized. These components are "internal;" that is, they occur within the agent. The agent externalizes them when he or she decides to bring about the new state of affairs, activating a causal chain that will potentially or actually make it possible to achieve his or her goal. The events in the causal chain are "external;" that is, they are the effects brought about by the agent's action.

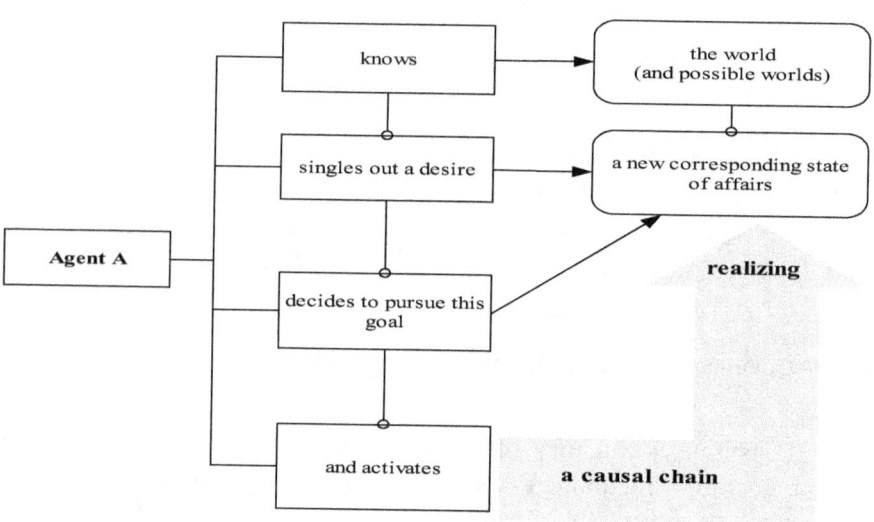

Figure 10. The structure of action (Rigotti 2005b)

As we have said above, communication is a particular kind of action: a joint action. Generally speaking, a joint action can take place when an agent is not able or does not want to pursue his/her own goal him/herself and negotiates with other people their engagement in the causal chain. The simple model presented above can now be used to assess the joint action system used by interacting agents in activating causal chains that make the realization of desires possible. The joint action might unfold as pure cooperation or involve a more or less prominent element of conflict of interests (Greco Morasso 2008), but in either case the outcome (successful or not) is dependent upon the abilities of the agents to communicate their needs and desires effectively.

3.1. Needs and desires

The last statement above implies that needs and desires are the common rationales behind interactions and that language is the vehicle that allows people to satisfy them. For the sake of the present discussion, a *need* can be defined as something required for some reason, and a *desire* as a wish or a longing for something (required or not). Both are forces that guide and shape human interaction. Since these words are often used synonymously in conversation, it is important to consider what sets them apart conceptually.

An initial difference can be seen in the fact that *desire* seems to refer to something more internal and personal than *need* does. For instance, in the sentence "Human beings need food and water to survive," the word *need* implies that external things (*food* and *water*) are required for physical survival. In the sentence *I need some money*, the implication is that money (again an external thing) is required to buy food, to pay off a debt, and so on. However, if one *desires* food or money, there is no implication of survival, but rather a longing, craving, or yearning for them. A second difference is the fact that it is illogical to desire something that is detrimental to one's wellbeing. Normally, one does not say "I desire to take this bitter medicine," but rather "I need to take this bitter medicine." The conceptual link between the two is, nevertheless, unmistakable. It is a fact that each human being needs food in order to live; so, the desire for food is, in a way, even more essential, because if one looses the desire for it, he or she will stop eating, even if he or she knows the dire consequences of such an action. Desire for an action is thus linkable to the notion of *responsibility*. Someone cannot be considered responsible for a state of affairs, an event, an incident, etc. that has occurred independently of his or her will. In fact, one cannot say: "You mean person, you should not be 1.70 meters tall!" or "I think you are wrong, you should not be Russian!"

The concepts of need and desire can also be analyzed in terms of conceptual metaphor theory (Chapter 2, §5.4). The source image schemas utilized in English to produce the two concepts—[container], [up/down], [impediment], [shape], [strength], [weakness], [intensity], [obscurity], [clarity], and [plants]—indicate that they share a common territory, as utterances instantiating the schemas reveal. However, there are several key conceptual differences between the two, as the utterances also show (? = probably invalid utterance):

(1) [the body or mind is a container of needs and desires]
    How many needs do you have (inside)?
    How many desires do you have (inside)?
(2) [needs and desires are entities that go up/down]
    His needs are constantly going up.
    His desires are also going up all the time.
(3) [needs and desires are impediments]
    Her needs are getting in the way.

Her desires are getting in the way.
(4) [needs and desires are pliable objects]
Your needs are distorted.
(?) Your desires are distorted.
(5) [needs and desires are entities having or lacking strength]
(?) She has strong needs.
She has strong desires.
(6) [needs and desires are luminescent or non-luminescent]
You have very clear needs.
You have very clear desires.
(?) You have dark needs.
You have dark desires.
(7) [needs and desires are plants]
His needs are growing.
His desires are growing.

Table 11, below, summarizes which source image schemas the two concepts share (√) and which ones, at least in part, they do not. A similar conceptual analysis of other languages reveals that these two concepts have both overlapping and distinctive meanings. Here are Italian examples that can be used in a comparative light:

(1) [the body or mind is a container of needs and desires]
How many needs do you have?
Quanti bisogni hai?
How many desires do you have?
Quanti desideri hai?
(2) [needs and desires are entities that go up/down]
His needs are constantly going up.
I suoi bisogni stanno sempre andando su.
His desires are also going up all the time.
Anche i suoi desideri stanno andando sempre su.

Table 11. Source image schemas underlying the concepts of need and desire

Image Schema	Need	Desire
[container]	√	√
[up/down]	√	√
[impediment]	√	√
[pliability]	?	√
[strength]	√	?
[luminescence]	√	√
[non-luminescence]	?	√
[plants]	√	√

(3) [needs and desires are impediments]
  Her needs are getting in the way.
  I suoi bisogni costituiscono un ostacolo.
  Her desires are getting in the way.
  I suoi desideri costituiscono un ostacolo.

(4) [needs and desires are pliable objects]
  Your needs are distorted.
  (?) *(No discernible Italian version)*
  (?) Your desires are distorted.
  (?) *(No discernible Italian version)*

(5) [needs and desires are entities lacking or having strength]
  (?) She has strong needs.
  (?) *Lei ha dei forti bisogni.*
  She has strong desires.
  (?) *Lei ha dei forti desideri.*

(6) [needs and desires are luminescent or non-luminescent]
  You have clear needs.
  (?) *Tu hai dei chiari bisogni.*
  You have clear desires.
  Tu hai dei chiari desideri.
  (?) You have dark needs.
  (?) *Tu hai dei bisogni oscuri.*
  You have dark desires.
  Tu hai dei desideri oscuri.

(7) [needs and desires are plants]
>   His needs are growing.
>   *I suoi bisogni stanno crescendo.*
>   His desires are growing.
>   *I suoi desideri stanno crescendo.*

Needless to say, the appropriate conveyance of needs and desires in IC constitutes a major source of misunderstanding. The following sample of dialogue was recorded at the University of Lugano during an exchange between one of the authors of this book (A) and a non-native speaker of English (B) during a seminar conducted in English at the university:

A: Do you need anything?
B: *I have a need. A glass of water is wanted by me.*
A: Do you really need one right now, because I think the cafeteria is closed?
B: *I need one. I can wait.*

Clearly, B's use of the term *need* in his first statement is in contrast with its conceptualization in English. A was aware of the conceptual calque in this case, and thus ignored it. The correct version of the dialogue is the following:

A: Do you need anything?
B: I'd like a glass of water.
A: Do you really need one right now, because I think the cafeteria is closed?
B: No. I can wait.

3.2. Points of view on events

In the last dialogue above, B used a passive sentence—"A glass of water is wanted by me"—which may not impact on meaning, but nonetheless comes across as awkward. This is an example of what can be called, simply, *stylistic interference*. It is thus instructive at this point to take a brief digression from the consideration of joint action and needs and desires, focusing briefly on the role of style in interactions of all kinds. Let's consider B's misuse of the passive further by considering the differential communicative effects produced by the active and passive sentences below:

(1) The chocolate bar was eaten by Debbie. It was not eaten by me, nor was it my intention to do so. The eating action was accomplished quickly. The chocolate was devoured by her.

(2) I put sodium together with chlorine. I knew I was going to get a reaction. I thought I would get salt. But it didn't work out for some reason. I need to investigate this further.

If told that (1) was part of a dialogue between friends and (2) part of a published study in a professional journal, we would tend to perceive both utterances as anomalous. The reason for this is simple—stylistic practices dictate that (1) should be phrased in active sentences and (2) in passive ones, with appropriate lexical and morphological adjustments. In English (and other languages), active sentences are used to emphasize the speaker as the actor in a direct relation with the goal (the person spoken to), whereas passive ones are used to de-emphasize the speaker as actor and highlight the goal as the "object" of interest. The requirement of "objectivity" in scientific writing, in effect, translates into the practice of using passive sentences and other syntactic and morphological structures, where the "goal-object" is highlighted over the "subject-actor." Reformulating both sentences by reversing their voice, and by making other modifications, rectifies their stylistic abnormalities:

(1) Debbie ate the chocolate. I didn't eat it, nor did I intend to do so. She ate it quickly. She devoured the chocolate.

(2) Sodium and chlorine were mixed, in order to attain the expected reaction. The anticipated outcome was salt. However, this outcome was not achieved for some reason. Further investigation was prompted by this unforeseen result.

As the foregoing discussion shows, more often than not, rules of syntax turn out to be rules of style, which mirror rules of action (as discussed above). The stylistic relation between an active and a passive sentence such as *He ate the apple* vs. *The apple was eaten by him* is called *conversion* and is based on a differentiation of point of view, or perspective. At the level of their denotative semantics the two conversive sentences have predicate-argument structures that are perfectly equivalent. This relation of *converseness* could be represented as follows:

to eat (x_1, x_2) = *to be eaten* (x_2, x_1)

What changes is the perspective from which the scene or frame denoted by the predicate is presented. The converseness relation has been the object of special attention in the *frame semantics* approach developed by the American linguist Charles Fillmore. He defines the conversness relation as follows:

> If there are two predicate words that belong to the same frame but occur in syntactic structures that require that the entities of the associated schema are mentioned in different orders, then those two words are converses of each other. *Buy* and *sell* are converses in this sense, as are *taller than* and *shorter than*, or *husband* and *wife* (Fillmore 2003: 255).

If we go back to our original example, we find that in the active sentence the subject x_1 (*He*) is in the foreground of the mind's eye, while the object x_2 *(apple)* is in the background. The action implicated by the verb (*eating*) is spotlighted as an action of the subject. The overall mental image schema that the active sentence conveys is, therefore, one of the subject as a perpetrator of an action. The passive sentence, on the other hand, implicates a difference in the position of the foreground and the background in the mind's eye. It brings the *apple* x_2 to the foreground, relegating the eater x_1 to the background *(him)*. The action of eating is now spotlighted on the object, or the receiver of the action. The conceptual shift between perpetrator and receiver is, clearly, built into the structure of each type of sentence. Passive sentences are hardly just variants of active ones, and vice versa. They encode, in actual fact, a different mental angle from which to see the same scene or frame conceptually.

This is perhaps why Wittgenstein, as mentioned, had characterized sentences as structures designed to mirror features of the world in the same way that pictures do. The lines and shapes of drawings show how things are related to each other; so too, he claimed, do the ways in which words are put together in sentences. A half century later, the psychologist Rudolf Arnheim (1969: 242) presented a similar pictorial account of sentences, explaining the raison d'être of function words such as prepositions and conjunctions as follows:

> I referred in an earlier chapter to the barrier character of "but," quite different from "although," which does not stop the flow of action but

merely burdens it with a complication. Causal relations are directly perceivable actions; therefore "because" introduces an effectuating agent, which pushes things along. How different is the victorious overcoming of a hurdle conjured up by "in spite of" from the displacement in "either-or" or "instead;" and how different is the stable attachment of "with" or "of" from the belligerent "against."

In effect, the way in which words are put together, the length of sentences, and the mode of sentence construction impart a certain "feel" to an interaction that interlocutors interpret in specific ways.

4. Interaction

As discussed above, a joint action (or interaction) can take place when an agent is not able or does not want to pursue his/her own goal him/herself and negotiates with other people their engagement in the causal chain. Two basic scenarios of joint action can be envisaged (Rigotti 2005b):

1. Both agents share the same goal. In this case we can speak of *cooperation*: one single action with two co-agents (when, for example, two agents cooperate in helping an injured person).
2. Each agent pursues his/her goal by realizing the goal of the other. We speak in this case of *transactive interaction*, or *interaction proper*. Two inter-agents having different goals leave the realization of their respective goals to the action of the other, relying on each other for the satisfaction of their desires.

Beside these two basic configurations of joint action, two other special cases need to be discussed because of their relevance for intercultural communication. The first is represented by *competitive*, potentially conflictual, interactions. The second, which could be called *benevolent interaction*, has an intrinsically problematic nature and, in practice, plays a critical role in many IC events, especially in the area of international cooperation and in social work contexts.

4.1. Cooperative and transactive interaction

The structure or flow of a cooperative interaction, in which the interlocutors are labeled *co-agents,* can thus be schematized as shown below:

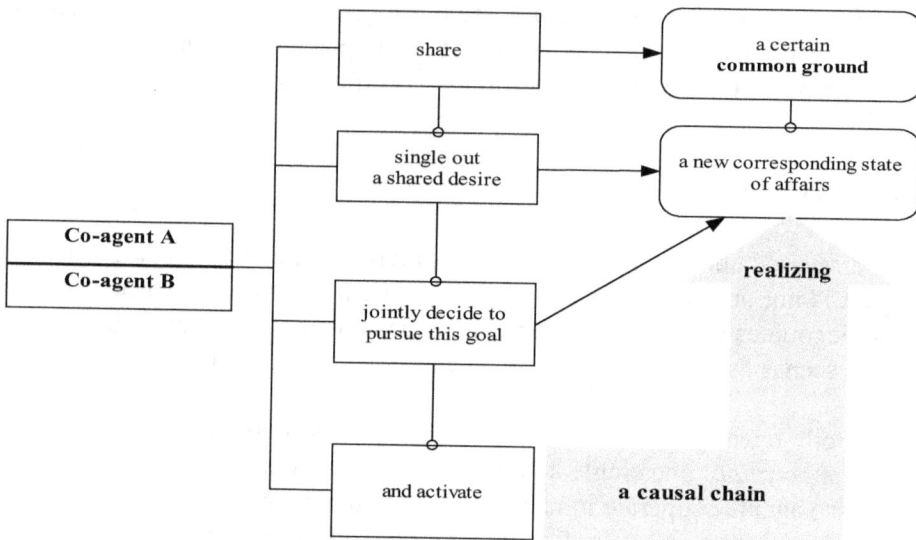

Figure 11. Cooperative interaction.

In such an interaction, the co-agents consciously share a desire (a "we-desire," as it may be called), and thus coordinate themselves to realize a joint causal chain for realizing it. In a sense, cooperation is the basis of the "we-ness," that is, of the awareness of belonging to a community. Cooperation requires maintaining a complex evolving common ground, which includes a (partially) overlapping picture of the world, a consciously shared we-desire, and a constantly monitored state of advancement of the joint causal chain.

Cooperation, in fact, is not simply defined as two agents pursuing the same goal. Indeed, two people may be pursuing the same goal without even being aware of each other's existence. But they are not co-agents in this case. For instance, A may be trying to get rid of a poster from a telephone pole on the street where he lives, by shredding it with a knife. Unknown to A, B may also want to get rid of the poster, contemplating the same action as A, at the same instant that A is carrying it out. Despite the fact that the goals of the two individuals are the same, they are not acting cooperatively, for they do not perceive their joint action as cooperation.

Cooperative interaction is not, however, the only possible mode for realizing a joint action. If someone goes to a store to buy a watch, with the desire to purchase a good but inexpensive watch, hence asking for a discount, it is unlikely that the storeowner would share that *same* desire. Rather, it is more likely that the owner would want to sell the watch at a profit. The owner may, of course, have other pertinent desires– he may be an artisan and may therefore desire that the watches he makes be appreciated by his customers seeing a discount as an affront; he may desire to keep the price as is because he knows that he needs all the financial help he can get to support his family; etc. The desires of the two interacting agents, thus, do not coincide. Nevertheless, neither of them can realize his or her particular desire without bringing about an appropriate action on the part of the other. So, the nature of the communicative exchange between customer and owner will still involve joint action, but it does not involve *pure* cooperation. This situation can be represented as shown in Figure 12.

Ideally, in a transaction the actions of each interlocutor should realize the desires of the other. But situations such as the one depicted above (which are actually quite common) involve a partial conflict of interests. While the resolution of the partial conflict of interests is in the interest of both inter-agents (if the watch does not change hands *both* will be unhappy), it is also true that each one will try to solve the conflict *in their own favor*. This situation will likely lead to the use of argumentation to solve the conflict in a "reasonable" way which is acceptable to both parties, and, at the same time, to the use of strategic communication, whereby each interlocutor attempts to realize his or her particular desire by affecting the actions of the other advantageously (Cf. also van Eemeren and Houtlosser 1999). So, for example, the customer (A) could produce an argument such as the following:

A: This watch is going out of fashion, and thus its price does not reflect its current worth. A small discount would rectify this, don't you agree?

The store owner (B) could respond strategically, with the following counterargument:

B: Yes, but it is a classic model and thus will even increase its worth eventually.

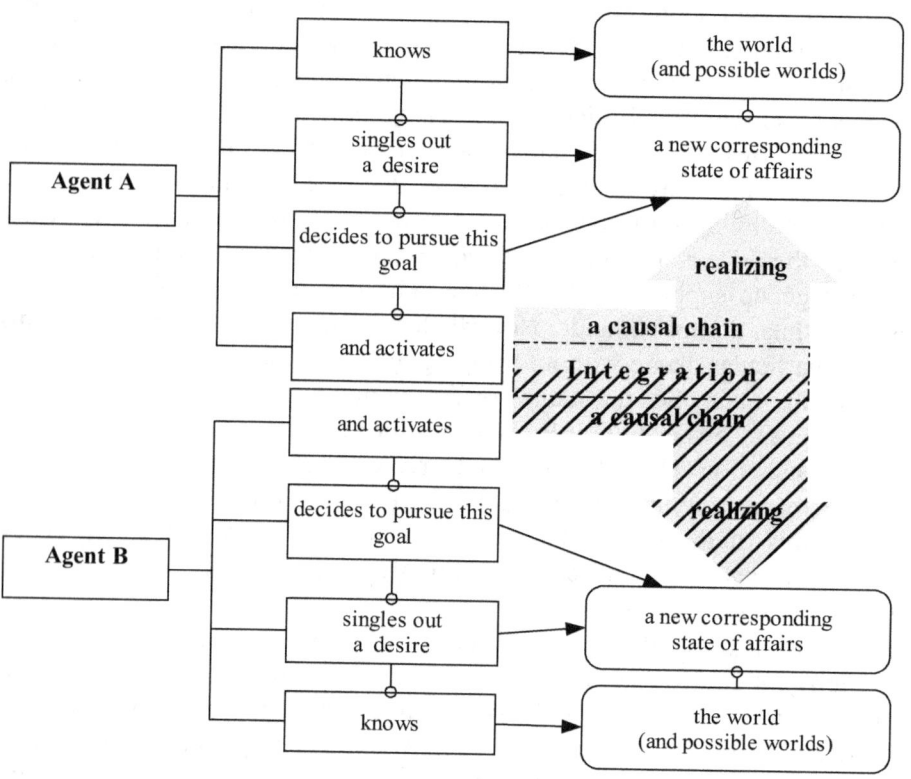

Figure 12. Transactive interaction.

Incidentally, this kind of strategic exchange is perceived as meaningful since it takes place in the *interaction field* (Rigotti and Rocci 2006b) of a store between interlocutors who are there for specific reasons. Resolving the stalemate requires that the desires or needs of one of the two become greater than those of the other for the situation to be resolved cooperatively. For example, the storeowner might expect to make more sales than usual and, thus, concedes to A's request by bartering a little. However, if A is a foreign visitor, then the interaction would be fraught with difficulties since a speech function such as bartering involves knowledge not only of the words to be used in an appropriate utterance but also of the rules of interaction of that particular *interaction scheme*, of its applicability to the interaction field at hand (e.g. bargaining is appropriate in a traditional souk while it is totally inappropriate in a supermarket), and of the relationally appropriate style (e.g. how do I bargain without looking rude or undignified?) that are designed to allow for such a joint action to be realized.

Consider, now, cooperative communication in another interaction field—a coffee shop. In the shop, a client desires a cup of coffee. So, she asks the server for a cup. He instantly provides her with one upon hearing the utterance *May I have cup of coffee, please?* This speech act sets in motion the following chain of actions and events:

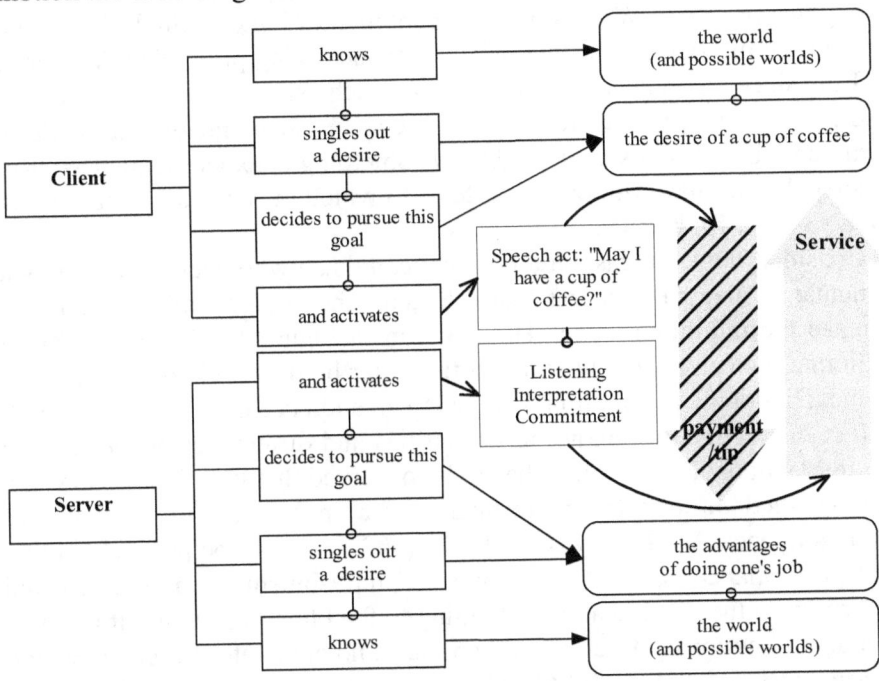

Figure 13. Asking for a cup of coffee. Zooming on the integration of the two causal chains via the production and uptake of a simple speech act. Note that in the interaction field of a coffee shop the client's speech act counts also as a commitment to pay for the coffee.

In this case, the utterance *May I have a cup of coffee, please?* pronounced within the appropriate interaction field triggers a series of events that allow the speaker to satisfy, almost automatically, her desire. Research on discourse suggests that many interaction fields are so standardized that the speech forms used in them tend to be highly formulaic. They amount to *routine procedures* (Clark 1996). The difference with respect to the previous situation is that the interaction field—a coffee shop—precludes bartering. It provides a common ground that allows for mainly formulaic or script-like communication as appropriate. Similarly, ordering from a menu at a restaurant tends to unfold in an analogous script-like manner ("Can I take your order?" "What do you recommend?" etc.). Such formulaic cooperative discourse is in line with the economizing principle (Chapter 1, § 3.1) since it makes interaction in such situations effortless and predictable. The predictable flow of events in such interaction fields is disrupted only when a server might say something unexpected such as "I'm so sorry, but we have run out of coffee," to which the customer might reply "Don't worry, I'll be back."

Consider, now, the case of a political candidate who decides to deploy a particular strategy in order to get elected—the strategy of promising to increase the minimum wage. The diagram in Figure 14 shows the causal chain that the candidate puts into motion after he or she utters "If you vote for me, I'll double the minimum wage" to an audience of potential voters.

It is instructive to look at the similarities and differences between these two interactions. First of all, it has to be observed that both interactions are accomplished through the performance of a speech act, in the sense of Searle's Speech Act Theory (Chapter 2, § 4.2). It has to be pointed out that such performance is, in itself, a joint accomplishment of the speaker and the hearer: without the hearer's attending to the utterance, taking it up in its intended illocutionary force and accepting it, no complete speech act would be accomplished (Clark 1996). The two examples partially differ in the type of illocutionary forces they deploy. In the coffee shop example the client's utterance is an obliquely formulated *directive* (*May I have a cup of coffee?*) accompanied by a little coda (*please*), which can be considered an *expressive* speech act in itself. The polite indirect phrasing and the addition of an expressive act aim to address the relational level of the interaction, making it smoother and more pleasant (or less unpleasant) for the subjects involved. The reason of the likely success of the directive does not reside primarily in the politeness strategy adopted, but in the structure of the interaction field itself: coffee shops are there to sell coffee, they are committed to that: it's their mission, so to speak.

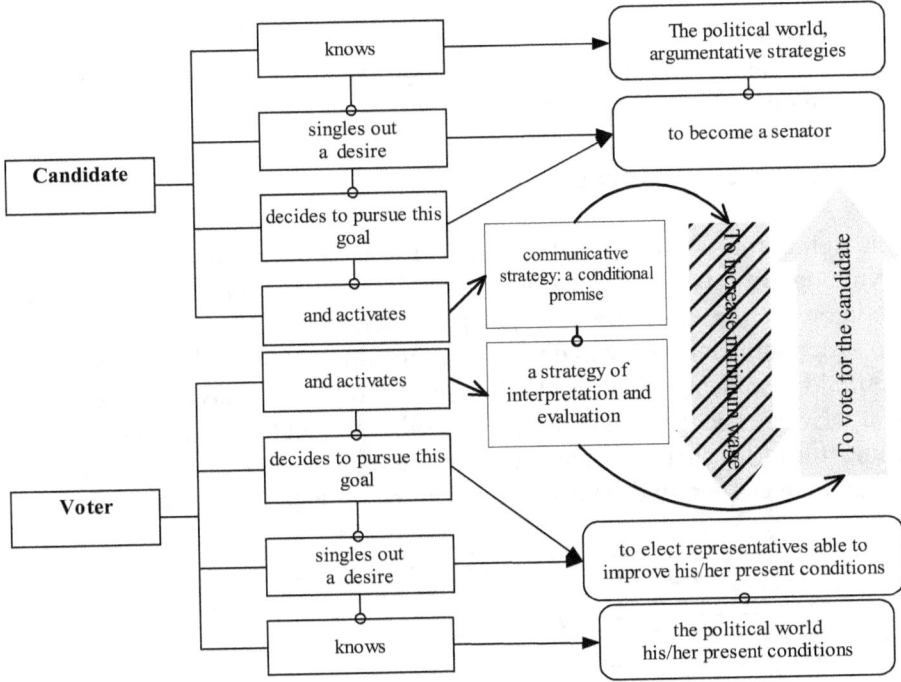

Figure 14. An electoral promise.

In the case of the election we have a directive – the request to vote for the candidate – accompanied by a commissive speech act – the promise of doubling the minimum wage. Here the interaction field does not bolster the success of the speech act: electors, at least in democratic countries, have no obligation to vote for a particular candidate. Rather the candidate tries to act on the beliefs and desires of the elector, by offering that promise as an argument supporting the expediency of the requested action. The realization of the interaction depends on the elector's evaluation of this argument and on his subsequent decision. Several aspects of the speech act of promising enter into the evaluation (Cf. Searle 1969):

- *Is the candidate sincere in her promise?* (sincerity condition)
- *Is the promised action really possible to carry out?* (preparatory condition)

- *Is the promised action really advantageous for me?* (another preparatory condition)

It is mind-boggling to think that complex social activities such as those discussed above are triggered by simple utterances. We rarely realize the consequences that our words have.

4.2. Competitive interaction

The counterpart of cooperative interaction is competitive interaction. The etymology of this term brings out what it implies. *Competition* derives from Latin *cumpetere*, meaning "two persons desiring to obtain the same object." Consider someone (A) who desires a large slice of cake, which may also be desired by someone else (B). Only one of the two can have a large slice— that is, if one succeeds in getting it, the other will not. The two agents are in competition for that slice and their joint action, in this case, is conflictual, rather than cooperative. The situation can be schematized as follows:

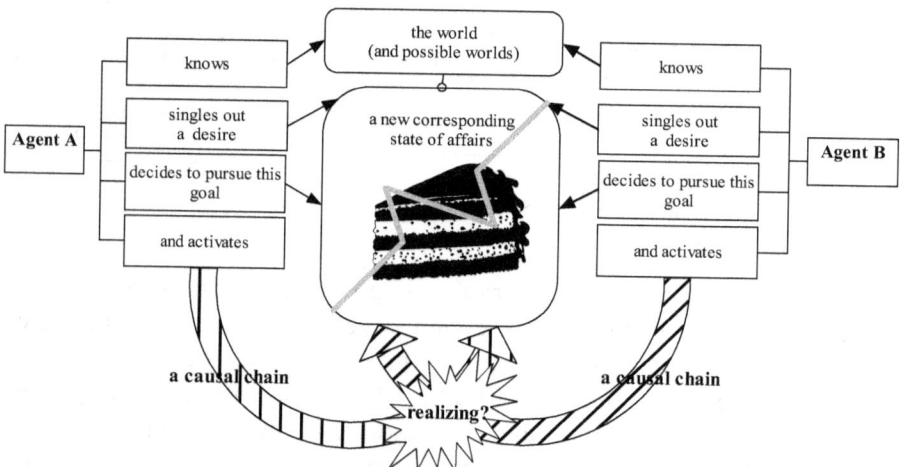

Figure 15. Competitive interaction

As this diagram brings out, the communicative resolution of the competition between two agents is likely to involve the deployment of argumentative strategies for obtaining the desired object through adjudication. Here is a possible start to a conflictual interaction between A and B:

A: I really should have that slice of cake, because I haven't had anything else to eat.
B: Neither have I, and moreover, I am much older than you are.

The arguments used by A and B, involve appeals to supposedly shared values such as justice, and to an established social order that institutes a hierarchy based on age.

There are different kinds of competition. For instance, consider a 100 meters *race* and a soccer *match*, both of which are competitive events. The difference between a race and a soccer match depends on the structure of the competition, which involves different rules for achieving victory. In the case of a soccer match, the team with the higher score (number of goals scored) wins; the other thus loses. The type of competition involved in soccer is encapsulated by the German term *Wettstreit* or the Latin *pugna*. In a race, a runner wins by coming ahead of the others. The fact that other runners also achieve results (second place, third place, national record, etc.) does not impede the achievement of victory. In this case, one could even speak of *emulation* (German *Wetteifer*, Latin *certamen*), rather than of *competition*.

Competition involves a strategic choice of words that allow one of the interlocutors to "win" the interaction. Suffice it to say here that this entails knowledge of a distinctive stock of verbal strategies. Take for example the strategy of tagging. As discussed in the previous chapter (Chapter 2, § 3.2), a tag is a word, phrase, or clause added to a sentence in a strategic fashion: "She's coming tomorrow, isn't she?," "That's a good cup of coffee, right?" etc. Tagging can, of course be interrupted by the other agent, but in general it ensures the full participation of the agent in what someone is saying. Hesitancy devices known as hedges—*yeah, uh-huh, well,* etc.—have a similar function. People use such strategies (consciously or not) to assert a position of dominance, to attract and maintain an audience, and to assert themselves when other speakers have the floor. It is in trying to gain the "upper hand" in competitive conversation that joint action strategies tend to break down seriously. Those with ineffectual verbal skills in such interactions will be compelled to accept defeat within the interaction field. As Eder (1990: 67) has observed, the way to "keep one's cool" during competitive exchanges is to deploy the strategy of not letting the opponent realize that one is wavering. Eder (1990: 74) points out that "the ability to respond to even personal insults in a non serious manner is a critical skill needed for successful participation."

Competitive interaction often involves the use of irony, making such interaction fraught with real danger in IC contexts. Deciphering the intent of an ironic utterance requires a substantial knowledge of the koiné being used in the interaction field. It is unlikely that such an utterance would have any meaning in any imaginable intercultural competitive exchange. Consider the following exchange between two students at the University of Toronto, one of whom was a foreign exchange student (A), whose native language was Korean, and who had studied English in Korea, and the other a native speaker of English (B). They were discussing term test results in the presence of one of the authors of this book:

A: Did you get your test back?
B: Yeah. Great results, let me tell you [with an ironic tone]!
A: But you failed?
B: Yeah, great.
A: I do not understand. I also got a low grade. I do not think it is so great.
B: Just kidding.
A: Oh!

Obviously, A had not grasped the ironic nature of B's initial comment. Although the dialogue ended in a friendly manner it nevertheless engaged the two interlocutors in a battle over the content of B's first utterance, which A found to be nonsensical. Fortunately, the outcome was resolved when B, sensing the source of the misunderstanding, "literalized" his chain of argumentation with "Just kidding."

4.3. Benevolent interaction

Communication that occurs in an interaction field whereby an interlocutor does not desire something for himself or herself, but rather for the other interlocutor, can be called *benevolent interaction*. The diagram in Figure 16 portrays such an interaction in ways that are similar to the other types of interactional models discussed above. In it, A loves B and knows that B desires something (x). A thus discusses x with B and sets off a chain of causality.

What does *benevolent* mean? It can be argued that, for an action to be purely benevolent, the agent should not perceive any personal advantage deriving from the performance of the action. So, can we conceive that some people (perhaps many) just desire the good of others? Or should we think of human beings as having only "selfish" needs, and performing typically "egoistic" actions, which may happen, by chance, to have "benevolent" collateral effects? In more philosophical terms, is *altruism*—the devotion to the welfare of others as the ultimate end for a moral action—a reality? Certainly, some relations are altruistic. For example, the bond that normally exists between a mother and her child or, more generally, among family members, is altruistic.

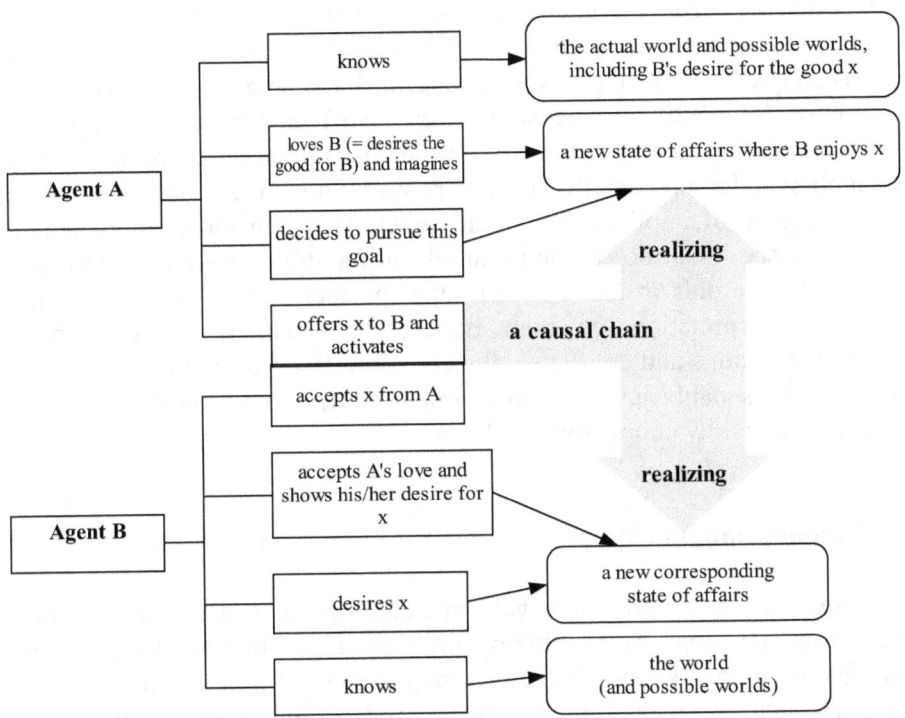

Figure 16. Benevolent interaction.

Apart from the issue of altruism per se, there are several other difficult questions that arise in connection with benevolent interaction. These are worth mentioning because they have practical consequences for certain IC contexts such as social work and international cooperation, as several international cooperators attending our IC courses in Lugano have explained to us.

One critical question is whether benevolence is a pattern of actions carried out by a single agent, or it is rather the result of joint actions. In other words, is the acceptance of a benevolent action also an action? With regard to the diagram above, one can ask whether B is an agent in the strict sense of the term. It must be noticed that there are many initiatives which may be considered benevolent from the point of view of intentions, but which are simply not received or accepted by the intended beneficiaries. If B does not accept A's action, as may be the case, complex negotiations may ensue that are designed to allow A to figure out if his or her offer is effectively related to B's desires (that is if it is really benevolent). There appear to be two possibilities: either B explicitly asks for something, and A responds to an explicit request; or A takes the initiative in doing something for B. In the latter case, A must be sure that what he or she offers is in fact good for B.

This situation raises a series of further questions. Does the offer of a benevolent action necessarily imply imposing it upon the beneficiary with a certain degree of implicit or explicit force? This is a rather fundamental question since it can be claimed that education at all ages and in virtually all contexts unfolds in this way. Despite the fact that people may assign different interpretations to their benevolence—which undergird many misunderstandings and conflicts—the common desire of good and the need to give a reasonable justification to one's choices may induce people to engage in a healthy cooperative dialogue.

5. Verbal communication

In Chapter 2 we delved extensively in examining how dialogues function and create meanings by mobilizing different kinds of knowledge in the dialogue participants: knowledge of grammar, of discourse strategies and discourse genre systems, knowledge of word meanings and connotations, knowledge of culturally shared metaphors, knowledge of socially relevant contexts, and knowledge of non-verbal semiotics systems. Speaking of semantics, we have also seen that meaning is a relationship between language and the world – not only in the restricted sense of what *is* the case, but also including what *may be* the case, the possible worlds. Semantics deals with the way people use language to speak about the actual and possible world as they "grasp" it.

In the present Chapter we have deepened our understanding of communication in another direction, by expounding its actional, "pragmatic" dimension (from the Greek *pragma* = 'action'). We examined communication as a form of joint action, enabling all sorts of interactions in different interaction fields. It is now time to see how the semantic and the pragmatic dimensions of verbal communication are linked.

Pragmatically, a text or speech represents a complex action – or, more precisely, an articulated proposal of a joint action to be realized with the participation of the addressee. Semantically, a text establishes a developing representation of states of affairs which hold true in some possible world. Studying these semantic representations is not alien to the study of discourse as social action. A large part of the perlocutionary effects of a text, that is its power to persuade, arouse emotions, entertain, in a word, its 'appeal', is mediated by its ability to plausibly evoke in the mind of the addressee the representation of a world fragment. Tannen (1989) devotes a whole chapter of her fortunate book on involvement in discourse to the effects of details that bring the addressee to imagining an experienced world.

In order for a dialogue to bring about a joint action, both interlocutors need to know how to represent the world, both actual and possible (desired or feared). Without this shared know-how, joint action is impossible (or at least unattainable). But there is more. Combining predicates (modes of being) and arguments (entities) our discourse can refer to the states of affairs that make up the world, including events, actions, and, more specifically, communicative actions. But when it comes to communicative actions, the predicates manifested by language can do more than just *describe* the world. Consider the following examples:

(1) I *apologize* for not attending the meeting.
(2) I *promise* I will double your wages.
(3) I *thank* you for your assistance in this matter.
(4) I'll *bet* you a couple of bucks she will arrive first.
(5) I *warn* you, the dog will bite you.

They have a special quality in that they are not just descriptions of actions. By uttering (1) the speaker does not describe an *apology*, she apologizes, respectively she promises and she thanks. The same in (4) and (5), which do not describe the communicative actions of *betting* and *warning*, but simply *perform* them. It was John L. Austin who observed that when used in the first person of the present indicative, verbs like *promise, apologize, thank, bet* and *warn* can be used *performatively* to realize an illocutionary

act. We can say that these verbs, which Austin calls *performative*, are a kind of *pragmatic predicate* (Rigotti 2005c), a predicate that does not describe a mode of being, but brings about those particular modes of being that are the communicative actions. We can represent the predicate-argument structure of the speech-act in (2) as follows:
Promise (x_1, x_2, x_3) — a triadic predicate

x_1 = the speaker, the one who makes the promise
x_2 = a future action of the speaker ("I will double your wages")
x_3 = the hearer, the one to whom is promised

There is then a deep constitutive link between semantics and pragmatics, between predicates and communicative actions, which has several important implications for intercultural communication. The first concerns the semiotic manifestation. Each language has its own means to express pragmatic predicates in an appropriate, idiomatic way.

For instance, in English, (6) below is a more appropriate way of making a hospitable offer than the blunt utterance in (7):

(6)   How about a beer?
(7)   Have a beer!

But in other cultures this may not be the case. Wierzbicka (2003: 62) points out that those who may not be acquainted with the semantic-pragmatic conventions of English speaking-cultures, might well interpret (6) as a genuine question rather than an invitation, and would certainly consider (7) a more appropriate type of utterance. In Italian the closest to (6) one can have is shown below in (8). However, this comes through as suspiciously similar to English and thus, in all likelihood, is the result of a calque or an imitation:

(8)   *Che ne dici di una birra?*
       Literally: "What do you say about a beer?"

5.1. Pragmatic predicates

The second, perhaps even more important, consequence of the constitutive tie between semantics and pragmatics is that the method of semantic analysis that we used for ordinary predicates can be applied for pragmatic predicates as well. Consider the conditions of the apology that we mentioned in Chapter 2, § 4.2. They can be expressed elegantly in a semantic analysis of the pragmatic predicate *to apologize* (x_1, x_2, x_3).

to apologize (x_1, x_2, x_3).
Presuppositions:
- PERSON (x_1) & PERSON (x_2) & ACTION (x_3) & PAST (DO (x_1, x_3)) & BAD (x_3, x_2)

Implications:
- RECOGNIZE (x_1, PAST (DO (x_1, x_3)) & BAD (x_3, x_2))
- REGRET (x_1, x_3)
- PROMISE (x_1, x_2, FUTURE (~DO (x_1, x_3))
- ASK (x_1, x_2, FORGIVE (x_2, x_1, x_3))

The semantic analysis of the pragmatic predicate *to apologize* reveals its relationships to a number of other predicates that appear as components of its meaning, like *regretting, forgiving,* and *promising*. For instance, we can develop further our analysis by unpacking the meaning of *promising*, as Searle did in his groundbreaking essay on speech acts (Searle 1969). A semantic analysis of the act of promising should look like that:

to promise (x_1, x_2, x_3).
Presuppositions:
- PERSON (x_1) & PERSON (x_2) & ACTION (x_3) & GOOD (x_3, x_2) & POSSIBLE (FUTURE (DO (x_1, x_3))) & ~ NECESSARY (FUTURE (DO (x_1, x_3)))

Implications:
- WANT (x_1, FUTURE (DO (x_1, x_3)))
- OBLIGED (x_1, x_2, FUTURE (DO (x_1, x_3)))

The semantic trait OBLIGED signals a commitment that must be exchanged between interlocutors in the dialogical performance of the act of promising. We could say that as a result of the speech act, such a commitment is added to a specific part of the common ground, sometimes called the *commitment store*, affecting the relationship between the speaker and the hearer, until the obligation is fulfilled, or the promise is retracted by the speaker, or else deemed to be impossible to fulfill.

Thus, along these lines, semantic analysis can become a powerful tool for unraveling the network of concepts that lies behinds communicative actions in a given culture, and – to the extent to which we find cross-culturally valid meaning components – to compare one culture to the other.

It is important to keep in mind that each of the pragmatic predicates examined above realizes the *proposal* of a joint action. This proposal is oriented towards what Bakhtin called the "responsive understanding" of the addressee. As Clark (1996) emphasized, in order to be complete the joint action needs that the addressee takes up the proposal of the speaker. The fullest, more explicit form of uptake is the actual response in a dialogue, where the addressee becomes the speaker in his/her own turn at speech. Consider again some of the examples of pragmatic predicates examined above:

(1)
A: I apologize for not attending the meeting.
B: I accept your apology.

(2)
A: I'll bet you a couple of bucks she will arrive first.
B: Fine with me!

It is only thanks to the uptake of B that the communicative actions in (1) and (2) are fully realized. B's utterance by explicitly accepting A's proposal realizes a minimal joint action. Conversation analysts (cf. Sacks, Schegloff and Jefferson 1974) have observed that the succession of turns in conversation is not a random, unpredictable affair, but is characterized by regularities that can be described in terms of *adjacency pairs* (*question-answer*; *request-acceptance*, etc.). Such adjacency pairs represent minimal joint actions within the ongoing joint activity of the participants.

It is interesting to notice that the coherence of the adjacency pairs in a dialogue depends on the congruity of the utterances with the pragmatic predicates involved. For instance, one cannot say

*I accept your apology, but I won't forgive you.
As we have seen through the semantic analysis, the act of apology entails a request of forgiveness, and by accepting it the interlocutor commits him/herself to forgiving the other.

The aim here was to show the general relevance of semantic tools for studying interactions across cultures. And indeed, the above is but a brief and very limited foray into a vast and rapidly expanding domain of research in verbal communication, emerging from the application of semantic tools to the analysis of pragmatic relationships in a dialogue (Rigotti 2005c).

6. The relational dimension

Consider the following example of interaction, recorded at the cash counter in a shop (from Hewitt 2002):

A: thirty-four pounds <u>please</u>
B: how can I pay you? - Visa?
A: yes – <u>Visa's fine</u>
(B gives Visa card to A)
A: <u>kyu</u>
B: <u>thank you</u>
(B runs Visa card through credit-card machine.)
A: <u>thank you</u> – there's your receipt
B: <u>thank you very much indeed</u>

Generally speaking, the speech acts exchanged by the participants in this episode are functional to realizing a very specific and highly routinized interaction scheme within a tightly defined interaction field. Paying at the counter is a cooperative interaction which is, in turn, part of a broader transactive interaction: the purchase of goods or services. If we look more closely at what the two participants say, however, we can see that not everything relates to the goal of the interaction in the same fashion. While an utterance such as *how can I pay you? - Visa?* is directly functional to carrying out the transaction, the utterance *thank you very much indeed* and the other underlined bit are not.

In fact, when we communicate, be it in routine or in exceptional situations – as strongly intercultural communication typically is – we always do two things at once: we take care of the business at hand (that is to say of the goals one has to reach in the interaction, and of the instrumental shared goals one has to commit to in order to create a common realization chain) and we take care of the overall interpersonal relationship with the other inter-agents. Brown and Yule (1983: 1) speak of *transactional function* for the first dimension of verbal communication and of *interactional function* for the second aspect, where language is used "in expressing social relations and personal attitudes". This view is further developed by Geis (1995) who distinguishes between the *transactional* effects of a speech act and its *interactional* effects (which we might call, more precisely, *relational* effects). For instance a question might have at the same time the transactional goal of seeking information and the – possibly unwanted – interactional effect of embarrassing our interlocutor. As noted by Geis (1995: 35), interactional effects influence both *what* people say (greetings, compliments, apologies and other expressive speech acts are typically performed in view of reaching an interactional effect) and *how* they say it (as we observed in the previous chapter, the use of honorifics, the choice of register, the recourse to connotative language can all express a particular kind of interpersonal relation). For the sake of clarity we prefer to use here the term *relational* function and *relational* effects, instead of interactional, because in the previous pages we used the term interaction in a broader and more literal sense, inclusive both of the relational and of the transactional dimensions.

Often the amount of communication necessary to realize a routine interaction is minimal, and most of the words exchanged by the participants have a relational function, addressing their relationships as human beings and members of a community *beside* their roles in the transaction taking place. An extensive study of client-shopkeeper interactions, conducted by a research group in Lyon (France), revealed that most of the words exchanged were not strictly necessary for the commercial transaction proper to take place but were rather addressing the interpersonal relationship (Cf. Kerbrat-Orecchioni 2005: 241-242). More precisely, as Kerbrat-Orecchioni explains, the transactional part of the interaction is largely based on the non-verbal actions of the participants (e.g. the client points to the products) and the information available in the context (e.g. prices are displayed on price tags). The role of verbal language is to "lubricate" the functioning of the transaction by taking care of the relational dimension.

6.1. Politeness

Most of this relational communication aimed at "polishing" the gears of transactions falls under the rubric of *politeness*. Politeness is both a universal phenomenon and, at the same time, an eminently culturally variable one (Kerbrat-Orecchioni 2005: 295). All human societies know polite linguistic forms and polite discourse strategies aimed at preserving the social harmony and taking care of the relationship between the interlocutors. They however differ greatly, as Kerbrat-Orecchioni observes, in the *conditions* of application of politeness (who has to be polite, towards whom, in what kinds of situation?) and in the *forms* that politeness takes (what kind of language and behavior is perceived as polite or impolite in a given situation?). For instance, while the French research cited above found out that politeness plays a major role in conversations between shop clerks and clients in France (accounting for about half of the verbal material exchanged), parallel researches carried out by Kerbrat-Orecchioni's group in Syria, Tunisia and Vietnam have revealed a variety of situations. In particular, in Vietnam clients do not use polite forms (like, in English, *please*) when asking for a product, and shopkeepers do not thank clients for their purchase. Interestingly, thanking would not only sound too polite but it would be even interpreted as insulting, because it would imply that the client was taken in by the shopkeeper and paid an unfair price. In fact, as observed by Kerbrat-Orecchioni, the dominant metaphor under which small commerce is seen in Vietnam is a little bargaining "war" between the client and the shopkeeper. Within such a frame, it is rather appropriate for the seller to look unhappy and "defeated" so that the client feels he was able to bargain well.

6.2. Politeness theories

Only recently *politeness* has become an important focus of scientific research in the study of language, culture and society. Of course, politeness has been for many centuries the object of a vast literature comprising treatises and manuals aimed at teaching good manners according to the fashion of the time and place. In Italy, for instance, early examples include the treatises *Il Cortegiano* ('The Courtier', 1528) by Baldassar Castiglione, which focuses on courtly life and is not limited to good manners, and the influential *Galateo* (1558) by Monsignor della Casa (from the title of the latter book comes the Italian word *galateo*, which simply means 'rules of good manners').

This kind of literature is still flourishing, in English as in many other languages, but it has usually held a rather peripheral place with respect to the development of philosophical and scientific thinking on social interactions and its focus is usually simply *prescriptive* (what you should do) rather than *descriptive* (what people actually do) and *explanatory* (why people do what they do). It is in the late 1970s that, under the influence of the sociologist Erving Goffman, researchers in sociolinguistics and pragmatics begin to systematically address politeness as one of the key dimensions of the study of language in interaction (Cf. Kerbrat-Orecchioni 2005: 189-190).

The most influential theory of politeness, put forth by the sociologist Erving Goffman (1967) and perfected by the linguists Penelope Brown and Stephen Levinson (1978) is based on the concept of face. Face, according to Goffman includes:

- The desire to be appreciated by others;
- The desire to be free and not interfered with.

Goffman calls the first desire *positive face* and the second desire *negative face*. Negative face, therefore, for Goffman does not mean losing one's face or lack of positive face. It means the need or desire not to be disturbed and preserve one's own territory. According to Goffman the function of politeness is to minimize and repair to *face threatening speech acts* (FTAs) that might occur in an interaction. For instance, the act of criticizing what someone did or said may be perceived as threat to his/her positive face, particularly if it is performed in front of other people. A directive speech act, such as a command or a request, on the other hand, can be a threat to the addressee's negative face inasmuch it places a burden on him/her.
The communicative work aimed at preserving the face of the interlocutors gives rise to two kinds of politeness:

- *Solidarity politeness*: showing goodwill and appreciation in order to protect the positive face.
- *Respect politeness*: minding not to infringe the other's personal domain, thus protecting the negative face of the other.

Interestingly, there can be conflicts between the two kinds of politeness. Consider, for instance, the act of offering. The insistence in offering food to a guest might be seen either as an act reinforcing positive face (it shows the goodwill of the host towards the guest), or as an act menacing negative face (it constrains the freedom of the guest). A further problem in such a situation would be to determine what should be proper polite reaction to such a behavior, should the guest accept or (politely) decline the offer? Acceptance would reinforce the positive face by showing one's appreciation of the host's hospitality, but might impinge on the host's territory by consuming his resources. Different cultures resolve these potential conflicts in different ways, giving priority to one or the other aspect of politeness. In this situation English-speaking cultures tend to put an emphasis on the negative face of the guest and on respect politeness while other cultures give priority to goodwill politeness. For instance, a standard English phrase for offering food, such as *Help yourself!* would sound rather cold and inhospitable in many Southern and Eastern European cultures.

Another interesting case of politeness dilemma is represented by the choice of the proper reaction to *compliments* (Cf. Kerbrat-Orecchioni 2005: 226-229 and Bettoni 2006: 100-111). If the addressee of a compliment refuses to acknowledge it he/she will imperil the positive face of the addresser. However, if the addressee accepts the compliment he/she would damage his/her own positive face by looking vain or conceited. Basically, there are three possible strategies in reacting politely to a compliment:

What a beautiful dress! You look gorgeous!
1. Graciously accepting the compliment. The acceptance may include thanking and/or reciprocation of the compliment (*You look gorgeous too!*).
2. Limited acceptance: the addressee minimizes the compliment or deflects the merit (*It just looks nice because the sun shines today*).
3. Refusal (*Oh no! You are way too kind! It's just a regular dress.*)

Again, different cultures solve the dilemma in different ways. A series of empirical studies (Cf. Bettoni 2006: 106-111) has shown that Americans typically chose to accept the compliment, while Chinese will refuse it most of the time and Italians will tend to minimize it or deflect the merit. Divergent reactions to compliments seem to show that relational needs, such as *agreeing with the interlocutor* and *looking modest*, have a different relative weight in the different cultures.

Brown and Levinson (1978), who investigated a sizeable sample of languages and cultures, extended Goffman's approach by developing a theory of the relationship between the intensity of the threat caused by the speech act and the corresponding linguistic politeness strategies. They have developed the following formula for "calculating" the intensity (weight, W) of the FTA:

$$W(FTA) = R + D + P$$

R = rate of imposition (according to a certain culture)
D = distance (the horizontal dimension of the interpersonal relationship)
P = power (difference in the vertical dimension of the interpersonal relationship)

While it is not obvious how to operationalize this hypothesis by giving numerical values to R, D and P and correlate values with the verbal strategies adopted, Brown and Levinson's formula remains a useful shorthand for expressing the factors involved in choosing politeness strategies. Brown and Levinson (1978) examine the options available to people when faced with the need of performing a FTA in an interaction. Basically, they can be reduced to the five options below, ordered according to their increasing degree of politeness:

1. Just perform the FTA, thus risking appearing impolite:
    - Girl to father: "Hey, Dad, lend me your car for tonight!"
2. Perform the FTA, using positive politeness:
    - "Hey, Daddy, lend me your car for tonight! I know I have the best daddy on Earth! Please, pretty please!"
3. Perform the FTA, using negative politeness.
    - "I'm sorry to ask you again, Dad. But wouldn't it be possible to, say, temporarily borrow your car, just for two or three hours tonight?"
4. Implicitly perform the FTA "off record":
    - "It's really a pity I can't join the others tonight for Tammy's birthday. If only I had a car to drive there!"
5. Renounce completely to perform the FTA.

If we look closely at the two types of politeness envisaged by Goffman (1967) and Brown and Levinson (1978) we can connect them to the respect of two minimal requirements of interaction itself as it has been envisaged in this chapter.

Positive politeness is connected to the fact that in order to interact a minimum of goodwill is required. After all, I am satisfying in some way my inter-agent's desire. If my hate of the other exceeded any other gain I might get from the transaction, there would be no reason to interact. Negative politeness, on the other hand, relates to the fact that interacting with someone else coincides with recognizing his/her own freedom of will, his/her freedom to decide whether to accept or to refuse the joint action we propose. We do not interact with *tools* not even with "intelligent" or "interactive" tools.

Consider the case of a routine transaction like ordering a coffee in a coffee shop or buying bread in a bakery. These interactions do not involve real negotiation of a common goal, they only activate pre-defined possibilities in the interaction field. As Clark (1996: 298) puts it, in these situations "equity is taken for granted" as "the participants know their roles, rights and duties and potential joint purposes". Nevertheless, politeness intervenes to a certain extent even in these interactions to signal, at least in a formulaic manner, the ultimately free nature of interpersonal relations: *please* means that I acknowledge the possibility for the other to say *No* to the proposed interaction, and that I rely on his/her goodwill.

Chapter 4
Culture

> *Culture, the acquainting ourselves with the best that has been known and said in the world, and thus with the history of the human spirit.*
>
> Matthew Arnold (1822–1888)

1. Introductory remarks

The word *culture* has been used throughout this book. Clearly, in the context of IC the question *What is culture?* is hardly a trivial one. Although interest in culture is as old as human history, the first scientific approaches to its investigation had to await the middle part of the nineteenth century with the founding of anthropology as an autonomous discipline. The first true scientific definition of cultures comes from the pen of the early British anthropologist Edward B. Tylor (1832-1917), who defined it in his book *Primitive Culture* (1871: 1) as "a complex whole including knowledge, belief, art, morals, law, custom, and any other capability or habit acquired by human beings as members of society." Tylor and other early anthropologists also differentiated between culture and society, which, to this day, are terms considered to be synonymous by many people. *Society* is a term referring to a specific collectivity or community of people who have come together historically for various political, economic, and other reasons. *Culture* is the system of meanings shared by groups of people as encoded in their language, music, arts, and other expressive and representational forms and systems. A society may, of course, encompass one and only one culture—hence the reason why the two terms are often confused as meaning the same thing. But more than one culture can exist in the same society. Switzerland, for example, is a single society, but it consists of four distinct linguistic and cultural systems within it—German, French, Italian, and Romansh. In an opposite manner, several societies can share the same general culture—for example, European culture, Asian culture, African culture, etc.

The study of culture comes under the rubric of several disciplines, including anthropology, semiotics, and cultural studies. It is also a central focus of several schools of linguistic science, as we have seen in previous chapters, especially the school called Cognitive Linguistics. In this chapter, we will take a general look at the role culture plays in IC. Needless to say, we cannot possibly go into any depth or detail here. In one chapter, all we can really do is scratch the surface of the many questions raised by the role that native cultures play in the global village. We will therefore be selective, highlighting only those ideas and frameworks that we consider to be relevant to GL, even if this entails leaving out many others whose influence on the development of a general theory of IC is hardly negligible.

2. What is culture?

In their classic study of culture decades ago, the anthropologists Kroeber and Kluckholn (1963) found more than 150 qualitatively distinct definitions of this term scattered throughout the scientific literature. Interestingly, they found broad consensus on two points: (1) that culture is a way of life based on some system of shared meanings; and (2) that it is passed on from generation to generation through this system. These core points are incorporated by the authors in their own formal definition (Kroeber and Kluckholn 1963: 181):

> Culture consists of patterns, explicit and implicit, of and for behavior acquired and transmitted by symbols, constituting the distinctive achievement of human groups, including their embodiments in artifacts; the essential core of culture consists of traditional (i.e., historically derived and selected) ideas and especially their attached values; culture systems may, on the one hand, be considered as products of action, on the other as conditioning elements of further action.

Culture is, in effect, a form of communal knowledge based on shared systems of communication and symbolism. It has often been compared to a "cradle," because of the fact that it functions, first and foremost, as a communal cradle welcoming a newborn into a community. The original meaning of the term bears this out. The Latin words *cultus* and *cultura* are derived from the verb *colere*, which means "to take care of", as in *agrum colere* "taking care of the field, growing crops, practicing agri-culture" and in *deos colere* "taking care of the gods, worshipping", which indicated a relationship of affect and devotion to the divinity. *Cultus*, thus, refers to the process of taking care of children within a community, which allows them to grow up and become complete human beings, possessing *cultus atque humanitas* "cultivated humanity" (Rigotti .2005a).

The term culture is thus used here in its anthropological sense, rather than its many colloquial senses of cultivation, breeding, refinement, and taste. That is to say, culture is understood in this book as a system of classification that satisfies human needs in particular ways through the use of symbols and language, and as imparted knowledge and values shared by the members of a certain community. Each culture shapes the way its members satisfy human needs. Humans have to eat, but their culture teaches them what, when, and how to eat. For example, Americans tend to eat larger breakfasts than Italians do (consisting of such items as eggs and toast). In many parts of the United States, people generally eat dinner at 5 or 6 pm (especially in winter), whereas most Italians would start dining a little later. Turks generally prefer strong coffee with the grounds left in the cup, but Australians will filter out the grounds for a weaker brew.

2.1. Cultural diversity and common human nature

The role of culture in IC is of obvious importance to GL. As living beings we depend on the atmosphere we breathe, which surrounds us providing a favorable environment. As humans we live in a *semiosphere*, as Estonian semiotician Jurij Lotman (1991) called language, music, myths, rituals, and the other semiotic systems that people learn during their upbringing. Lotman created the term semiosphere to emphasize how these systems pervade human lives largely affecting how humans come to understand the world around them, even though that same culture provides individuals with the cognitive resources for making changes as new needs and new opportunities arise. Cultures are not sets of fixed traits defining ethnic or national character. They are constantly being modified by new generations of artists, scientists, philosophers, and others to meet new demands, new ideas, new challenges. The Tartu school of semiotics, to which Lotman belonged, defined culture simply as the entirety of non-genetic information that is transmitted across generations (Lotman and Uspenskij 1973: 40). Simply put, culture is the memory of a community. This memory is not accepted passively by members of a culture, as is genetic information, but rather creatively. And this is why cultures change from generation to generation.

As mentioned (Chapter 1, § 3.1), cultures serve the classificatory needs people have through the languages they speak (the classificatory principle).

And these in turn affect perception. The implicit everyday workings of this principle can be seen even in the use of apparently simple particles of speech such as prepositions. In English, we say that something can be read *in a newspaper*, implying through the preposition *in*, that we unconsciously perceive the newspaper as a container of information into which we must go to seek it out. That is why we also say things such as: "We got a lot out of that newspaper story" or "There was nothing in it." On the other hand, Italian speakers use the preposition *su* ("on"), implying that the information is impressed on the surface of the pages through its words. In Italian, therefore, there are no expressions similar to "We got a lot out of that newspaper story" and "There was nothing in it." Such differences show that speakers unconsciously talk about the same world according to the linguistic categories that they have acquired in cultural context. The differences may be small and subtle, or large and incomprehensible. In other words, language categories produce mental filtering effects on how people perceive the topic they are discussing during an interaction. These can be called "Whorfian effects," for lack of a better term (alluding to the ideas of Benjamin Lee Whorf in this regard). The term refers to the fact that cultural relativity plays a direct role in the negotiation of meaning during speech.

The concept of Whorfian effects is, in no way, meant to preclude the possibility that interlocutors will come to a common understanding of the world, despite what languages they speak. People do this all the time by an instinctive "gap-filling" process. Specific languages have many conceptual gaps in them. But humans the world over have the innate ability to fill them any time they so desire. They do this typically by inventing new words, altering already-existing ones to meet new semantic demands, borrowing words from other languages, translating concepts across languages, and so on. So, although human beings are indeed shaped by the so-called Whorfian effects associated with the languages they speak, they are also endowed with gap-filling faculties that allow them to transcend them whenever they wish or need to do so.

In IC settings, cultural worldview – including Whorfian effects – will obviously play a direct role in shaping the causal chain involved by interaction. As shown in the diagram below (Figure 17), each inter-agent in the intercultural exchange has a particular (though partial) knowledge of different elements of culture that he or she may or may not share with the other inter-agent. This pool of cultural knowledge is complemented by the knowledge of shared or non-shared private experiences, which may well be cross-cultural. Using the interaction scheme already introduced in Chapter 3, we can model intercultural interactions as in Figure 17.

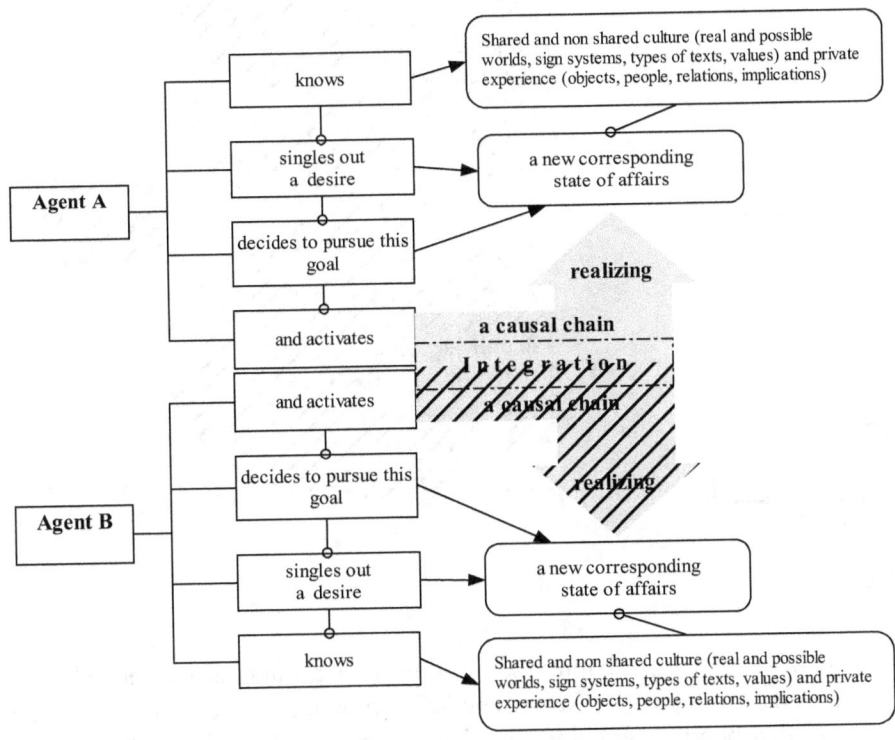

Figure 17. A model of intercultural interaction.

Inter-agents thus bring to an interaction their cultural and personal spheres of knowing, of which are only partially shared with the other inter-agent. The conscious overlap of the two spheres is the *common ground* (Chapter 2, §6.1), which can be further subdivided in *personal common ground*, based on the sharing of personal experience, and *communal common ground*, which is inferred on the basis of the belonging to a given cultural community (Clark 1996).

142 *Culture*

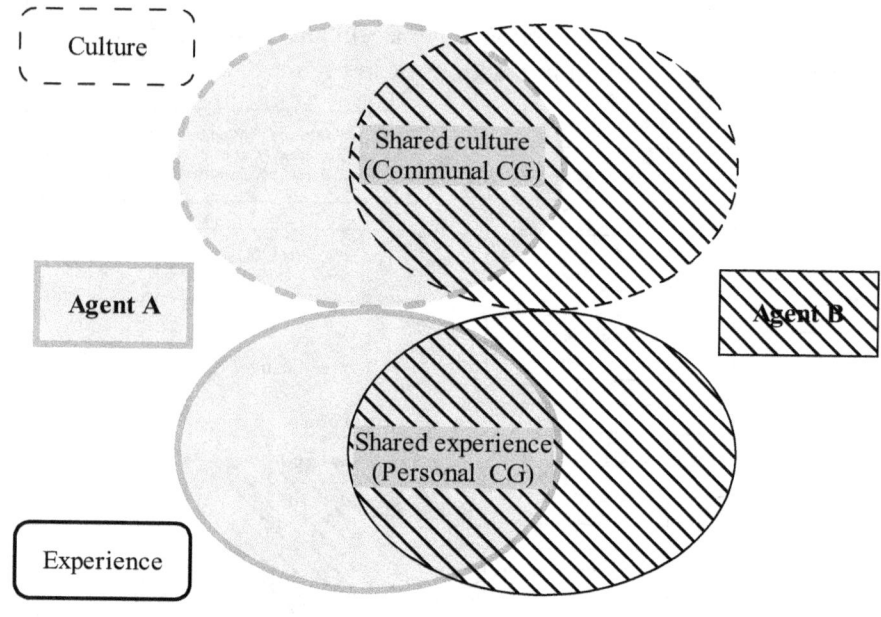

Figure 18. Common ground in IC

As we have seen in Chapter 2, the common ground is composed of an overlapping (but partial) set of beliefs, knowledge, desires, needs, and interests that people share and that they are aware of sharing at the moment of the interaction. The personal common ground contains what Clark (1996: 112) calls the set of "joint personal experiences," made up of "joint perceptual experiences and joint actions." For instance, the interlocutors may already have some knowledge about each other, about the background leading to the present interaction, about previous interactions, and so on. Other experiential domains include the set of *relationships* an interlocutor has established (and tends to establish) with other people, which are not necessarily coincident with those of the other interlocutor. Similarly, the cultural systems of the interlocutors taking part in a given IC interaction can also overlap partially. This overlap, or rather the joint construal of this overlap by the inter-agents, is the communal common ground. For instance, one may be a French-speaking person from Geneva, and the other an Italian-speaking person from Lugano. Both are Swiss citizens, but do not share the same mother tongue, they likely have different religious backgrounds – Protestant (Calvinist) in Geneva, Catholic in Lugano – and may possess subtly-different culture-specific conceptual systems.

In interaction people infers the information in the communal common ground from community membership. For instance, if I know that, Marcel, the colleague that I have just met for the first time, is from Geneva I can – as a fellow Swiss person – infer with reasonable certainty that he can speak French. However, from that alone I cannot tell whether he can also speak German or Italian, the other two Swiss national languages. It is only when I learn that his parents are both Swiss-German that I infer with a reasonable certainty that he can speak German and some form of *Schwyzerdütsch* – the Swiss-German dialect. Clark (1996) discusses the kinds of information that one can glean from shared community membership. The baseline is represented here by *human nature*:

> Whenever I meet other humans – adults from anywhere in the world – I assume as common ground that they and I think in the same way about many things. I may be wrong, but I would still draw the inferences and these would inform my actions as we tried to coordinate with each other (Clark 1996: 106).

Typically, we assume that other humans have the same perceptual access to the world (they can see, hear, smell, taste what we can), that they know some basic facts about the physical world (e.g. gravity) and the biological world (e.g. distinguishing between animals, plants and inanimate objects), we also assume a basic common ground regarding culture and society (e.g. people speak some language and have proper names) and the deeper moral world (e.g. mothers love their children). People may err in considering certain kinds of information as part of the universal common ground of human nature. The goal of GL is, in large part, determining which aspects of the communal common ground are specific and which are universal, in order to identify culture-based sources of misunderstanding and, thus, to attenuate potentially negative Whorfian effects (as we have called them here).

Among the possible contents of the communal common grounds shared by more or less specific communities Clark (1996) lists the following:

- Knowledge of the phonology, morphology, syntax, semantics and pragmatics of a common language (e.g. Italian or Korean);
- Knowledge of a shared jargon or specialized lexicon or nomenclature (e.g. mathematical jargon);
- A certain background of known facts concerning history, geography, literature, current events, etc. (e.g. *On October 12, 1492, Columbus landed at San Salvador*);

- Norms and conventions taken for granted (e.g. for British culture, waiting in queues at bus stops, driving on the left, etc.)
- Certain interaction schemes, scripts, and discourse genres (e.g. eating in a restaurant, a medical consultation, a newspaper article).

2.2. Two dimensions of culture: grammars and texts

The Tartu School semioticians draw an important distinction between two aspects of culture, cutting across the open ended list of cultural contents presented above (Lotman and Uspenskij 1987: 50):

- Culture as a set of rules to generate texts;
- Culture as a set of texts.

In the former perspective culture can be seen as a semiotic system, or better as a system of semiotic systems (Rigotti 2005a), including language, the system of discourse genres, register, together with iconic and gestural codes of communication. In this perspective culture is a *grammar*, a sort of "generative mechanism" enabling the construction of texts. As a semiotic system, culture also defines the categories enabling the members of the community to grasp reality and communicate their experience of the world. Seen as a semiotic system, culture is *virtual* in nature. It defines the rules for creating possible meaningful texts according to certain genres, the conceptual grid used to capture a range of possible human experiences.

According to the latter perspective cultures can be also seen in terms of the *texts* that they produce to preserve their traditions: sacred texts, legal texts, literary texts etc. These texts do not simply define virtual meaning possibilities in a language, they convey specific meanings. For instance, they tell the story of the previous generations or propose a specific hypothesis on how things are and how they should be.

2.3. Culture as hypertext

In general, the system of texts that constitute a culture, with their mutual relations and multilayer interrelationships, can be described as a *hypertext*. Consider the following important texts characterizing the culture of the United States of America:

- The Declaration of Independence, adopted by the Continental Congress on July 4, 1776, announcing that the thirteen American colonies then at war with Great Britain were no longer a part of the British Empire;
- The Emancipation Proclamation, issued by Abraham Lincoln on September 22, 1862, declaring the freedom of all slaves in Confederate territory;
- Martin Luther King's *I have a dream* speech in Washington on August 28, 1963, demanding civil rights for African-American U.S. citizens.

These texts not only mark important events in U.S. history, they also embody enduring values of American culture and remain part of its cultural common ground. Furthermore, they are not perceived as isolated but as linked one to the other in various ways and forming, together with many other texts, a coherent whole, a sort of macro-text telling the "American story" (Polanyi 1989). Sometimes the intertextual links are expressed explicitly through direct quotation and other forms of mention (Bazerman 2004). When Martin Luther King said

> I have a dream that one day this nation will rise up and live out the true meaning of its creed: "We hold these truths to be self-evident, that all men are created equal."

he explicitly quoted the preamble of the Declaration of Independence, using it as a shared premise in argumentation to support his demand of Civil Rights for black citizens (Rocci 2009). Sometimes the links are much more subtle, yet they are perceived as real in the consciousness of the members of the cultural community and can be activated in interaction. The cultural hypertext is not limited to famous texts. Countless everyday texts also participate in this interrelated network. Livia Polanyi (1989) analyzed stories told in conversation by American people – for instance autobiographical stories of foreign immigrants coming to the U.S.A. – and found that they reflect and distort in various ways a sort of "master narrative", which we could call the "American dream" or "the American story" reflecting cultural values such as "equality of opportunity" and "freedom to pursue one's happiness" (Rocci 2009).

The metaphor of hypertextuality that we use here comes out of the computer lexicon. It is a concept that is particularly useful as an analogue in describing how the cultural common ground is structured and how it is evoked in interactional situations to shape the course and outcome of interactions. Reading a printed page is, at the level of form (that is, deciphering the actual signs on the page), a one-dimensional process, since it consists in understanding the individual words and their combinations in sentences in the framework of a specific text type or genre (a novel, a dictionary, etc.). Information on any specific sign in the text must be sought outside the text: for example, if one wants to follow-up on a reference in the text, one has to do it by consulting other printed texts or other sources. This is of course what must be done when, for instance, one wants to look up the meaning in a dictionary of a word found in a printed text. The computer screen has greatly facilitated such tasks, by introducing hypertextuality, which is arguably the most useful feature of the World Wide Web (Cantoni and Tardini 2006). The term *hypertext* was coined in 1965 by Theodor Holm Nelson to describe an interlinked system of texts in which a user can jump from one to another. This was made possible with the invention of hyperlinks—portions of a document that can be linked to other related documents. By clicking on the hyperlink, the user is immediately connected to the text specified by the hyperlink. Web pages are written in a simple computer language—currently, HTML (Hypertext Markup Language). A series of instruction "tags" are inserted into pieces of ordinary text to control the way the page looks and which can be manipulated when viewed with a Web browser. Tags determine the typeface used in a text or act as instructions to display images, and they can be used to link up with other Web pages. Hypertextuality permits the user to browse through related topics, thus allowing him or her to follow the multiple semantic connections that exist between them. For example, navigating among the hyperlinks to the word *language* in an article contained on a website might lead the user to the *International Phonetic Alphabet*, the science of *linguistics*, samples of *languages*, etc.

Computer hypertextuality mirrors how the mind processes discourse. The human mind, indeed, does not just decode and store in memory the propositional content of a given text, but places the text being processed within an ever evolving network of intertextual connections linking it in multiple ways to other texts stored in the individual or cultural memory. During conversations, people do not process the ongoing conversational text only linearly, but also link the unfolding components of the content of a conversational text to the network of the other texts, which are implicit in the common ground. The conversation is, thus, produced in relation to its hypertextuality (previous conversations, culturally-significant texts such as novels, etc.), according to a series of cognitive, aesthetic, ethical, and other value-based conceptual modes of construction.

The notion of hypertextuality thus can be considered to be a productive metaphor for understanding how dialogue unfolds and how culturally-relevant textual content is brought to bear on the dialogical situation itself. In other words, hypertextuality serves as an analogue for understanding intellectual activity in conversations and in textual traditions more broadly. Some of the latter are:

- foundational and reference texts, such as sacred texts, historical rituals, foundational myths, charters, sayings, monuments, literary works, festivities, culinary traditions, and the like
- verbal (written and oral) and nonverbal historical texts, including texts that are designed to preserve the ongoing history of a community
- texts recording and ensconcing civic obligations and ethical principles
- texts that record and encode constitutions, laws, and other verbal and nonverbal systems for everyday interactions
- implied texts, which are the written and unwritten rules of interaction and discourse.

Those texts considered to be foundational for a community, insofar as they provide the historical foundations of the social system that they undergird, are particularly relevant in any analysis of the cultural component in IC. In Switzerland, for example, the story of William Tell – summarized below – conveys values such as independence, unity, and freedom to this day.

> William Tell was the legendary Swiss patriot of the Fourteenth Century who, according to tradition, refused to humiliate himself before Bailiff Gessler, a despotic Austrian governor of what is now central Switzerland. Gessler then forced Tell to shoot an apple off his sons head with his crossbow. Tell accomplished the feat, but he openly declared that he had prepared a second arrow to shoot the governor in case he would have hurt the child. Tell was then imprisoned. Upon escaping, he killed the governor. The slaying is said to have sparked the Swiss uprising against their Austrian rulers. The first written version of the legend appeared in a Fifteenth-Century ballad.

This mythic narrative reverberates (albeit largely in a latent way) in rituals, stories, laws, and other texts that constitute Swiss culture. It is a key element in the hypertext that composes this particular culture. All cultures have such narratives, typically "shuttling" back and forth through the boundary between history and myth. Other kinds of foundational texts are founding constitutions, such as the recent constitution of the Russian Federation (1993), which was drafted at the end of the Soviet Union with the precise aim of reconstructing Russian traditions, highlighting the common fate uniting all Russian peoples. It is worthwhile reproducing it here, since it brings out how a foundational text records human aspirations:

> We, the multinational people of the Russian Federation, united by a common destiny on our land, asserting human rights and liberties, civil peace and accord, preserving the historic unity of the state, proceeding from the commonly recognized principles of equality and self-determination of the peoples honoring the memory of our ancestors, who have passed on to us love of and respect for our homeland and faith in good and justice, reviving the sovereign statehood of Russia and asserting its immutable democratic foundations, striving to secure the wellbeing and prosperity of Russia and proceeding from a sense of responsibility for our homeland before the present and future generations, and being aware of ourselves as part of the world community, hereby approve the Constitution of the Russian Federation. (Constitution of the Russian Federation 1993)

The notions expressed in such foundational texts are found throughout the domain of discourses that make up the daily conversational texts of a society. These texts constitute points of reference for the community, either because they represent an implied value system, or because they are considered to be sources for inspiration as authoritative cultural benchmarks. In the former case, referring to the texts in question is considered to provide *inherent proof* to support a certain claim in argumentation (this role is sometimes played, for instance, by the Bible in Christian communities and by the Quran in Muslim communities); in the latter case, allusion to the texts in question is considered to enrich and confer depth and aesthetic value to one's discourse because they have become widely recognized as being particularly meaningful to the culture (this role is played, for instance, by Shakespeare's plays, which are perceived as critical for understanding and picturing the world by members of Anglo-American culture). Such texts are perceived to constitute a "repository of wisdom," which is often echoed in all kinds of conversations.

Using argumentation theory, it can be said that hypertextuality provides a hidden set of textual premises that underlie conversational arguments. Many of the rhetorical devices used in conversations have such textual-argumentative function. The following were recorded in Toronto by one of the authors during several lectures at different conferences:

(1) This has an Oedipal quality to it.
(2) In this case, it was freedom of speech that was jeopardized.
(3) That idea fell from academic grace a long time ago.
(4) That was a Promethean task.

Extending in an imaginary sense the computer notion of "clicking," one could say that in (1) and (4) the relevant clicking was on Greek mythical texts (involving the mythical figures of Oedipus and Prometheus), while in (3) it was the Bible, and (2) the American constitution. This "mental clicking" is part of an unconscious presupposition system used by speakers. However, it cannot be assumed to be operative wherever a common ground does not exist. It has happened several times to one of the authors who, in lecturing in English to a non-native group of scholars, has had to intervene by explaining these cross-references to implicit texts, and thus paraphrasing them in terms of more understandable or common-ground predicate structures.

3. Culture, perception and cognition

Cultural competence involves knowledge not only of hypertextuality, but also of a series of interdependent codes, or "grammars", forming a complex whole (Cf. § 2.2 above). Culture can thus be characterized, following the Tartu School, as a semiotic metasystem in which the language system plays a primary role (Gatti 2003). Language and culture are, in this model, intertwined completely. Language is an expression of culture at the same time that culture constitutes the metasystem of meanings that can be expressed through language. Since culture affects perception and cognition, it is obvious that language is the trace system to how this occurs in actual fact. Some of the ways in which this takes place are discussed in the sections below.

3.1. Perception

As a metasystem, culture acts on perception to shape the interpretation of messages or representations of all kinds, linguistic and nonlinguistic.

Consider as a case-in-point the grid created by the Italian Renaissance architect and writer Leon Battista Alberti (1404-1472), which he used to exemplify the technique of perspective painting:

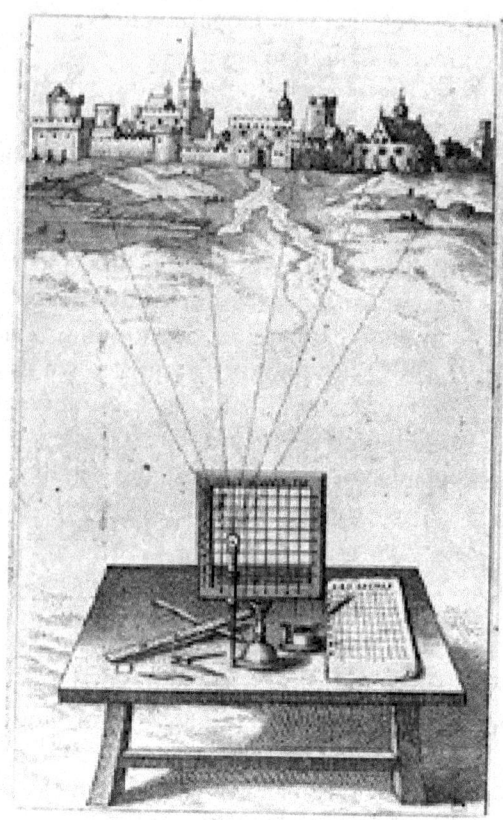

Figure 19. Alberti's perspective grid

As mentioned, Alberti's primary goal with the grid was to show that perspective in visual representation can be made to simulate the elementary laws of optics, and in particular the fact that distant objects appear smaller and less distinct than near objects. The grid can be applied to understand how objects appear optically to grow smaller as they recede in the distance. The flat surface of an image is known as the picture plane; the horizon line is the horizontal or so-called eye-level line that divides the scene in the distance; and the vanishing point is located on the horizon line where parallel lines in the scene appear to converge.

The technique of perspective creates powerful simulations of optical reality. In the following plane figure there are 12 lines. The way they are put together, however, makes us believe that they represent a three-dimensional box:

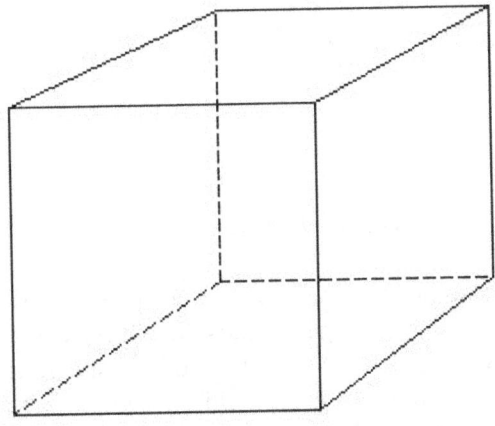

Figure 20. Perspective drawing of a box.

The figure has been drawn with straight lines drawn on a two-dimensional surface (the page). Yet we cannot help but interpret it as a three-dimensional box. This is because of the perspective drawing technique, which us to see objects as three-dimensional on a two-dimensional surface.

The way we view and interpret pictures is hardly based on physical vision alone. It is influenced by the culture-specific system of visual representation to which people have become accustomed. Interpretation of any visual text is thus culture-specific. Clearly, each sign or text to which someone is exposed requires knowledge of the cultural metasystem in which it was constructed. Consider the following figure:

Figure 21. Drawing representing the expression *a bright idea.*

What does it mean? The answer to someone living in a Western culture is *a bright idea*. How does it present this meaning? It does so by showing a light bulb inside a bubble. Why is this representative of its meaning? Answering this last question entails unraveling the cultural roots of each component of the visual text hypertextually. The use of light in the figure is consistent with the general view in Western culture of light as an analogue for intellect and intelligence. This can be seen as well, for instance, in such expressions as *to become enlightened, to shed light on something*, and so on. The use of a bubble to enclose the light bulb (the source of light) is derived from the comic book tradition of putting dialogues and thoughts into bubbles. In an intercultural context, therefore, interpreting this simple figure can be problematic if the addressee has never been exposed to comic books and has no familiarity with the [light is knowledge] conceptual metaphor. In an encounter with a student in Toronto of Asian background with only a rudimentary knowledge of English, one of the authors (A) used this figure to explain the notion of "enlightenment" during a question-and-answer period after a class, receiving the response recorded below:

A: Do you see that the figure stands for a bright idea?
B: Sorry, professor, but why a bubble?
A: It is the same figure as in comic books.
B: I don't see the connection.
A: Oh.

A then went on to explain the expression in various other ways, at the end of which B remained somewhat perplexed because the [light is knowledge] conceptual metaphor also existed in his language but without any use of vehicles such as light bulbs. He explained that the tradition is to use natural sources of light in explaining such matters.

3.2. Cognition

What is a concept? Take the word *blue* in English (Danesi 2004a). As a concrete concept, *blue* was probably coined in reference to a pattern of hue found in natural phenomena such as the sky and the sea, and then by noting the occurrence of the same hue in other things. The specific percept of *blue* that comes to mind will, of course, be different from individual to individual. But all percepts will fall within a certain hue range on the light spectrum. In a phrase, the word *blue* allows speakers of English to talk and think about the occurrence of a specific hue in a concrete way. But that is not all it does. Speakers use the very same word to characterize emotions, morals, and other abstractions. Consider, for instance, the two sentences below:

(1) Today I've got the *blues*.
(2) That piece of information hit me right out of the *blue*.

The use of *blue* in (1) to mean "sad" or "gloomy" is the result of a culture-specific process, coming out of the tradition of "blues" music, which is perceived typically to evoke sadness or melancholy through its melodies, harmonies, rhythms, and lyrics. The use of *blue* in (2) to render the concept of "unexpectedness" comes, instead, out of the tradition of ascribing unpredictability to the weather. In other words, the denotative functions of words such as *blue* are expanded in culture-specific ways through a metasystem of hypertextual associations. In so doing we produce our everyday concepts. Incidentally, both of the above utterances were used during a university lecture by one of the authors and, at the end of the class, a student of Slavic background asked him about their meaning, indicating that she had never heard the use of the color term *blue* in such a way, that is, as a predicate referring to sadness and surprise.

Naming the world of objects, events, things, plants, flowers, animals, beings, ideas, etc. allows people to organize the world conceptually, that is, to remember it in the mind through words. The accumulated store of concepts is part of what we commonly call *cognition*. Without words, the world would not have parts to it, at least in cognitive terms. Linguistic labeling practices bring out what parts are useful or necessary to specific cultures. Every culture thus develops specialized vocabularies over time according to need (or even whim). These serve specific social and cognitive reasons (Chapter 1, § 3.1). In Shinzwani (a language spoken in the Comoro Islands of the Western Indian Ocean), the word *mama* refers to both *mother* and *aunt* (Danesi 2004b). The reason for this is that the two individuals perform similar kinship duties.

Naming family members and relatives constitutes, actually, a classic case used by linguists to show how language and classification mirror socio-cognitive organization. In English, the primary kinship relations are encoded by the words *mother, father, brother, sister, grandmother, grandfather, grandson, granddaughter, niece, nephew, mother-in-law, father-in-law, sister-in-law,* and *brother-in-law*. English vocabulary also distinguishes between *first* and *second cousins* and *great-aunts, great-uncles,* etc. However, it does not distinguish lexically between younger and older siblings. Moreover, English distinguishes a *nephew/niece* from a *grandchild*. But the latter distinction is not encoded in other languages. In Italian, for example, *nipote* refers to both "nephew/niece" and "grandchild." This conceptual contrast in kinship conceptualization came out in the following conversation recorded by one of the authors (A) and an Italian-Canadian woman (B) who spoke English rather well. The conversation shows a semantic calque from Italian, whereby she obviously assumed that one word *niece* was applicable to cover kinship relations that English codified instead with two terms *niece* and *granddaughter*:

A: Who is Claudia?
B: She is my niece.
A: But I thought she was your daughter's daughter.
B: Yes, my *nipotina*, you know, little niece?
A: You mean granddaughter?
B: Same thing.

Kinship terms indicate how the family is structured in a given culture, what relationships are considered to be especially important, and what attitudes towards specific kin may exist. In the Hawaiian kinship system, all relatives of the same generation and sex are referred to with the same term—the term used to refer to *father* is used as well for the father's brother and the mother's brother (for which we use *uncle*). Similarly, the mother, her sister, and the father's sister (for which we use *aunt*) are all classified together under a single term. Essentially, kinship reckoning in Hawaiian culture involves putting relatives of the same sex and age into the same category. On the other hand, in the Sudanese system, the mother's brother is distinguished from the father, and mother's sister is distinguished from the mother, as well as from the father's sister. Each cousin is distinguished from all others, as well as from siblings.

Color terminologies are similarly specialized. Experts estimate that we can distinguish perhaps as many as 10 million colors. Our names for colors are, thus, far too inexact to describe accurately all the colors we actually see. As a result, people often have difficulty trying to describe or match a certain color. If one were to put a finger at any point on the spectrum, there would be only a negligible difference in gradation in the colors immediately adjacent to the finger at either side. Yet, a speaker of English describing the spectrum will list the gradations as falling under the categories *purple, blue, green, yellow, orange,* and *red.* This is because such a speaker has been conditioned by the English language to classify the content of the spectrum in specific ways. There is nothing inherently "natural" about our color scheme; it is a reflex of English vocabulary, not of Nature. What is a shade of color in one language is a distinct color in another. Vocabulary is a guide to what is "out there." And vocabulary is really the verbal means by which cultures come to understand the world.

Speakers of Shona, an indigenous African language divide the spectrum up into *cipswuka, citema, cicena,* and *cipswuka* (again), and speakers of Bassa, a language of Liberia, segment it into just two categories, *hui* and *ziza.* So, when an English speaker refers to, say, a ball as *blue,* a Shona speaker might refer to it as either *cipswuka* or *citema,* and a Bassa speaker as *hui.* What a Shona speaker would consider as shades of *cicena,* the English speaker would see as two distinct colors, *green* and *yellow.* But such differences do not stop speakers of the above languages from relating their color notions to those of the other two languages. This is, indeed, what a teacher of English would have to do when he or she imparts the new color system to students with Shona and Bassa backgrounds. Moreover, in all languages there exist verbal resources for referring to more specific gradations on the spectrum if the situation should require it. In English, the words *crimson, scarlet, vermilion,* for instance, make it possible to refer to types of *red.* But these are still felt by speakers to be subcategories or shades of red, not distinct color categories on their own. Similar kinds of resources exist in Shona and Bassa.

Clearly, as Laroche (2007: 13) aptly puts it, "Color is interesting to linguists who study language differences in different cultures [because] such study can illumine the idea that since we think in words, we can think only about what we have words for or, as Ludwig Wittgenstein put it, 'The limits of language are the limits of my world.'" In 1969, American anthropological linguists Brent Berlin and Paul Kay decided to study the relation between color systems and cognition more extensively than had ever been done in the past. Their study has become a point of reference in discussing the Whorfian effects and the function of specialized vocabularies ever since, because it apparently shows that differences in color terms are only superficial matters that conceal universal principles of color perception. On the basis of the judgments of the native speakers of widely-divergent languages, Berlin and Kay came to the conclusion that there were "focal points" in basic (single-term) color vocabularies, which clustered in certain predictable ways. More specifically, they asked speakers of 98 languages to sort 329 color chips into categories that could not be subsumed within any other class. In this way, Berlin and Kay were able to identify eleven universal focal points, corresponding to the English words black, white, red, yellow, green, blue, brown, purple, pink, orange, and gray. Not all the languages they investigated had separate words for each of these colors, but there emerged a pattern that suggested to them a fixed sequence of color naming across cultures.

- If a language had two colors, then the names were equivalents of English *black* and *white*.
- If it had three color terms, then the third one corresponded to *red*.
- A four-term system had a term for either *yellow* or *green*, but not both.
- A five-term system had terms for both of these.
- A six-term system included a term for *blue*.
- A seven-term system had a term for *brown*.
- Finally, terms for *purple, pink, orange,* and *gray* were found to occur in any combination in languages that had the previous focal terms.

Berlin and Kay had in effect found that languages with, say, a four-term system consisting of black, white, red, and brown did not exist. Despite gaps found in the sequence, and various arguments made against it over the years, the Berlin-Kay study has had profound implications on several counts. First, it shows that the contrast between *light* and *dark* is the basic distinction made by human beings across the world. So, a specialized color vocabulary with the lowest number of terms will turn out to be a two-term vocabulary. Second, it suggests that languages go through stages in the naming of the other colors and, thus, that color vocabularies are a product of human perception, not language traditions. Cultures provide the contexts in which the sequence develops—but the sequence remains universal.

But many problems remain to this day with the conclusions reached by the study. For one thing, some of the terms Berlin and Kay listed turn out to be borrowings, which somewhat undermines the empirical backing of their theory. More importantly, the fact that the eleven focal colors posited by Berlin and Kay correspond to the color terms of their own language (English) colors the outcome (no pun intended) of the study. Could the researchers have been predisposed by their own language to gloss all other terms according to the English categories? The exceptions to their universal sequence that have accrued over the years seem to bear this out. Moreover, color vocabularies seem to have originated from specific experiences, not from the operation of innate perceptual mechanisms. In Hittite, for instance, words for colors initially designated plant and tree names such as *poplar, elm, cherry, oak*, etc.; in Hebrew, the name of the first man, *Adam*, meant "red" and "alive." No wonder then that the study of color has become its own area of investigation today (Biggam, Kay, and Pitchford 2006, Maclaury, Paramei, and Dedrick 2007, Plümacher, and Holz 2007).

The gist of the foregoing discussion is that culture, language, and cognition are dynamically intertwined in human beings. When the setting for communication is intercultural, it is obvious that difficulties in understanding messages often are due to basic differences in this dynamic.

4. Conceptual calquing

The foregoing discussion implies that language is at the basis of how people living together come to conceptualize the world and, then, to act in it. It also implies that many of the interferences found in IC are bound to be the result of what can be called *conceptual calquing*. This is defined as the transfer of native-language concepts to the koiné words, phrase, and structures. The result is the use of the forms of the koiné as bearers of native concepts.

Consider the ways in which bodies of water are named in English. In this language, terms such as *lake, ocean, river, stream, sea, creek*, among many others, are part of the English-speaker's lexical repertoire for referring to such bodies. This indicates bodies of water have cultural salience, perhaps because of the presence of such bodies in English-speaking societies. On the other hand, people living in the desert have very few words for such bodies, for obvious reasons. Because of their importance in English, further differentiation criteria such as size enter the classificatory system (*ocean* versus *lake*), as does width and length (*river* versus *stream*). Now, when an interlocutor does not have access to such conceptual differences, he or she will tend to use native concepts instinctively when speaking about bodies of water. For example, one student in Toronto of non-English background would consistently refer to Lake Ontario as an *ocean* because in his language any large body of water was conceptualized in terms of a single word that corresponded to English *ocean*. So, he would refer to the body of water as *Lake Ontario*, when naming it, because that is the term he learned. However, when talking about it an abstract way, he would refer to it as an *ocean*.

4.1. Lexical calques

Technically speaking, the set of terms used to designate bodies of water is called a *lexical field*. This is defined as a collection of lexical morphemes that are used to refer to a single domain of reference. Color terms, kinship terms, among many other kinds of terms, form lexical fields. Lack of knowledge of lexical fields is often the source of miscommunication in IC. The following dialogue, for example, occurred in Lugano between two students (and recorded by one of the authors). Both students were non-native speakers of English: one was of Slavic origin (A) and the other of Japanese origin (B):

A: Did you bring your writing board?
B: My pad?
A: Not your pad, this lecture is important. We have to take lots of notes.
B: Yes, I use my pad.
A: OK, same thing.

Needless to say, a *writing board* makes little sense to a speaker of English. On the other hand, the choice of *pad* is appropriate in the given interaction field. Writing materials and instruments are culturally important to English-speaking societies (and many others, needless to say), probably because of the enormous industry developed over time to produce such objects, as well as the crucial role that writing plays in such societies. Here are just a few common examples of how English vocabulary is specialized in this domain:

Table 12. Writing materials and objects in English

Object	Distinguishing Features (among others)
sheet of paper	allows for writing on two sides
pad	bound assemblage of sheets
agenda	bound assemblage of sheets marked for calendar entries
book	bound pages for specialized writing
pen	ink-based writing instrument
pencil	instrument for erasable writing
notebook	writing pad specialized for note-taking functions
marker	felt-tip pen for making marks
highlighter	felt pen with transparent colored ink for marking passages
eraser	device (usually made of rubber) for erasing something written
diary	book for keeping a personal record of events in writing

A's error above can be called, simply, a lexical calque. It reveals that A probably used a native concept that he calqued as the English phrase *writing board*. Such calquing occurs at all levels of language, from simple literal lexical-item substitutes, such as the example above (*ocean* for *lake*), to the use of invented terms such as *writing board*. Often the lexical calque is a figure from some textual tradition—as in *He pulled a Machiavellian trick on me*, which refers to the Italian philosopher Niccolò Machiavelli and, especially, his treatise titled *The Prince*, in which Machiavelli seems to suggest that expediency in achieving a desired goal is to be given prominence over ethical behavior and morals. Knowledge of such textually-based lexical forms and more generically of lexical fields is part of conceptual fluency (Danesi 2003). This can be defined more specifically as the ability to access lexical fields, so as to come up with items that are appropriate semantically and argumentatively in a given interaction field.

4.2. Metaphorical calques

Research on intercultural dialogue, especially in classroom situations (Danesi 2003) suggests that interlocutors show virtually no traces of conceptual fluency, even after several years of study, especially in the area of metaphorical language use. The reason for this is not that they are incapable of learning the conceptual metaphors of their second language (or koiné, as the case may be), but rather that they have never been exposed to them in systematic ways.

During a graduate summer course one of the authors gave to Italian-speaking high school teachers of English at the University of Perugia, which he conducted in English (for obvious pedagogical reasons), a dialogue ensued between the author (A) and a student (B):

B: How many years do you have *(Quanti anni ha)*?
A: I have many of them *(Ne ho tanti)* (Delivered ironically, but not understood by B in an ironic sense).
B: But you carry them well *(Ma li porta proprio bene)*.
A: Thanks.

The student was clearly using English words to deliver Italian conceptual metaphors. Being himself of Italian origin, A understood what the student was saying and attempted to be ironic by answering back with a similar metaphorical calque (which the student did not grasp). In effect, B was thinking in Italian and using English words to convey her thoughts. This kind of metaphorical calquing is typical in all kinds of intercultural settings.

In order to point out what this entailed, A used the occasion to help the student-teachers to prepare explanatory, grammatical, and activity materials, that showed conceptual differences between English and Italian. The following conceptual contrasts were discussed at length:

- *Quanti anni hanno i tuoi amici e come li portano?* = How old are your friends, and how do they look for their age?
- *Chi ha più/meno anni di te?* = Who is older/younger than you?
- *Quanti ne hanno?* = How old are they?

Without going into details here, suffice it to say that the Perugia experience showed that the notion of conceptual fluency is as teachable and usable as is any other notion. By simply discussing conceptual metaphorical differences and then by presenting the appropriate grammatical and lexical patterns of the language as reflexes of these, the result was extremely positive. By the end of the course previously-used metaphorical calques had virtually disappeared from dialogical interactions.

5. Intercultural contact

As mentioned in the opening chapter (§ 2.1), the study of IC within linguistics can be traced to the work on contact phenomena that was conducted in the early 1950s and, thus, long before the present proposal to make the study of contact a primary target of GL. The contact linguists looked at the language-culture link in very specific, yet enlightening ways. One of these was the investigation of calquing across languages and another was the study of the role of borrowing in contact situations. The overall question their line of research raised continues to be a fundamental one for GL today: Why do people borrow from other languages? The most common motivation for borrowing, it would seem, is to fill conceptual gaps. The words that are borrowed are called, logically, *loanwords*. In English, loanwords such as *naïve* (from French) and *memorandum* (from Latin) entered the language ostensibly because no English morpheme existed at the time for expressing the concepts that such forms encode (and still does not). Borrowing is thus a practical strategy. When speakers of a language do not have a word for something that they wish to identify, they can either create one for it or else borrow the word from a language that does. The latter happens more frequently than one might think, probably because it takes less cognitive effort to do so.

Since IC involves languages in contact, it is worthwhile taking a look at contact study in a general way. Such study is a model for how GL should develop its *modus operandi*. One of the characteristics of the GL approach is that it is not limited to considering strictly lexical and grammatical borrowing, but broadens the scope of the investigation to what we could call *textual borrowing* between cultures. This is consistent with the twofold approach to culture as semiotic system (text generative mechanism) and as an interconnected set of texts (hypertext) that was outlined above in § 2.2.

5.1. Loanwords

One of the key notions developed by contact linguists is that of loanword. When *denotative* conceptual gap-filling is the raison d'être behind a loanword, then it is called a *necessary loan*; if the reason is social and *connotative*, such as the use of a foreign word in place of a native one for prestige, then the loanword is called a *luxury loan*. Other terms have been used in the relevant literature, but these will suffice for our purposes since they designate the most common kinds of loanwords. There are many luxury loans in English. Some of these are listed below:

Table 13. Luxury loans in English

Luxury Loan	Native Term
au courant (French)	up to date
ad hoc (Latin)	on the spot, without deliberation
RSVP *(Répondez s'il vous plaît)* (French)	reply politely requested
machismo (Spanish)	masculinity
memorandum (Latin)	written reminder
gusto (Italian)	taste, zest

Whereas luxury loans retain their original morphological structure, and are pronounced according to their original phonology (as best one can), necessary loans are typically adapted to the morphology and phonology of the borrowing language as they gradually gain currency—a process referred to as *nativization*. Among the words that English has nativized from Italian, one can mention *alarm* (from *allarme*), *bandit* (from *bandito*), *bankrupt* (from *bancarotta*), *carnival* (from *carnevale*), *gazette* (from *gazzetta*), and *sonnet* (from *sonetto*). These now have English word-structure and are pronounced according to English rules of phonology.

In 1973, the *Oxford English Dictionary* conducted a computerized survey of about 80,000 words. According to that survey, the source languages of English loanwords were as follows:

- French = 28.3%
- Latin = 28.24%
- Germanic = 25%
- Greek = 5.32%
- Others = 8.31%

What this shows is that without borrowing, a language like English would probably be rather limited in its vocabulary resources. English has also borrowed affixes. The suffix /-er/ *(waiter, baker*, etc.) was borrowed from Latin, and the verbal suffix /-ize/ *(customize, regularize*, etc.) comes to English (via Old French) from Greek. English is, of course, also a "lending language" to many languages today. In the area of computers, for example, many languages simply use English terms *(software, hardware,* etc.) without nativization. These are not luxury loans, however. They are often direct loans, and do not replace any existing native lexemes. This indicates that it is easier to take an existing word from another language, rather than create a new one (or a paraphrase), again reflecting an inherent economizing principle in language (Chapter 1, § 3.1).

Borrowing and nativization is characteristic of immigrant communities. Immigrants tend to settle in ethnic communities within the larger society to which they have emigrated for a simple reason—so that they can communicate with others of their own linguistic and cultural backgrounds. The language used is therefore the language of origin. But this language changes almost overnight, borrowing considerably from the dominant language of the host society.

A well-documented case-in-point of this phenomenon is the Italian language spoken in North America. After World War II, there was a large immigration from Italy to English-speaking countries (England, United States, Canada, Australia). In these countries, Italians settled into ethnic communities, known appropriately as "Little Italies." Within these communities, Italian constituted the code for carrying out daily interactions within the family and with others of Italian backgrounds. However, being in daily contact with the English language, the Italian spoken by the immigrants came to be characterized by a large infusion of nativized words borrowed from English. Predictably, most of the loanwords were nouns and verbs filling conceptual gaps. In nativization, nouns are assigned grammatical gender through the addition of final vowels and verbs are assigned to the first conjugation (ending in /-are/)—that being the most regular and the most frequent one in the Italian verb system:

Table 14. English loanwords in the Italian of immigrant ethnic communities in North America.

English Loanword	Nativized Form	Standard Italian Form
mortgage	*morgheggio*	*mutuo, ipoteca*
switch	*suiccia*	*interruttore*
fence	*fenza*	*recinto*
to push	*pusciare*	*spingere*
to smash	*smesciare*	*frantumare*
garbage	*garbiccio*	*immondizia, rifiuti*
to squeeze	*squisare*	*spremere*

In addition to borrowing, the Italian of the immigrant communities was, predictably, replete with calquing:

Table 15. Calques in the Italian of immigrant ethnic communities in North America

English Loanword	Nativized Calque	Standard Italian Form
downtown	*bassa città*	*centro*
it looks good	*guarda bene*	*sta bene*
to make a call	*fare il telefono*	*telefonare*

The primary reason why loanwords and calques are so plentiful in immigrant community languages is, as mentioned, conceptual gap-filling tied to everyday communicative need. They are the result of people desiring or needing to refer to the objects and ideas in their new physical and social environments with facility. Lacking an appropriate word for *mortgage* in his or her own language of origin (usually an Italian dialect), for instance, Italian immigrants adopted the English word and made it their own linguistically.

5.2. Translation as textual borrowing

In a sense, the study of loanwords and calques in immigrant contexts is a study in the raison d'être of translation. In this way the network of a cultural hypertext is enriched, incorporating texts originating from other cultures. Throughout history, the role of translation in developing scientific knowledge and in re-shaping cultural identities cannot be overestimated. The translation of critical cultural texts, such as scientific treatises, novels, tales, and poetry, has led over the centuries to attempts on the part of people of different cultures to understand each other and, more importantly, to enter into a meaningful intercultural form of communication—long before the advent of the global village. Translation can be considered in itself as a *textual borrowing*. This form of borrowing does not work at the level of the linguistic system, but touches the level of culture as an hypertext. By translating, in fact, one adopts a text elaborated in another language and in another culture.

To show what translation implies, interculturally and conceptually, one of the authors of this book (Danesi 2003), gave the following passage to several classes of advanced students of Italian at the University of Toronto, totaling 48 students. They were asked to translate it into Italian:

> Jack is a real cool cat. He never blows his stack and hardly ever flies off the handle. What's more, he knows how to get away with things. Of course, he is getting on, too. His hair is pepper and salt, but he knows how to make up for lost time by taking it easy. He gets up early, works out, and turns in early.

This passage is, clearly, rich in metaphorical content and thus poses a truly difficult translation task. Needless to say, all the students found it, initially, very hard to conceptualize how the passage would be rendered in Italian. However, with the help of the instructor and the guided use of reference materials (dictionaries, phrase books), the students were gradually able to translate it in ways that reflected appropriate Italian versions of the text to various degrees of fidelity, as native speakers confirmed subsequently by reading and assessing the translations.

One student made the following analogies (Table 13 below), allowing her to reconceptualize the text in a culturally-appropriate manner. Her analogies rendered the text much more literal, yet still appropriate conceptually. The word "literal" is used in a relative sense, because most of the words chosen by the student were, in effect, either latent metaphors or had metaphorical derivations. For example, the word *cavarsela*, which she chose to render the concept of "to get away with something," is formed with the verb *cavare*, which means "to dig out, to take out/off," thus having a latent metaphorical meaning. As such, it is an instantiation of a conceptual metaphor. Indeed, it was in making such explicit comparisons that the student was able to translate the passage in a conceptually-appropriate manner:

Table 16. Analogies between English and Italian expressions

English	Italian
to be a (real) cool cat	*essere una persona molto calma*
to blow one's stack	*perdere l'auto-controllo, arrabbiarsi*
to fly off the handle	*arrabbiarsi fortemente*
what's more	*per di più*
to get away with something	*cavarsela*
of course	*certo, naturalmente*
to be getting on	*invecchiarsi*
pepper and salt	*capelli un po' grigi*
to make up for something	*riprendere, riacquistare, rifare*
lost time	*tempo perduto*
to take it easy	*stare calmo, non preoccuparsi*
to get up	*alzarsi dal letto*
to work out	*fare esercizio, fare ginnastica*
to turn in	*andare a dormire la sera*

This led her to produce several drafts that she then edited for grammar and style. The end result was a translation text that delivered the same message as the English one, but in conceptually-appropriate Italian.

The above discussion provides a few implicit insights into understanding interferences in IC. The main is that when interlocutors of different cultural backgrounds speak not only are two language systems in contact—the native and the koiné—but also two conceptual systems. The relevant systems can be symbolized as follows:

L_1 = the native language
CS_1 = the native conceptual system
L_2 = the common language (or koiné)
CS_2 = the conceptual system of the target culture

Now, the main problem in intercultural contact can be traced to a clash between conceptual systems. Successful communication in IC involves the ability to express oneself in the L_2 while utilizing the CS_2, rather than relying on the CS_1. Knowledge of the CS_2 is not simply a question of familiarity with unique cultural concepts, such as the Spanish bullfight, the Tibetan practice of sand painting, or the Italian *passeggiata*. Rather, it implies being able to participate in a system of concepts without unconsciously relying on the native CS_1 to decipher conversations or dialogues.

It is entirely possible, of course, that interlocutors will produce grammatically and conceptually native-like utterances, even though they are relying on the CS_1. The reason for this is positive conceptual transfer, whereby L_2 expressions result as native-like because the CS_1 and CS_2 overlap in a specific domain. Clearly, the individual concepts shared by two conceptual systems in contact will vary, depending on the particular languages and cultures in question. It is safe to assume, however, that there will indeed be some overlapping, and that this is a possible source of positive conceptual transfer for inter-agents in IC. In terms of congruity theory (Cf. Chapter 2, § 5.1), what seems to happen frequently in intercultural contact situations is the use of CS_1 predicates that are lexicalized in L_2 but maintain the predicate-argument-frame and congruity requirements of CS_1 predicates. This asymmetry creates incongruities when the text is semantically interpreted in terms of CS_2 by the addressee. Consider the following utterance, recorded by one of the authors (A), which was spoken by an native English student of Italian (B), attempting to say that he was *hot* during a very warm and humid day:

A: *Come stai?* ("How are you?")
B: *Oggi sono caldo.* ("I am hot.")
A: *Hai caldo, vero?* ("You're hot, aren't you?")
B: *Sì, sono caldo.* ("Yes, I am hot.")

Clearly, the student was unaware that the expression *to be hot* in English translates to *avere caldo* (literally, "to have heat") and that *essere caldo* ("to be hot") in Italian implies something different—it is used for example, when one has a fever. B had, in effect, used a predicate *to be hot* (x_1) from his native CS_1 thinking that he was relaying a certain message rather than another one.

This is a conspicuous case of conceptual interference. In the Italian CS_2 the verbs *avere* ("to have"), *fare* ("to do, make"), and *essere* ("to be") are used in expressions that are linked to various situations in which "coldness" and "hotness" are conceptualized differentially:

(1) *Fa freddo/caldo fuori.* ("It is cold/hot outside.")
(2) *Lui ha freddo/caldo.* ("He is cold/hot.")
(3) *Il caffè è freddo/caldo.* ("The coffee is cold/hot.")

168 Culture

The different verbal selections, together with the underlying conceptual system that occasioned them, can be shown in diagram form below (L_1 = English, CS_1 = English conceptual system, L_2 = Italian, CS_2 = Italian conceptual system):

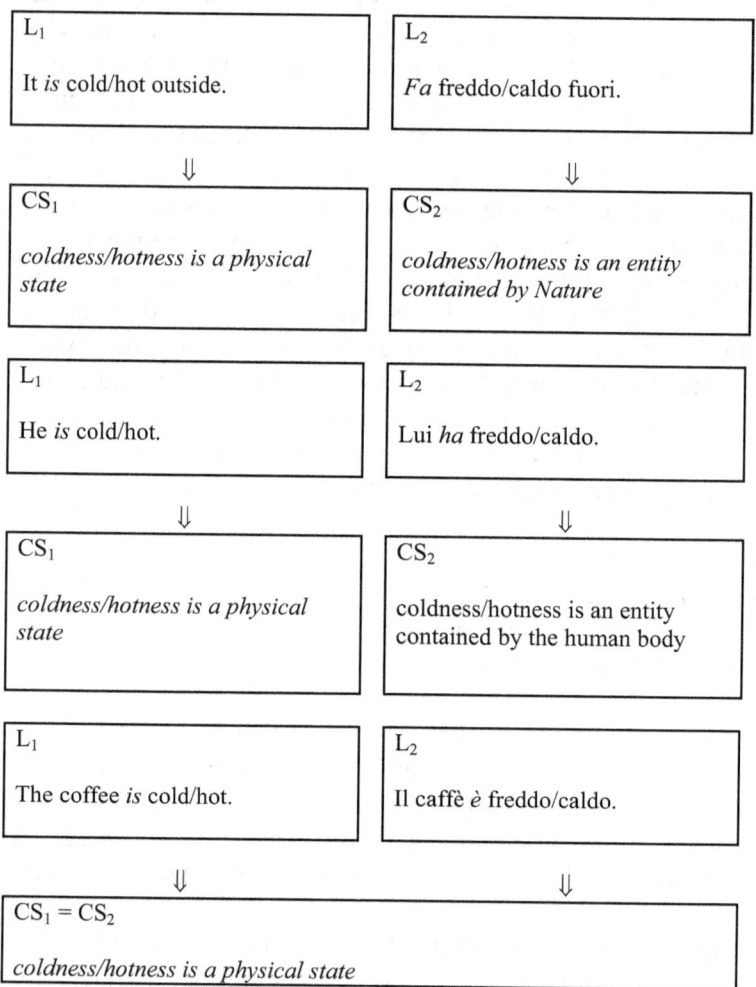

Figure 22. Conceptual systems in contact.

In Italian, the verb *fare* is used with respect to a weather situation—*fa freddo* (literally) "it makes cold," *fa caldo* (literally) "it makes hot." The physical state of "coldness" or "hotness" is conveyed instead by the verb *essere* when referring to objects (*è freddo* "it is cold," *è caldo* "it is hot") and by *avere* "to have" when referring to people (*ha freddo* "he/she is cold", *ha caldo* "he/she is hot"). The use of one verb or the other—*fare, essere,* or *avere*—is clearly motivated by an underlying image schema of bodies, objects, and the environment as containers and the states of "coldness" and "hotness" as entities. The container and entity schemas are the sources of the differential verbal selections. If the container is the environment, then the entities ("coldness" and "hotness") are *made* by Nature *(fa freddo, fa caldo)*; if it is a human being, then the individual's body *has* them *(ha freddo, ha caldo)*; and if it is an object, then the object *is* their container *(è freddo, è caldo)*. No such conceptual distinctions are required by the English CS$_1$.

6. Cultures in context

The foregoing discussion should not be construed as implying that people have one and only one conceptual system and, thus, exclusively embrace one cultural identity. On the contrary, the very fact that people of different cultural backgrounds enter into daily communication is evidence that people wish to embrace each other, regardless of cultural backgrounds, and that they are capable of understanding the conceptually-different ways of viewing the world. Throughout history, many countries have institutionalized different cultural realities through legislation. Called "multicultural," such societies bear witness to the fact that contact is (or could be) a cooperative form of interaction (of the type discussed in Chapter 3). The linguistic study of multiculturalism, in all its modalities, should thus constitute another area of relevance to GL.

The example of a country like Switzerland clearly demonstrates how diverse cultural identities can characterize individuals (Cf. Figure 23). The political personality of the nation (a confederation of 26 cantons-states) is composed of distinct cultural identities according to specific linguistic communities. Switzerland is subdivided into four linguistic regions (German, French, Italian and Romansch) each one of which has historical and cultural links with the corresponding societies who speak the relevant languages—Germany, France, Italy, and the northeast area in Italy where the Ladin and Friulian languages are commonly used (both being related to Romansch in origin) (Cf. Table 17, below).

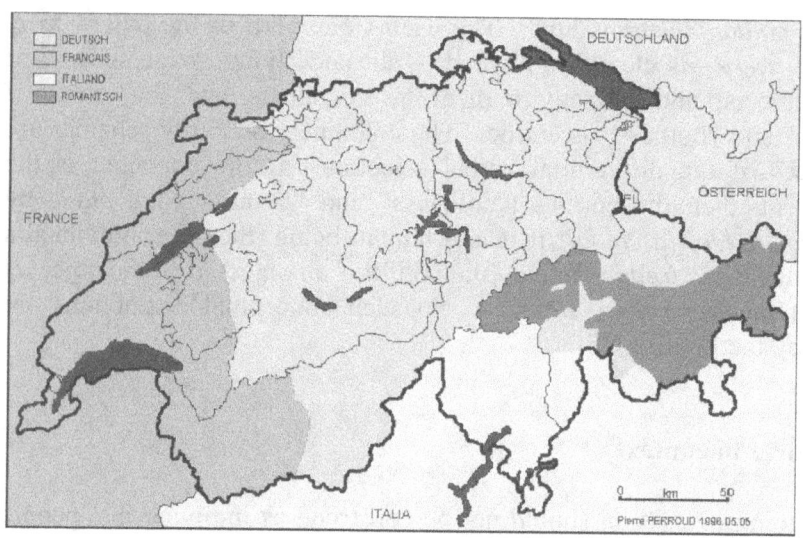

Figure 23.   Linguistic geography of Switzerland.

Table 17. Languages spoken in the Swiss Confederation (Lüdi and Werlen 2005:8)

Language	% of Population
German	63.7
French	20.4
Italian	6.5
Romansch	0.5
Other	9.0

A person born and raised in Geneva is Swiss by national identity, but, at the same time, belongs to a community of native speakers of French (wherever they might live). In effect, that person shares the L_1 with individual born and raised in France, but his or her conceptual system is different in many ways, and thus can be symbolized as CS_2. Switzerland is also characterized by the historical presence of two main religious traditions: Catholic and Protestant. About 42% of the Swiss population are Catholics, while Protestants amount to 35% of the population (Bovay 2004). While nowadays religious practice and the influence of churches in the daily life of Swiss people has significantly decreased, the presence of these two traditions has profoundly shaped Swiss identity. Interestingly, the borders the historically prevalent religious traditions do not match linguistic borders. For instance, the French speaking Canton Geneva was the birthplace of Calvinism, and the German speaking Canton Zurich is characterized by the Protestant tradition of Zwinglianism, while Catholicism is historically associated, for instance, with the German speaking Canton Lucerne and the bilingual (French-German) cantons of Fribourg and Valais, as well as with the Italian speaking Canton Tessin. Local exceptions abound: the Italian speaking Val Bregaglia, for instance, is proud of its Protestant heritage and is located in the tri-lingual canton of Grisons. Recently, the historical multiculturalism of Switzerland has become even more complex due to massive immigration (currently about 20% of the resident population of Switzerland is represented by foreigners) bringing new languages and religious traditions to the Swiss territory.

The criss-crossing of national, linguistic and religious boundaries should remind us that cultures are not impermeable bubbles enclosing totally separate semiospheres, they are, like living cells, permeable structures where osmotic phenomena are the norm. The overlapping of cultural boundaries also shows that each of us belongs to several cultural communities at once (Cf. Rigotti 2005a).

The number of overlapping cultures increases considerably if we take into account variables such as the profession (e.g. being a linguist, as opposed to, say, a stock exchange broker), the institution where we received our education (e.g. being an alumnus of a particular university), other institutions in which we participated (e.g. having served in the military), affiliation to groups and movements (e.g. political parties) and furthermore hobbies and sports (e.g. being part of the surfers' culture), belonging to particular "urban tribes" or subcultures (e.g. being a Goth), to online communities (e.g. being a player of World of Warcraft). From a linguistic and communicative viewpoint each of the above cited communities brings with it its specialized lexicon, and, more generally its discourse system, its common ground of values and shared beliefs. It is clear, however, that this overlapping of multiple "identities" does not make a person schizophrenic: everyone of us has a hierarchy of interests, desires and affective relationships, and can identify which cultural communities are crucial for his/her identity with regard to the specific issues that he/she is involved in.

The discomfort that immigrants often feel when they have contact with an unfamiliar culture is commonly called *culture shock*. But this usually passes if an immigrant stays in the new culture long enough to understand it and get used to its ways. Over time members of immigrant communities may tend to give up their old ways and become part of the dominant culture. The process by which they do this is called *assimilation*. Through assimilation, a minority group eventually disappears because its members lose the cultural characteristics that set them apart. In a multicultural society, however, assimilation is attenuated considerably. Such a society espouses the view that preserving cultures is a desirable objective, so as to strengthen the overall society. The United States, for example, is a multicultural and multilingual society, albeit not officially (as are Switzerland and Canada). In the US millions of people speak both English and the language of their ancestral culture. Most prominent amongst the "other" languages of the US is, of course, Spanish, which is spoken at home by more than 34 million people (according to the U.S. Census Bureau 2007). For the purposes of GL, the study of multicultural societies, and cultures in contact generally, will clearly provide a case-in-point against which ideas and assessments of IC can be assessed and compared.

Chapter 5
Argumentation

> *Our only choice is between reason and violence.*
> (Karl Popper 1902-1994)

1. Introductory remarks

We have already introduced in Chapter 1 the topic of argumentation and we have discussed both its centrality for IC and its problematic nature (Chapter 1, § 2.2 and 4.2). Threading the footsteps of the Amsterdam school of argumentation, we can define argumentation as a social and rational activity aimed at resolving a difference of opinion reasonably, that is by putting forth arguments (reasons) supporting a standpoint in a way that would be acceptable to a reasonable critic (van Eemeren & Grootendorst 2004). Van Eemeren and Grootendorst observe that for argumentation to be carried out meaningfully and with any hope of success the discussants need a common starting point, something that they already share and can agree upon.

Interestingly, the starting point of argumentation is nothing else that a particular specification of the general notion of *common ground*, which we introduced in Chapter 2 (§ 6.1). We can think of arguing as trying to lead somebody to assent to a standpoint, making it follow inferentially from arguments (also called *premises*) that are already accepted as part of the common ground. Every bit of information that is in the common ground can be virtually used as an argument to make a point: this includes recollections of shared personal experiences (*personal common ground*), but also, and crucially the *communal common ground* that stores the shared cultural propositional information. In Chapter 4 we referred to this declarative aspect of culture as the cultural *hypertext*. In intercultural situations we may well expect the starting point of argumentation to be shakier than in situations where a good deal of the hypertextual network is shared. Van Eemeren and Grootendorst (2004) also make a distinction between the *material* starting point of argumentation – the cognitive representation and affective evaluation of the world that they share – and the *formal* starting point, that is the shared rules of the game that will be used to adjudicate the point in doubt. As we will see presently these two different starting points lead to different communication problems in IC.

An ancient art long neglected, argumentation has recently gained widespread interest among scholars of different disciplines and has become a vibrant cross-discipline, encompassing not only linguistics, but also communications, philosophy, rhetoric, law, logic and even computer science and artificial intelligence (see Walton 2007 on the latter). In a way, the development of argumentation theory across disciplines parallels the emergence of the global village and reflects the perceived need of laying down the logical foundations of the ongoing discussion in this village.

In this chapter, we will take a closer look at argumentation theory, since it is, in our view, fundamental for gaining a solid understanding of some of the problems that constantly arise in IC and, in particular, of the deepest problems that range from socio-pragmatic failures to full fledged intercultural conflicts. As in other chapters, however, we can only scratch the surface here as well. The objective is, simply, to delineate the main notions associated with argumentation theory so as to be able to include them into the broader framework of GL.

2. Discussions: freedom and responsibility

If we want to understand how argumentation works as a form of socialized reasoning it is natural to start from a *discussion*. A discussion is a form of dialogue in which argumentation takes place. In fact, all arguments, even those that appear in monological texts, like, for instance, newspaper editorials and opinion pieces, are to be understood – at least implicitly – as interventions in a virtual discussion. We can say that argumentation theory subscribes to a version of Bakhtin's *dialogical principle*, which we introduced in Chapter 2 (§ 2).

Let us examine a mini case-study to see what the key components of a discussion are and how argumentation may unfold from them. Let us suppose that Mary and John are discussing about animal taxonomy, perhaps just after biology class, and Mary advances the following standpoint: *Whales are mammals*. John is not convinced and casts doubt on the standpoint: *No I don't think so.* John's expression of doubt functions as a challenge to Mary to defend her standpoint. In a reasonable discussion the *burden of proof* is on whoever advances a standpoint. John, in his turn, may or may not advance his own standpoint. If he does – for instance by saying *I'm pretty sure the whale is a fish* – he will have in his turn to support it with arguments. Van Eemeren and Grootendorst (2004) propose that our argumentative discussions can be better understood and evaluated if we compare them against an ideal yardstick, which they call *the model of critical discussion*. A critical discussion is simply a discussion where the participants cooperate to solve their difference of opinion *on the merits*, that is by testing the standpoint against the evidence that is accepted by both parties as part of the starting point. The ideal of critical discussion is not something entirely extraneous to argumentative realities. After all, when people engage in argumentation it is because they try or at least pretend to do exactly that: cooperate to solve the difference in a reasonable way. If this were not the case argumentation would leave the place to other more violent and coercive means of settling a dispute. In Chapter 3 we have seen that indeed any form of communicative interaction needs an element of cooperation in order to realize the goals of the inter-agents.

Van Eemeren and Grootendorst (2004) posit that cooperating in solving a difference of opinion entails the respect of certain rules. The Amsterdam scholars established 10 rules that define a "code of conduct" for reasonable discussants. One of them is the *freedom rule*. This rule says that "parties must not prevent each other from putting forward standpoints or casting doubt on standpoints" (van Eemeren, Grootendorst and Snoeck Henkemans (2002: 110). If in our hypothetical discussion John says to Mary *Oh, shut up, girl! I'm your older brother* the discussion will not move forward towards a reasonable solution. The same happens if Mary refuses to deal with John's doubt, by saying something like *You always criticize what I say. You are really mean. I think I'm gonna cry.*

There are countless social situations in which the freedom rule is, if not completely negated, at least severely limited or bracketed. For instance, studies of problem-solving discussions in corporate contexts (Cf. van Rees 1994) have shown that consideration of corporate hierarchy and authority can severely limit the ability of advancing standpoints on the part of the discussants, or lead participants to formulate standpoints indirectly and tentatively in the format of a question, at the risk of being ignored or misunderstood. These violations of the freedom rule severely limit the problem-solving potential of a discussion.

In the perspective of intercultural communication, it is important to focus also on the deep human relational implications of violations of the freedom rule. Van Eemeren, Grootendorst and Snoeck Henkemans (2002: 111) observe:

> Restricting the other party's freedom of action is an attempt to dismiss him as a serious partner in the discussion. Two ways of doing this are (a) to put him under pressure not to put forward a certain standpoint or objection or (b) to discredit him in the eyes of the public by casting doubt on his expertise, integrity or credibility.

The simplest way of putting pressure on a discussant is through the use or the threat of violence. A threat, blatant or subtle, aimed at preventing someone to advance a standpoint is called the *fallacy of the stick*, that is, using the traditional Latin terminology, *argumentum ad baculum*. Often threats are rather indirectly formulated. For instance, a corporate representative might say to the editor of a newspaper:

> Of course you are free to write about our company however you think fit. I don't want you to be influenced by the fact that we are your main advertiser!

Appeals to pity are another way to put pressure on the addressee in situations where the social power relations are in favor of the latter, who is in any case supposed to maintain a benevolent attitude towards the discussion partner. For instance, a student may complain about a failing mark by writing an e-mail like the following:

> I have just read your evaluation of my paper and I am now heartbroken. I am truly desperate and I do not know what to do. (Authentic e-mail message translated from Italian)

Mary's "threat" to break in tears, in our fictitious case, is another example of an attempt to constrain the freedom rule by playing on the feeling of the addressee. This is a sort of emotional blackmail. In a world characterized by power imbalances, intercultural communication is particularly exposed to the risk of threats, but also of appeals to pity.

John's strategy in the same example corresponds to the second option: discrediting the discussant. According to him, as a girl and as a younger person she is not entitled to present her point of view. In many interpersonal arguments the discredit of the source often takes the form of a personal attack (*argumentum ad hominem*). In intercultural communication, however, the potentially most dangerous form of discredit happens when discussants are excluded on the basis of their belonging to a category of people (gender, ethnicity, nationality, social class, level of formal education, etc.), which is disqualified as a whole as unreliable, stupid, ignorant, etc.

Another way of limiting the freedom of advancing standpoints or expressing doubts that is particularly relevant in the context of IC is preventing discussion by declaring a standpoint *sacrosanct* or, conversely, by declaring it *taboo*. The second strategy is the one adopted in the following example:

> I don't think you should say that Grandmother shouldn't have remarried. One should not speak ill of the dead. (van Eemeren, Grootendorst and Snoeck Henkemans 2002: 111)

This very problem is felt in IC, in particular, when the partner of a discussion resents a standpoint or the expression of a doubt as offensive or even threatening for her very cultural identity. Such a situation represents a standstill in the intercultural discussion that is very difficult to ease out. Here intercultural communication faces a thorny dilemma: can the mere discussion of a standpoint be *in itself* a threat to someone's culture? Are there limitations to be imposed to the freedom of discussion?

In the model of the critical discussion the freedom of advancing a standpoint is always accompanied by a responsibility that comes with it: a party who puts forward a standpoint is obliged to defend it if asked to do so. This is called the *burden of proof rule*. Conversational gambits aimed at evading it are all too common:

A: Journalists get more subjective every day.
B: How come?
A: Well, maybe you can explain that they are as objective as they used to be!
(From van Eemeren, Garssen & Meuffels 2003)

3. Discussions: plausibility and relevance

If we suppose that neither Mary nor John try to evade the burden of proof that comes with their opposite standpoints, they will advance arguments in order to support them. After a series of verbal exchanges between the discussants we might come to a situation such as the one represented in the diagram in Figure 24, below.

In examining the statements that Mary and John have supplied as arguments in order to support their respective standpoints one should consider two independent aspects that affect reasonable persuasion: their *plausibility* and their *relevance*. Both aspects can be a source of criticism or further questioning in the unfolding of the argumentative discussions.

Considering the plausibility of an argument means asking whether its content is accepted as true by both the discussants – i.e. is firmly part of the common ground – or can be at least regarded as likely or expected in view of the same common ground. For instance, argument AJ1 can be considered plausible if Mary and John do agree that, as a matter of fact, whales do live their entire lives in the water.

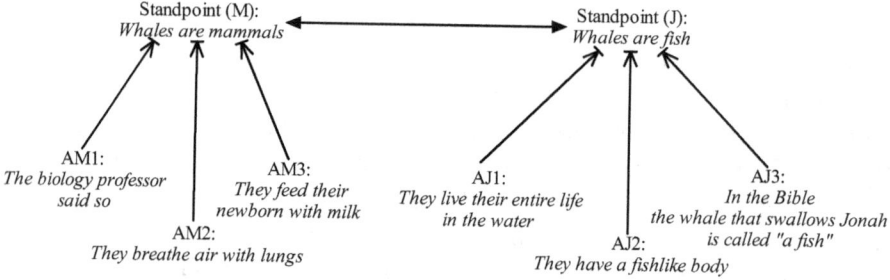

Figure 24. Standpoints and arguments supporting them in a discussion on the classification of whales.

Conversely, Mary may criticize argument AJ2 as not entirely plausible. Whales look roughly like fish, but there are also important differences: for instance, their tail fins are horizontal rather than vertical. Similar questions of plausibility might concern what exactly the biology professor did say about whales (AM1), or the exact text of the book of Jonah in the Bible (AJ3). The plausibility of the argument is a necessary condition of reasonable persuasion. However, plausibility alone is not sufficient.

One should also ask if the arguments that have being supplied, apart from being plausible in themselves, are indeed *relevant* for supporting the particular standpoint advanced by the discussant. In the critical discussion this is called the *relevance rule*. To be relevant as an argument, a statement must really impinge on some aspect of the standpoint. More precisely, they must relate to the standpoint in a way that guarantees the transfer of certainty – or at least of plausibility – from the argument to the standpoint.

Such a relevant relation is called an *argumentation scheme* (Cf. Walton 2006), or, following the traditional Latin terminology, a *locus* (Cf. Rigotti 2009). In Latin *locus* (pl. *loci*) means "place", and stands for a metaphorical place where we can look for arguments when we design an argument, a place whence arguments come, a logico-semantic relation from which they draw their persuasive force. Interestingly, the English word *commonplace* comes from an ancient technical term of argumentation theory: *locus communis* "common place". Originally the term was meant to indicate a basic relation that can be used to argue reasonably on a variety of subjects and is not tied to a particular science or branch of knowledge. As the particular sciences acquired more and more prestige, and the art of argumentation began to be forgotten or associated with *mere* rhetoric, the term *commonplace* gradually acquired its current derogatory meaning.

The relevance of arguments to their standpoints may depend on a wide variety of relations (*loci*). For instance, argument AJ2, in the whale example, depends on an *analogy*, an implicit relation of similarity between whales and other animals that are indisputably fish (like, say, salmon, shark, trout, tuna, etc.). Argument AM3 is different as it directly relies on an explicit system of categorization, which is culturally dependent. Walton (2006: 128-132) calls this *locus* "argument from verbal classification". The reasoning of AM3 works if we accept that, according to modern biology, feeding newborns with milk is a *sufficient condition* for being classified as a mammal. A discussant whose cultural background does not include the category system of modern biology but relies on other, implicit or explicit, cultural criteria in order to classify animals would not find the argument of milking cogent and could even consider it outright irrelevant. In fact, before the taxonomy of Carl Linnaeus (1707-1778) became widely accepted in Western cultures, the folk taxonomy gave much more importance to the *place* where animals lived in classifying them, as in the Biblical verse "The fish of the *sea*, the birds of the *heavens*, the beasts of the *field*, all the creeping things that *creep on the earth*..." (Ezekiel 38:20). If place is indeed the central criterion, then John's statement AJ1 *They live their entire lives in water*, becomes a perfectly relevant argument from verbal classification. If John and Mary happen to rely on different category systems, as it is often the case in intercultural communication, their disagreement about the whale cannot be solved immediately. They need to engage in a meta-discussion on the merits of the taxonomy systems, in order to find out which one is more insightful, or simply which one is more convenient for their present purpose.

Arguments such as AM1 and AJ3 can be also examined with respect to their relevance. In AM1 Mary, by referring to the authority of the biology teacher, invokes a locus called "appeal to expert opinion" (Walton 2006: 84-91). Appeals to the authority of an expert are a perfectly legitimate form of reasoning, and even a necessary one in many social circumstances where people are called to take pressing decisions that concern them but do not know all the relevant facts, and collecting and evaluating them would be practically unfeasible. For instance, global warming is an issue that concerns everybody on the planet, but we cannot realistically expect every single person to check all the relevant facts on her own in order to make up her mind. We must rely on the opinion of experts.

Different cultures and societies may differ in their attitudes towards the authority of the expert and with respect to whom exactly they regard as an expert (scientists, priests, businessmen, etc.). All cultures, however, know the argument from expert opinion. In its simplest form, this scheme of argumentation coincides with the respect for the authority of the elders: those who have lived longer than me and know more than me. They are experts of life. Systems of honorification such as the one found in the Korean language (Cf. Chapter 1, § 4.1) express exactly this kind of traditional values. As Yoon (2004: 197) observes, *noin* "old people" are thought to have had "abundant valuable experiences through their life-long activities and incidents [...] which have given them special knowledge". In fact, we can say that the very notion of culture as knowledge that is passed from generation to generation entails a sort of argument from expert opinion.

In modern societies the role of the expert has changed dramatically but has not diminished its importance. Due to the complexities and rapid pace of change of the global village, elders have lost their privileged status as experts of life to a host of "specialists" of different domains. Checking whether an expert that has been appealed to in a discussion is really an expert in the *relevant domain* is one of the most important ways of checking the relevance of this kind of argument. Had Mary appealed to the authority of the president of the World Bank to back up her opinion that whales are mammals, her argumentation would have been wholly irrelevant. The president of the World Bank may be an expert on how a financial crisis might affect developing countries, but he is hardly an authority on marine mammals.

Argument, AJ3, where John cites the Book of Jonah in the Bible is similarly an appeal to an authoritative opinion. In the perspective of IC, this kind of appeals may be examined at two levels. First, we might ask if the Bible is recognized as a "foundational text" in the cultural common ground of both discussants. If this is not the case the interlocutor might still appreciate the elegant simplicity of the story of Jonah and the whale as a literary work, but would not feel compelled to accept it as an authoritative source.

If the biblical narrative of Jonah is indeed accepted as a cultural "foundational text" by both discussants, it remains to be seen what is exactly the intended significance of the story of Jonah and the whale: is it meant to convey a spiritual teaching through a symbolic narrative or to provide an appropriate classification of marine animals?

In these first two sections we have provided an overview of argumentative discussions, tackling the pragmatic and social aspects of argumentation from the "normative pragmatic" viewpoint of the Amsterdam school. In the following sections we will sharpen our understanding of argumentative relevance throwing light also on the logico-semantic and cognitive aspects of argumentation.

4. Reasoning

4.1. Of gates and guardians

Argumentative discussions such as the one between Mary and Peter involve *reasoning* or, to use a roughly equivalent term, *inference*. Discussants do not simply try to get their discussion partners to accept their standpoint; they try to do that in a particular way, that is by inviting their discussion partners to infer the standpoint from an accepted starting point (Rocci 2006, Rigotti and Greco Morasso 2009). As Pinto (1996) puts it, arguments are "invitations to inference": by presenting an argument we invite our interlocutor to reason from the premises provided to the conclusion (or standpoint) we want to support.

Even though we are not consciously aware of it, we constantly take decisions by using logical reasoning based on given information. Making judgments, weighing the advantages or disadvantages of certain actions, deliberating about what to do about some situation, are all decision-making processes that depend on the utilization of appropriate reasoning for their outcome. Clearly, reasoning is a crucial aspect of human interaction. What is it? It is something that we know intuitively, yet find very difficult to define concretely.

A practical example might be instructive as an initial vehicle for understanding what it implies. Consider an adventure story, in which a heroic character finds herself before the entrance to two caverns, X and Y. She knows that one leads to a sought-after treasure, and the other to certain death. Each entrance is protected by a guard. Of the two guards, the heroine knows that one is a truth-teller and the other a liar, but she does not know which one is which. As a heroine with great intellectual skills, she comes up with an ingenious question to guard A, which will help her identify the appropriate cavern, no matter if that guard is a truth-teller or a liar. She asks A: "If I were to ask your fellow guard (B) which cavern leads to the treasure, what would he answer?" If A is a truth-teller, he would answer sincerely that his partner would tell her a lie; if he was a liar he would also tell her that he would lie (since he is a liar and would never admit that the other guard would tell her the truth). Here's what our heroine's clever question accomplishes:

Reasoning Scenario I:
Based on the assumption that A is a truth-teller.

A would answer the heroine's question as follows:
"B will say to take cavern X, but don't believe him."

In this scenario, A has given the heroine the correct advice. In so doing, he has identified (by the process of elimination) cavern Y as the one that has the treasure. But she cannot assume this, since she does not know that A is a truth-teller. So, let's go ahead and assume that A is a liar instead. Here's what the same question accomplishes in this case:

Reasoning Scenario II:
Based on the assumption that A is a liar.

A would answer the heroine's question as follows:
"B will say to take cavern X, and you should believe him."

In this scenario, A has given the heroine incorrect advice, since he would never admit that B is a truth-teller and give her a truthful answer—

namely, that Y is the cavern with the treasure. In so doing, however, he has again identified cavern Y as the one she should enter (by inverse logic). The outcome of her simple question is, in sum, that she should enter cavern Y, no matter if A is a truth-teller or not.

Incidentally, this type of reasoning scenario was given a popular puzzle format in the 1930s by the British puzzlist Hubert Phillips, who concocted many ingenious reasoning puzzles of this nature under the pseudonym of "Caliban" for the *New Statesman* and "Dogberry" for the *News Chronicle* (Danesi 2002). As can be seen, such logical puzzles involve setting up hypothetical situations and then reasoning about their logical conclusions or outcomes. As such, they can be used to model how everyday reasoning is used in all kinds of activities and interactions. Such reasoning may not always be as clever, but it has the same kind of logical structure within it— a structure which is based on formulating premises (or hypotheses), and then following them to a logical conclusion.

4.2. Induction, deduction and abduction

Reasoning takes various forms. Of these, there are two types that are of direct relevance to the study of IC. They are known as induction and deduction. The former involves reaching a general conclusion by observing a recurring pattern (or premise); the latter involves reasoning about the consistency or concurrence of a pattern (or premise). Aware that other types of logical processes existed (such as those found in poetry, the arts, music, etc.), the ancient Greek philosophers argued that induction and deduction were particularly crucial in mathematical reasoning. Take, for example, the fact that the number of degrees in a triangle is 180. One way to arrive at knowledge of this fact is, simply, to measure the angles of hundreds, perhaps thousands, of triangles and then assess if a pattern emerges from the measurements. Assuming that the measuring devices are precise and that errors are not made, we are bound to come to the conclusion that the three angles add up consistently to 180^0. This "conclusion-by-extrapolation" process is the sum and substance of inductive reasoning.

The expert mathematician would, however, claim that such thinking is not 100% reliable, because one can never be sure that some triangle may not crop up whose angles will add up to more or less than 180^0. To be sure that 180^0 is the sum of the angles for *all* triangles one must use a deductive method of reasoning. This inheres in applying already-proved concepts (or premises) to the case-at-hand. Without going into the details of the *proof* (as it is called) here, suffice it to say that it consists in using previously established proofs and the fact that a triangle is basically a straight line, which is an angle $180°$ segmented into three parts and "folded" together to form three lines connected to each other in the triangle form. Since the triangle under consideration is a general one, we would have proved the pattern true for *all* triangles. This "conclusion-by-demonstration" process is the sum and substance of deductive reasoning.

Induction and deduction play a significant role in the formation of many kinds of concepts and in reasoning about various things. But they hardly explain how the entire range of human reasoning unfolds. In mathematics itself, hunches and guesses play a much more central role in the origination of mathematical ideas than is often assumed. It was the American philosopher Charles Peirce (1839-1914), himself a mathematician and logician, who emphasized that many, if not most, of our originating concepts are formed by a type of inferential process that he called *abduction*. He described it as follows (Peirce 1931-1958, V: 180):

> The abductive suggestion comes to us like a flash. It is an act of insight, although of extremely fallible insight. It is true that the different elements of the hypothesis were in our minds before; but it is the idea of putting together what we had never before dreamed of putting together which flashes the new suggestion before our contemplation.

The reasoning used by our fictional heroine above is really an act of insight thinking that comes about as a "flash," as Peirce characterized it. Most mathematical discoveries occur in this way. Once an insight is attained, it becomes useful to "routinize" it, so that a host of related problems can be solved as a matter of course, with little time-consuming mental effort. Such routinization is a memory-preserving and time-saving strategy. It is the rationale behind all organized knowledge systems. Such systems produce *algorithms*—routinized procedures—for solving problems that would otherwise require insight thinking to be used over and over again.

4.3. Arguments and proofs

Argumentation in discourse shows several similarities with the form and structure of mathematical proofs. Arguments have four properties in common with proofs: they are *discursive*, *inferential*, *formal* and *critical* (Cf. Rigotti and Greco Morasso 2009).

As in mathematics, argumentation in interactional situations is *discursive*: it involves a step-by-step process where each step amounts to a discourse move. A static linguistic or semiotic *representation*, however complex, cannot be an argument. Argument requires discursive dynamics. As we have seen above, both proof and argument are *inferential*: the conclusion derives its truth value from the already ascertained truth value of the premises. If somebody claims, for instance, that William Shakespeare wrote *Othello* in 1678, we could object that this is surely not possible, since we know for a fact that Shakespeare died in 1616 and we are also pretty sure that a person cannot be dead and at the same time write a play.

We touched the issue of the truth value above, by introducing the requirement of plausibility for arguments in a critical discussion. Truth depends on what is out there in the world. Plausibility is a weaker requirement and depends on what is accepted as true or likely in the common ground. Arguments also need to be *relevant* to the standpoint. Now, it is interesting, and also a bit surprising, to observe how the relevance of an argument to a standpoint is connected with the abstract logical *form* of the argument. For instance, many arguments can be reconstructed as having the form of a *syllogism*. The form of the syllogism, which is the cornerstone of classic Aristotelian logic, consists of a major premise, a minor premise, and a conclusion:

(1) A valid syllogism:
Major premise: All animals that feed their newborn with milk are mammals.
Minor premise: Whales feed their newborn with milk.
Conclusion: Whales are mammals.

Such reasoning is *valid*, i.e. its form guarantees that it leads to a conclusion that must be true if all the premises are true. Argumentative validity, therefore, depends on the *form* of the argument, not on its content. Consider this second argument, which is also based on true premises:

(2)
Major premise: All mammals breathe air with their lungs.
Minor premise: Whales breathe air with their lungs.
Conclusion: Whales are mammals.

Here the form of the reasoning does not correspond to a valid syllogism and the conclusion happens to be true just by chance. The form of (2) cannot really vouch for the truth of the conclusion given the truth of the premises. In fact, using this same pattern we might as well conclude, always using true premises, that iguanas are mammals:

(3)
Major premise: All mammals breathe air with their lungs. (True)
Minor premise: All iguanas breathe air with their lungs. (True)
Conclusion: All iguanas are mammals. (False!)

What we lack in (2) and (3) in order to have a valid syllogism is a proper *terminus medius* ("middle term"). This is called the *fallacy of undistributed middle*. A terminus medius is a term that occurs in both premises but not in the conclusion. In order to ensure the validity of the syllogism the middle term has to be taken at least once in its full extension (e.g. *all those who breath air with their lungs...*). Let us examine the reasons of this requirement. There is a very common deductively valid pattern, traditionally called *figure I* of the syllogism, where the terminus medius occurs in the subject of the major premise and in the predicate of the minor premise. For instance, in (4) below *human being* is the middle term:

(4)
Major premise: All **human beings** *are mortal.*
Minor premise: *Mary is a* **human being**.
Conclusion: *Mary is mortal.*

The logical role of the terminus medius in a valid figure I syllogism like (1) or (4) can be highlighted if we represent the syllogistic form schematically:

(5) Underlying form of (1) and (4):
Major premise: All **A**s are B.
Minor premise: c is **A**.
Conclusion: Therefore, c is B.

In (4) the letter A stands for the terminus medius. Its crucial role could easily be explicated in set theoretic terms (Figure 25): A is a (proper or improper) subset of B, and c belongs to A. Therefore we must conclude that *c* also belongs to the superset B. No such set-theoretic translation is possible for the invalid pseudo-syllogisms (2) and (3).

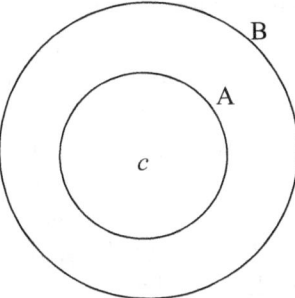

Figure 25. Set theoretic representation of valid syllogisms (1) and (4).

Looking at the formal validity of an argument can be a powerful tool to assess its relevance to the standpoint under discussion. The relationship between formal validity and the broader dimension of relevance can be stated as follows: an argument is directly relevant with respect to a standpoint that has been put forth in a discussion when (a) I can reconstruct the argument as (part of) a formally valid inference chain (e.g. a syllogism) (b) whose conclusion coincides with the standpoint under discussion. Our syllogism in (1) is both valid and relevant. If no formally valid inferential chains can be established – such as in (2) – the relevance of the argument is, to say the least, doubtful. At the same time, a perfectly valid inference that proves a conclusion that is not the standpoint of the discussion is equally irrelevant. Walton (2006: 268) observes that the latter form of irrelevance is routinely exploited by politicians in interviews and debates: "The speaker is wandering from discussing the issue he is supposed to discuss [...] Instead, he is trying to gain the favor of the audience by arguing for a proposition they all enthusiastically accept.". A typical conversational gambit to introduce irrelevant argumentation is the following:

Before answering your question, *I do have to mention that...*

This is the fallacy of irrelevance, also called *ignoratio elenchi* in the classical terminology. Interestingly, accusations of irrelevance abound in intercultural argumentative discussions, as shown in empirical studies (FitzGerald 2002: 87). The allegation of irrelevance is part of a broader array of negative appreciations of the logical quality of argumentation by people from different cultural backgrounds, which have been recorded in intercultural situations.

Cross-cultural research on argumentative writing has provided interesting data in this respect, but it has initially struggled to find a consistent interpretive framework for them. Robert Kaplan (1966, 2001), an American linguist who initiated the comparative study of written texts produced by members of different cultures – a pursuit which he named *contrastive rhetoric* – had initially drawn rather extreme conclusions with respect to the way in which different languages and cultures define relevance in written texts. By studying English essays produced by foreign students, he came to the conclusion that different languages favored discourse structures that departed markedly from the English idea of a "linear" text. For instance, he observed that Spanish and Italian discourse models were far more tolerant than English in allowing for digressions and introduction of "extraneous" material. As for the Russian discourse model, he famously remarked:

> [The structure of the Russian sentence] is made up of a series of presumably parallel constructions and a number of subordinate structures. At least half of these are irrelevant to the central idea of the paragraph..." (Kaplan 1966: 13-14).

Kaplan (1966) concludes that the different cultural discourse models correspond to "cultural thought patterns" rather than simply to rhetorical patterns or patterns of text organization, suggesting a deep difference in reasoning processes (Rocci 2006). Should we conclude that Italian speaking or Russian speaking people are *less relevant* than English speaking people when it comes to arguing a standpoint in written form? The early conclusions of Kaplan (1966) have been criticized by many subsequent studies (Cf. Connor 2004 for a synthesis), including the self criticism and clarifications of Kaplan (2001), where the author explicitly rejects culturally dependent differences in cognitive abilities.

In interpreting Kaplan's early observations on how people from different cultures organize written texts we should bear in mind that *digressing* is not the same thing as being argumentatively irrelevant. Being argumentative irrelevant means *pretending* to provide arguments in support of a standpoint, while in fact presenting an argument that supports a different standpoint or no valid argument at all. Digressing means temporarily abandoning the main track of the discourse in order to deal with something loosely related or altogether unrelated. A digression, as long as it is presented and understood as such, is not a fallacy of irrelevance (*ignoratio elenchi*) because it does not *pretend* to be a relevant argument. So, that certain cultural discourse models give more leeway to add digressions in texts does not means that these cultures are less relevant when it comes to actually argue a point.

In fact, the impression of irrelevance provoked by arguments presented by people from different cultures may derive from two sources:

(a) The first is a difficulty in identifying the standpoint being argued for. This difficulty is particularly connected with differences in the order of presentation of arguments in different cultures (Cf. Scollon & Scollon 2001: 86-105).

(b) The second is a difficulty in reconstructing a valid scheme of inference supporting the argument (Rocci 2006).

In this section we have examined what is common to argument and proof. Eventually, the most important feature that the two have in common is the adoption of a *critical* attitude. The adjective *critical* does not refer here to a polemic attitude; it evokes rather the commitment to find adequate reasons for one's own actions, decisions, beliefs, theories, etc. Two pillars sustain this critical approach: fidelity to evidence and correct reasoning.

4.4. Arguments vs. proofs

We have seen that argument and proof share a number of basic properties: discursiveness, inferentiality, formality and critical attitude. Arguments, as reasoning we apply in our everyday interactions, however, also depart from mathematical proof in equally crucial respects (Cf. Rigotti and Greco Morasso 2009).

Argumentative discussions are embedded in the human semiosphere (Lotman 1991). They are situated in a social context of communication and are functional to the realization of a variety of particular human interactions and, more indirectly, to the broader human endeavor which we could call *the construction of social reality* (Searle 1995).

Argumentative discussions intervene not only in the adjudication, negotiation or mediation of disputes within and between human communities; they also play an essential part in the definition of common goals and values of communities and organizations, and enter decision-making processes at crucial joints within the interaction schemes (Rigotti and Rocci 2006) of deliberation and collaborative problem solving. Mathematical reasoning is clearly not enough to reason in the human semiosphere, where human freedom, desires, affections, emotions, and personal relationships intervene. Determining if something belongs to someone rather than to someone else, if an action is right or wrong, whether to get married or not, whether to vote for a certain political candidate or for an opponent, whether to go to university or not, whether to accept a certain job, and so on, are hardly conclusions that can be just proven. In intercultural communication the insufficiency of proof is particularly striking. More often than not, the success in an intercultural argumentative discussion does not depend on the ability of *correctly deducing* the standpoint from shared premises, but on the heuristic ability of *discovering* profound shared premises despite the apparent absence of a cultural common ground between the interlocutors.

Mathematical proof typically aims at establishing general laws of reality (speed of light, relations between angles in triangles, etc.). Argumentation applies to the human sphere, and can try to evaluate also the particular data: whether a certain territory belongs to a country or to another one, whether to get married or not, etc. In their introduction to the study of argumentation Rigotti and Greco Morasso (2009) remind us that for Aristotle —the originator of the syllogism— argumentation was the domain of *things that could also be otherwise*. It requires a typically human capacity of evaluation.

The examples we have just briefly evoked remind us also that argumentation is *pragmatic* in nature. Argumentative discussions are communicative actions or, more properly, interactions (Chapter 3, § 3) affecting not only cognitive, but also social aspects of human life (Cf. Eemeren & Grootendorst 2004). This also means that argumentation is always oriented towards decisions, addressing a decision-maker. Aristotle made this point forcefully in a passage of his *Rhetoric*:

> The use of persuasive speech is to lead to decisions. (When we know a thing, and have decided about it, there is no further use in speaking about it.) This is so even if one is addressing a single person and urging him to do or not to do something, as when we scold a man for his conduct or try to change his views: the single person is as much your "judge" as if he were one of many; we may say, without qualification, that any one is your judge whom you have to persuade. Nor does it matter whether we are arguing against an actual opponent or against a mere proposition; in the latter case we still have to use speech and overthrow the opposing arguments, and we attack these as we should attack an actual opponent. Our principle holds good of ceremonial speeches also; the "onlookers" for whom such a speech is put together are treated as the judges of it. Broadly speaking, however, the only sort of person who can strictly be called a judge is the man who

decides the issue in some matter of public controversy; that is, in law suits and in political debates, in both of which there are issues to be decided. (Aristotle, *Rhetoric*, Book II Chapter 18, translated by W. Rhys Roberts)

One always argues to persuade some decision maker, a single person or a group: the board of directors of a company, the jury of a criminal trial, the citizens who will vote in the election, the audience of a talk show, etc. Arguments are oriented towards the decision-maker. Not only they draw premises from a starting point accepted by the decider, but also take into account the preferences and needs of the decision-maker in strategically designing the whole argumentative text. This strategic design is particularly difficult and subject to error in IC, when the arguer must take into account beliefs, values, desires and concerns that might differ markedly from her own.

Everyday argumentative discussions are conducted in *ordinary language* rather than in the technical languages typical of proofs in mathematics or geometry. Using human languages with all their flexibility and metaphorical potential makes everyday arguments both powerful and slippery. The polysemic potential of words can be used to express novel concepts, but can be used also to deceive. This deceptive use of polysemy is called the *fallacy of equivocation*. A condition of the formal validity of the syllogism is that it must utilize words unambiguously. Consider the following invalid syllogism based on the homonymy of the word *law*:

Major premise: All *laws* are made by our Parliament.
Minor premise: $e = mc^2$ is a *law* of physics.
Conclusion: Therefore, Parliament made $e = mc^2$.

The term *law* is the problem here. It can refer to a physical law or to legislative law. As a result, this syllogism has four terms instead of three, introduced by semantic processes, making it thus invalid.

Semantic ambiguity often turns out to be a source of mistakes and fallacious reasoning, which is particularly dangerous in IC. Important cultural keywords (Wierzbicka 1997, Rigotti and Rocci 2005) such as *liberty*, *progress* and *democracy* are remarkably vague and can be understood in radically different ways across different cultures, societies, ideologies and political systems. It is relatively frequent, then, to talk at cross purposes when using them. Before 1989, in the Cold War era, both the Western countries and the countries of the Soviet Bloc qualified themselves as *democracies* – take for instance the official name of Eastern

Germany: Deutsche *Demokratische* Republik (DDR) – while their political systems were completely different. Sometimes it is not expedient for the arguers to clarify the confusion, so that they can get the addressee to agree on the basis of the powerful positive *connotation* (Chapter 2, § 5.3) associated with the word. Communist parties in Western Europe, at times, exploited strategically this ambiguity to gain broader acceptance in public discourse. Metaphors are another source that can be exploited by the fallacy of equivocation. The word *war* can be used metaphorically to mean a systematic and sustained struggle against a situation that is negatively evaluated. Thus one can declare, for instance, *war on poverty* and gain broad consensus. In this context, the expression *war on terror*, as initially used by the U.S. Administration on the wake of the tragic terrorist attack against the World Trade Center, allowed both this broader metaphorical interpretation and the more literal one that turned out to be the case.

Not only everyday arguments are phrased in potentially ambiguous language, they are also largely *implicit* as concerns the manifestation of their inferential structure. Mathematical or geometrical proofs ideally tend to make every passage explicit, or to refer to already demonstrated statements. Arguments leave implicit what is not strictly necessary for comprehension. In particular, premises that are deemed to be part of the cultural common ground are routinely left implicit. Thus syllogistic arguments are usually communicated in an abbreviated conversational form, called *enthymeme* (Jackson and Jacobs 1980, Rocci 2006). Consider an argument like (1) below:

(1) He's a traitor. Therefore he deserves to be put to death.

Imagine that this argument was uttered in a social and cultural context where it is known to everybody – it is common ground – that treason of the type at hand is customarily punished with the death penalty. (This is not necessarily part of the cultural common ground of most modern societies, but it was in many historical periods, and still is in many subcultures – just think of the Mafia.) It would be natural to reconstruct (1) as a more implicit (enthymematic) version of the full fledged syllogism in (2).

(2)
Major premise: *Traitors* deserve to be put to death (implicit premise)
Minor premise: He is a *traitor*
Conclusion: He deserves to be put to death

Note that *traitor* – a cultural keyword – plays here the role of the terminus medius of the enthymeme. In fact, if someone was to make explicit every single inferential step in an argument, she would look incredibly pedantic, or stupid or patronizing towards the addressee – as if she treated him like a little child. In intercultural situations the common ground is shaky or, at best, limited. As a consequence, leaving premises implicit in the argument exposes the communicator to the risk of misunderstanding. Thus, in IC the arguer is caught in a dilemma: is it better to leave things implicit at the risk of misunderstanding, or to make everything explicit at the risk of looking patronizing towards the "poor foreigner" or (alternatively) of being labeled as stupid?

Another trait that sets argumentation apart from proof concerns the status of its premises as plausible (or probable) assumptions rather than as incontestable truths like the axioms on which a mathematical theorem is based. This feature of argumentation has been evoked since the beginning when we introduced the loose requirement of *plausibility* for arguments.

In human interaction, premises may also include shared beliefs, opinions, assessments, and other plausible statements. Due to the *probable nature of premises*, conclusions of the argumentative discourse are also typically probable or tentative rather than certain, even if the reasoning procedure is in itself logically sound.

In the end, we can say that the critical attitude characterizing argumentation is not a pure, or even the less mechanical, application of *rationality*, conceived as logical soundness. Arguments are the product of human *reasonableness*.

5. Reasonableness

As observed in a study by Rigotti, Rocci and Greco (2006), based on an extensive corpus, the English word *reasonable* is normally used to refer to good enough arguments in a variety of social contexts. Expressions such as *reasonable argument, reasonable grounds, reasonable evidence* are common. These are expected to lead to *reasonable conclusions*. Other common constructions are the following:

(1) It seems reasonable to infer / conjecture / predict / guess that...
(2) It is reasonable to believe / assume / expect / hope / doubt...

It is clear that *reasonable* is an important keyword, not only of argumentation theory (Cf. van Eemeren and Grootendorst 2004: 10-19) but also of everyday argumentative practice: people use this word to evaluate positively argumentative moves. It is also clear that arguments do not need to be demonstratively conclusive to be reasonable. What are then the components of reasonableness?

First, reasonableness does include *rationality* as one of its components. Reasonable discourse avoids contradictions. This is why, during a critical discussion, statements are assessed as to their consistency, while inconsistent ones are challenged, modified or discarded. More precisely, rational discourse does not only avoid inconsistency, but it is also developed constantly under the "threat of inconsistency" (Rigotti and Greco Morasso 2009), and therefore legitimates the acceptance of a statement every time this acceptance is necessary in order to avoid inconsistency.

In most situations, however, avoiding inconsistencies is not a sufficient criterion for taking decisions. Often many alternative decisions remain consistent with the data. Consider the case of a physician who must diagnose a disease on the basis of visible or manifest symptoms. The physician decides that these *probably* or *most likely* are indicative of a specific ailment or disease. Not until the therapy or treatment chosen has brought about the desired consequences, will the physician's assessment of the symptoms be considered as definite. The physician faces a risk when proposing a diagnosis, and the patient assumes this risk when accepting the remedial strategy given. The physician's original decision was *reasonable*, rather than strictly logical. Often *time constraints* are a key element in defining what is a reasonable course of action. There are a lot of situations where decisions are taken in a race against the clock and one cannot wait to have all the necessary evidence to decide because the lack of decision would have *certain* negative consequences – for instance for the health of the patient. There are similar constraints that concern other kinds of resources necessary for problem solving, like economic or cognitive resources. Scientific experiments, for instance, can be very costly at times. A reasonable scientist would try to assess whether the knowledge gain hoped for justifies the expenses for a particular experimental procedure.

In many concrete decision situations being reasonable also means taking into account the *broader picture*. Or, in other words, to strive to consider all the relevant factors involved in a decision. A decision or conclusion that appears to be perfectly logical if one considers only its narrow context can turn out to be unreasonable in a broader context. A student who is learning a foreign language, say, German, would certainly expect to be corrected from time to time, so as to learn the proper forms of the language. However, is it reasonable for the teacher to correct the student every single time the student makes a mistake? This method of teaching, in effect, would risk being counterproductive, if the student becomes discouraged and eventually decides to give up studying the German language—an outcome that both the teacher and student presumably would want to avoid.

Being able to evaluate the side effects of a course of action is a key component of reasonable decision making. This often involves being able to put into perspective the different goals that we have when we act. One needs to bear in mind the hierarchy of goals (*teleological hierarchy*) that motivates one's action (Cf. Rigotti and Greco Morasso 2009). For instance, let us suppose I want to get rid of the rats that infest my basement. Would I ever consider dropping an atomic bomb on the house? That would be insane. Certainly the bomb would kill the rats, but the negative side effects of my action would greatly overwhelm any good that I might have hoped from it. Put into perspective, the goal of getting rid of the rats is not an absolute goal, but rather an instrumental goal subservient to higher level goals, like, say, living healthily at home. A key feature of the *reasonableness principle*, as it may be called, is the capacity of interlocutors to assess logically what the main goal of an action is (such as living healthily at home) from various sub-goals (getting rid of the rats). Sub-goals are, of course, part of the causal chain activated during discourse in order to realize an overarching goal (Cf. Chapter 3).

Sometimes, in cases of conflict, the goals that the arguers declare do not actually correspond to their real ultimate goal. In their classic treatment of negotiation and conflict resolution, *Getting to Yes*, Fisher and Ury (1981) distinguished accordingly between real goals (or *interests*) versus declared goals in discourse (*positions*).

5.1. Categorical adequacy and a feeling for context

When we speak, we are implicitly categorizing the world, whether we realize it or not. This is in line with the classificatory principle (Chapter 1, § 3.1). This invariably comes into play into any perception of the reasonableness of an interaction or an action. The two are perceived as intrinsically intertwined. When we examined the case of John and Mary discussing about whales we saw that the reasonableness of the arguments offered by the discussants crucially revolves around the categorical system employed. Different cultural categorization systems focus on different descriptive traits —e.g. where whales live as opposed to their reproductive system – and obtain different categories. We choose to focus to certain traits and consider them more relevant than other traits. Or, as Umberto Eco's (1999) would put it, we cut reality along different lines. Culturally and linguistically encoded categories provide us with the default system to organize our experience of the world. At the same time we cannot say that one categorization is as good as another. A system of categorization can be judged as more or less reasonable along two dimensions: its suitability for its purpose and its adherence to reality itself. While it is true that we can cut reality along different lines, it is also true that not all lines are equivalent and that reality offers us certain "lines of resistance" (Eco 1999) along which it is more natural to cut. Moreover, experience can prompt us to redefine our categories, as if engaging in a dialogue with reality itself.

Eco (1999) gives an illuminating example by reconstructing the story of the discovery of the platypus (*Ornithorhynchus anatinus*). The discovery of this egg-laying, venomous, duck-billed, beaver-tailed, otter-footed Australian animal, whose bizarre appearance seems to be made just to flout categorization systems, lead biologists to revise the definition of what a *mammal* is. In fact, unlike all the then known mammals, the platypus lays eggs instead to giving birth to live youngs, but like all mammals it feeds them with milk.

The purpose of categorization is also important. Consider another case-in-point. A professor can categorize students in his or her class in a variety of ways (in principle). The professor can do it by the color of the students' hair, by the sound of their voices, by their height, or by the seat they normally occupy in a classroom. But these are not reasonable ways to categorize them in a university context, although they may be reasonable if the learning context is, for example, a hairdressing school, a vocal training school, or a basketball court. Each of the categories may thus be reasonable in certain contexts. But they would not be perceived as reasonable in the context of a university class. Classifying students by height, hair color, and the like, can also be construed negatively and lead to an uncomfortable situation.

The German historian Walter Demel (1992) wrote a book provocatively entitled "How the Chinese became yellow" (*Wie die Chinesen gelb wurden*). The book critically reconstructs the origin of racial theories in XIX Europe, which would provide a justification to the emerging racist ideologies that would tragically mark the following century. Arguably, prejudice towards other peoples and cultures has always haunted human minds, but systematic prejudice based on "racial" categorization is a relatively recent invention. Demel shows how an unessential feature of human beings – the color of their skin – was "discovered" and transformed into a distinguishing feature at a certain time in history, in connection with the legitimation of established power relationships. This process becomes even more grotesque when, in order to make every human group fit the classification based on skin color, the racial ideologies resort to perceptually improbable color labels. Early European travelers and missionaries who visited China from the XVI to the XVIII century described the Chinese as similar to Europeans in complexion. It is only in the XIX century that Chinese, and East Asians in general, begin to be described as *yellow*. Should we attribute that to a sudden change in the perception of colors on the part of the Europeans? In fact, the significance of this "color" is symbolic rather than perceptual. Being intermediate between *white* and *brown*, *yellow* denotes an intermediate place of Asians in a hypothetical racial scale where Europeans would occupy the highest position and Africans the lowest. Demel concludes his argument with a poignant metonymy: far from being the product of the vast expanse of the Asian steppes, the "yellow race" was in fact born in the stifling rooms of European racist theorists.

The term used to identify the appropriate reasonable use of categories in a given context in discourse theory is *categorical adequacy*. This implies also the choice of a level of granularity of the categorization that is adequate to a given discourse situation. If the choice is too "case-specific" or too "generic", then one risks being perceived as unreasonable. Consider a few cases-in-point. One concerns an episode that happened during a course taught by one of the authors of this book. A student in class claimed that Southern Italians generally shied away from work and that this was ingrained in their culture, basing his argument on linguistic evidence: in many southern Italian dialects the word for "to work" is *faticare*, a verb that also means "getting tired" or "experiencing difficulties". His argument was based on a true linguistic fact, but it was also an irrelevant one if looked in a broader perspective. In fact, it turns out that the same association between work, tiredness, and being in trouble is present as a single category in many other languages and cultures. Interestingly, the root of the Spanish word *trabajar* and of the French correspondent *travailler*, for instance, is to be found in Latin *tripalium*, which designated a form of torture, suggesting that working is painful. This meaning is found analogously in the English word *laborious* which derives from Latin *labor*, but has a negative connotation built into it, as does the German *Arbeit*, which derives from *Erbe*, referring to an orphaned heir who is forced to work in order to survive (Benveniste 1969). The level of abstraction of the student's statement about Southern Italians was, clearly, inadequate, because it was too low.

The use and intentional misuse of adequacy requirements is a phenomenon that is found across all discourse phenomena. Consider the following statement:

(1)   Selling cigarettes to teenagers must be forbidden, because otherwise the companies making cigarettes would earn too much money.

In this case, an implicit rule [companies making cigarettes should not earn too much] is applied to a specific situation which, actually, suggests that other reasons would be more appropriate in the course of an argumentation. It might be true that such companies earn too much. But, is using the profit motive as a premise in argumentation a truly reasonable one without taking into consideration other probability factors, such as the health reasons why teenagers should not smoke in the first place? The above statement could be a convincing one in a context where the profit motive is assumed to be an evil force in society (such as it is construed to be among radical politicians of a certain ideology). Indeed, as this brings out, an argumentative strategy that is unreasonable in a certain context might be adequate in another, where the common ground shared by the audience and the arguer provides the material starting point for the strategy. Furthermore, argumentative moves that are adequate for certain *interaction schemes* (Rigotti & Rocci 2006) may be unfit or even fallacious in the context of another scheme. Now, consider the following statement:

(2)   If you do not agree with me, I am leaving.

It is unlikely that this would be uttered by a mathematician to another mathematician during an interaction whose goal is solving a problem. The move would not provide any relevant argument and would constitute an *ad baculum* fallacy (§ 2 above). However, it would be construed as perfectly admissible as a rhetorical strategy by mediators involved in a conflict resolution process—the mediator can threaten to quit the process and let the parties go to court (and face all the risks inherent to a lengthy and costly trial), as a means to convince them to provide the minimum level of cooperation that is required to solve the conflict through mediation (Princen 1992, Greco Morasso 2007, 2008). Here the "threat" is not unreasonable because it helps the discussants to focus on their real options in the conflict resolution. In many ways, the level of adequacy of an argument is determined by a "feeling" for its appropriateness in a given context. This "inner sense" is based on previous experience and a grasp of communicative appropriateness. As we have seen, an argument based on the use of references to an authoritative source to support it is often a useful strategy and a very practical and often necessary way of taking decisions (Cf. the notion of argument from expert opinion in § 3, above):

(3) It's aunt Debbie's recipe for making Thanksgiving turkey! Stick to it!

However, the same type of argument may be inapplicable in other contexts, either because the authority is not acknowledged as such (which is likely to happen in an intercultural context, since different cultures acknowledge different authorities), or because the considered activity type is such that appealing to an authority is meaningless. It would be absurd to contend, in the context of geometry, that a theorem holds because of Pythagoras' authority.

In concluding our attempt to capture the manifold notion of reasonableness it is worth going back to van Eemeren's and Grootendorst's notion of a *critical discussion*, which we introduced at the beginning of this chapter. Because a reasonable attitude also involves the commitment to find a resolution of the difference of opinion that is worthy of the human quality of interlocutors, respecting both their freedom and their reason. As we have seen, a critical discussion involves both the freedom of advancing standpoints and the responsibility of defending them starting from what is accepted by both interlocutors. The arguer does not want the assent of her interlocutor at any cost, but what Jacobs (2000: 264) calls "*warranted* assent, *reasoned* adherence, *voluntary* and *informed* acceptance". A long time ago Cicero (*De Officiis* I, 50) had observed that the possibility of engaging in argumentative discussions, using reason and discourse (*ratio et oratio*), is what distinguishes human beings from wild beasts, which, in his view, relied on aggression instead to obtain their ends.

6. Arguments in context

The role of context in identifying the meaning and force of an act of communication cannot be underestimated, as discussed several times above and in previous chapters (for example in Chapter 2, § 6.2). Context can be defined as a situation, a set of cognitively salient cues, a recognizable mode of interaction, etc. that constrains the meaning of an act of communication.

Consider a discarded cigarette or soft drink can (Danesi 2007). If one were to come across such a thing on a sidewalk on a city street, the tendency would be, no doubt, to interpret it as a piece of garbage or rubbish. But if one saw the very same can on a pedestal or in a frame displayed in an art gallery, "signed" by some artist, and given a title such as "Waste," then one would be inclined to interpret it in a vastly different way—as a work of art symbolizing a throw-away or materialistic society. Clearly, the can's physical context of occurrence—its location on a sidewalk vs. its display in an art gallery—will determine how it will be interpreted. The art gallery is, in effect, a socially sanctioned situation, or, in other words an *activity type* (Levinson 1979). Anything that is put on display within it is assumed to be art. Not possessing knowledge of this activity type, children would hardly be inclined to interpret the soft drink can as an art form; they would see it as a can, no matter where it is located. As children grow, and become familiar with the activity type, they will also become accustomed to interpreting objects in galleries, such as cans, differently.

To put it in other words, the identification, naming, and grouping of the "objects of reality" is a contextualized semiotic process. However, once the objects have been encoded by language (or some other code) they are perceived as necessary or natural discoveries of reality, not just convenient signs.

6.1. Contextualized argumentation

From the outset we considered argumentation in its socio-pragmatic dimension (as well as in its logico-semantic aspects). As we have seen, the socio-pragmatic perspective is embedded in the very notion of a critical discussion introduced the Amsterdam school. Argumentative discussions do not occur in a social vacuum and it is not surprising at all that the social context of communication (Cf. Rigotti and Rocci 2006b) in which the critical discussion takes place affects the argumentative strategies that arguers devise.

A key element of communication context is defined by the *activity type* (Levinson 1979, van Eemeren and Houtlosser 2005, Rigotti and Rocci 2006b). Several examples of activity types have already been discussed in the previous chapters (Cf. for instance Chapter 1, § 3.1, Table 2). Examples of activity types involving argumentation include parliamentary deliberation, debate in court, family mediation, real-estate negotiation, and countless others. Each activity type has two fundamental components (Rigotti and Rocci 2006b): (1) the *interaction field* where the critical discussion takes place (parliament, court, family, the real-estate market...), and (2) the *interaction scheme* employed (deliberation, debate, mediation, negotiation...). Each interaction field also defines a number of *social roles* and *communication flows* that obtain between them. A school, for instance, is an interaction field; the communicative roles assigned in this case are those of *pupil, teacher, principal, non-teaching staff*, etc.

In the same field, moreover, other role players might intervene legitimately (family members, officials of various types, etc.). Among them, other communicative flows are set in motion. For instance, teachers and pupils will interact with each other in a "pedagogical communication" style, which determines the kinds of arguments that can be employed in a specific interaction field such as a math class. This field determines what is reasonable in the ensuing dialogue and what is not. Discussing television programs during a math test would be illogical; but discussing how grades are assigned is not. Teachers, however, are obligated to answer any kind of question from their pupils, even during a math test, because it is the role of teachers to do so, even if the question is seemingly out of context.

Let us focus on the second fundamental component of the activity type: the *interaction scheme* that is activated within a certain interaction field in order to fulfill a specific goal. Interaction schemes are like communicative "recipes" for solving particular kinds of communication problems. They are part of a culture and also form a body of expert knowledge. Some people may be better "cooks" than others with certain specific recipes to the point that their specialized communicative competence becomes a job. Mediators are case-in-point. Imagine an intercultural conflict in a North American primary school that might be brought about by the desire of the teachers of a certain class to organize a small reception before Christmas with their pupils, all of whom come from different religious communities and whose parents might perceive to be an imposition rather than a celebration. The principal may choose different routes to solve the conflict, deploying different interaction schemes. He might call a meeting with the families, and conduct it as a sort of *problem-solving* activity; or, if the situation has escalated into a serious conflict, the principal may decide to take the role of *arbitrator* and take a decision having listened to the parties' reasons, or to request a *mediator*, to help the parties autonomously solve their conflict through a *mediation* practice (Greco Morasso 2006, 2007, 2008, 2009). The kind of communicative practice chosen influences the parties' possible argumentation strategies (Cf. also Walton 1998). More precisely what happens is that in each interaction scheme the nature of the standpoint to be discussed critically changes, and with it the whole structure of the supporting argumentation. If the discussion is framed as problem solving, the only allowed standpoints are *proposed solutions to a common problem* like "I think the best option for us is...", "I think we should..." Here the difference of opinion is defined as a possible divergence on the best course of action to take. This is a very cooperative form of argumentation, but it will not work in situations where positions are already polarized in two camps – "us" and "them" – and there is no perception of a common problem. The scheme of arbitration creates (at least) three separate argumentative tasks: first the two parties will present their case to the arbitrator, then the arbitrator—the school principal – will have to justify his or her decision in front of the whole community. The risk with this trial-like scheme is that it allows the parties to present very polarized standpoints in the first phase and then places a very heavy argumentative burden on the arbitrator, whose decision risks to create winners and losers or to discontent everybody. Finally the mediation scheme obliges the parties to frame the critical discussion as the search for an acceptable compromise. Here the standpoints to be discussed are framed like *proposed compromises acceptable to everybody*. In conclusion, the interaction schemes function as constraints on the type of critical discussions admissible in a given situation. As observed by Jacobs and Jackson (2006: 130), one of the more promising applications of argumentation theory is *argumentative design*, that is the practical task of creating purposefully designed "systems for conducting discussions aimed at assuring reasonableness in the search for resolution of disagreement". These systems can take the ideal model of the critical discussion as a starting point, but then have to take into account a number of further restrictions dictated by the real social context in which the resolution system has to work. The creation of resolution systems geared towards various types of intercultural situations and conflicts appears as one of the main areas of practical intervention in which an applied discipline like Global Linguistics can prove its usefulness.

7. Culture-bound and universal components of argumentation

Some contexts dictate the use of highly formalized or formulaic argumentation—courtrooms, scientific conferences, etc. In turn, these entail a corresponding formal language style that is based on the traditions established within the specific interaction field. Other contexts dictate the use of less formal or completely informal argumentation—conversations between friends or colleagues, family arguments, etc. In turn, these entail a more colloquial style of argumentation. In intercultural contexts, problems in an interaction field might arise when the interlocutors cannot align style with context appropriately. Let's consider a hypothetical conversation between interlocutors of different backgrounds. The interaction field (or setting) is the University of Lugano in Switzerland. Researchers from universities across the world have been invited to take part in a two-day conference on the topic of IC in the Mediterranean region. During the day, the professors and researchers present papers and discuss their ideas at the Congress Palace. At night, they are invited to have dinner together, in the open air in the park surrounding the Congress palace. The organizing committee has intentionally placed professors of different language backgrounds at the various tables. Each participant had been previously asked to bring some typical food from his or her culture to the dinner, so that the other participants could enjoy it.

Now, let us focus hypothetically on a specific table, where an interesting conversation is unfolding among five scholars—a Spaniard, two Egyptians, an Italian, and a Chinese who works in France. All consider themselves to be gourmets. Each one has brought along a sample of native cuisine to the table (as asked to do). To the general astonishment of all present at the table, the two dishes brought by the Italian (A) and the Spaniard (B) appear to be quite similar, not to say identical, at a first sight. At that point, the Italian asserts: (A) "You all should try this very good Italian specialty! It is Parma ham!" Upon hearing what the Italian has just proclaimed, the Spaniard follows suit exclaiming: (B) "Have some of this delicious ham! It is Pata Negra!"

Given the tone in which they are delivered, the two utterances are perceived by all at the table as being antagonistic, making it appear that an argument is about to break out between the two scholars. Why? Consider how the arguments presented by the two are constructed. The standpoints of A and B are, clearly, analogous, and can be characterized as advice-giving arguments: "the quality of this ham is excellent, and, therefore, this ham is worth tasting". The arguments presented to support the standpoints are, respectively:

A: It is Parma ham.
B: It is Pata Negra.

It is easily recognizable that, in both cases, the *aspect of the standpoint* to which the argument refers is, in a broad sense, the *origin* of the ham. In argumentative terms, it can be said that both professors have constructed their argumentation on the basis of the *locus from the origin* (Rigotti 2009).

7.1. The logical force: loci and maxims

We have already introduced (see § 3, above) the notion of a locus or argument scheme, saying that it defines what kind of relevant relation is established between the standpoint and the premise and is exploited in the argument (Rigotti 2009). The locus from verbal classification, the locus from analogy and the locus from expert opinion are three cases-in-point.

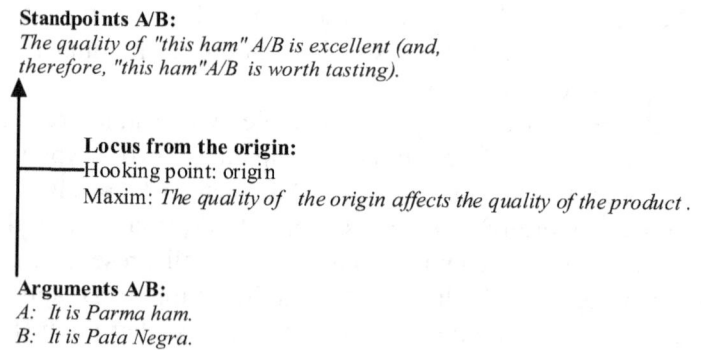

Standpoints A/B:
The quality of "this ham" A/B is excellent (and, therefore, "this ham"A/B is worth tasting).

Locus from the origin:
Hooking point: origin
Maxim: *The quality of the origin affects the quality of the product.*

Arguments A/B:
A: *It is Parma ham.*
B: *It is Pata Negra.*

Figure 26. A partial representation of the discussion concerning *ham*.

The *loci* – that is the kinds of semantic relation exploited by arguments – will vary according to their *hooking point*. The hooking point is the aspect of the standpoint the locus refers to. Ham is a product and every product has an origin, this aspect of the standpoint allows us to "hook" the standpoint with the locus – because the locus really impinges on the standpoint (for a complete account on possible hooking points giving rise to the system of *loci*, see Rigotti 2009). Now, let us show exactly how argumentation based on the *locus from the origin* works.

First, a general principle or rule, called *maxim* (Rigotti 2009), can be identified: *The quality of the origin affects the quality of the product*. The maxim gives the argument its logical force, "translating" in the form of a rule the semantic relation that makes up the locus: if the origin of a product is good, then the product tends to be good, whereas if the origin is not good, the product is not good. This kind of argumentation is not particularly abstruse. If we look at advertisement we can see that the *locus from the origin* is one of the most intensively exploited: just think of Swiss watches, and Swiss chocolate as an example.

The maxim itself provides a rule-like major premise to the argument, and a pretty general one at that. In fact, we can see very well that both the Italian and the Spaniard exploit the same maxim to argue their (different) standpoint. The general notions that are typically exploited by *loci* like origin, cause, goal, similarity, part-whole etc. seem to be shared by most if not all human cultures, even if they are not explicitly lexicalized in the languages – see in this respect the our remarks on the notion of causation in the Inuit language (Chapter 1, § 3.1). We may well hypothesize that these relations represent a culturally universal component of argumentation. As for the argument from expert opinion, which exploits a more complex and indirect relation than most other topics, we have already seen that it has a special relation with the notion of culture itself and it is deeply embedded in a number of languages through the system of honorification.

Does this mean that there are no cultural differences with respect to the use of loci? Probably not. Recent studies (Hornikx 2006) conducted on relatively close European cultures – French and Dutch – have shown that people belonging to different cultures have slightly different expectations and preferences as regards the right loci to employ in a given context (e.g. a persuasive health brochure produced by a government agency). It turned out, for instance, that French brochures make a moderate use of arguments from expert opinion, while Dutch texts use it only very rarely. At the same time, a parallel experimental study showed that the French are more persuaded than the Dutch by certain types of expert evidence. While empirical cross-cultural research on argumentation is beginning to cast light on preferences and fine differences between cultures in the use of loci, the evidence is still too spotty to draw any conclusions on the big picture. Research on fine variation connected to loci is also made more difficult by the fact that there is another, far weightier, factor that impacts on the cultural variation of argumentative strategies. Let us examine what this factor is about.

7.2. The common stock of opinion: *endoxa*

We have observed above that in our example the Italian professor and his Spanish colleague use the same locus and the very same maxim: *The quality of the origin affects the quality of the product*, or, to phrase it as a syllogistic major premise: *If the origin of a product is good, then the product will be good.* Interestingly, the maxim cannot be in itself a source of persuasion. For our maxim to generate the desired conclusion (i.e. *The quality of ham A/B is excellent*), the following minor premise is also necessary: *The origin of ham A/B is excellent.* This minor premise is not spelled out in the argument of the two professors. What I have instead are premises saying:

Ham A is from Parma.
Ham B is Pata Negra.

The move from these explicit premises to the required minor premise (*The origin of ham A/B is excellent*) is obtained through a second line of reasoning, backed by a major premise that differs, in nature, from the abstract rule expressed by the *maxim*: this premise, according to the rhetorical terminology is called the *endoxon* (plural *endoxa*).

The Greek word *endoxon* (from *en* 'in' + *doxa* 'opinion, fame') means a both a generally held belief and reputable opinion, held in high esteem. Thus *endoxa* are propositions that are part of the communal common ground of a cultural community and that are evaluated as authoritative by members of that cultural community. In the *Topics*, Aristotle gives an articulated definition of the *endoxa*:

> [*endoxa* are those opinions] which commend themselves to all, or to the majority, or to the wise – that is or to all of the wise or to the majority or to the most famous and distinguished of them" (*Topics* I 100b 21-23).

In our example the two competing endoxa that we need respectively for arguments A and B can be phrased as follow:

A: Everyone in Italy knows that / Every self respecting gourmet should know that: *the members of the Parma consortium produce the best possible ham*;

B: Everyone in Spain knows that / Every self respecting gourmet should know that: *Pata Negra is the best variety of Iberian ham; and Iberian ham made with the Iberian pig breed is the best possible ham.*

7.3. Cultural keywords

We can observe that the two endoxa remain implicit in the respective arguments. As we have already observed this kind of implicitness is rather typical of arguments in ordinary language. As observed by Aristotle, it is their status of *endoxa* that makes it possible to leave them implicit: "for if any one of these is well known, there is no need to mention it, for the hearer can add it himself" (*Rhetoric*, I, 1357a). Of course, this kind of availability of endoxa fully functions only *within* a culture.

What happens is that our endoxa, functioning as major premises are combined with the *data* explicitly mentioned by the two professors: *This is Parma ham*, and *This is Pata Negra ham*. The latter are minor premises and are the only explicit part of the whole argument. Note here that the name of the origin (*Parma* or *Pata Negra*) works in each argument as a *terminus medius* in the syllogistic structure. Within the relevant cultural community names such as *Parma ham* or *Pata Negra* will function as argumentative cultural *keywords* (Rigotti and Rocci 2005) and will be sufficient to activate the implicit endoxon in the mind of the culturally savvy hearer.

The work of Raymond Williams, as presented in his influential dictionary *Keywords: A Vocabulary of Culture and Society* (Williams 1976), is perhaps the best known contribution to the study of keywords from a sociological and cultural viewpoint. Williams (1976: 20) defines keywords as "significant, binding words in certain activities and their interpretation; they are significant, indicative words in certain forms of thought".

Another interesting take on cultural keywords, fully rooted in the anthropological linguistic tradition, is offered by the Polish-Australian semanticist Anna Wierzbicka (1997). Wierzbicka's research on keywords follows the footsteps of Edward Sapir (Cf. Chapter 1, § 3.1) in making the hypothesis that in certain areas of the lexicon there are language specific distinctions that reflect specific ways of living as well as "ways of thinking". In turn, these distinctions have, historically, shaped their communities and perpetuate the ways of living they reflect.

Many of the words analyzed by Wierzbicka, both prestigious, like *liberty*, and colloquial like the typically Australian verb *whinge* contain an embedded evaluative connotation (Cf. Chapter 2, § 5.3). Consider, for instance, her characterization of *whingeing* in Australian culture:

> What exactly is 'whingeing'? Clearly, it is a concept closely related to that expressed by the word *complaining*. But, first, *complain* is neutral, and does not imply any evaluation of the activity in question, whereas *whinge* is critical and derogatory. Furthermore, *complain* is purely verbal, whereas *whinge* suggest something that sounds like an inarticulate animal cry. Being purely verbal, *complaining* can be seen as fully intentional, whereas *whingeing* can be only seen as semi intentional and semi-controlled. Finally, *whingeing*, like *nagging* and unlike *complaining*, suggests monotonous repetition. (Wierzbicka 1997: 215)

Basically, the word *whinge* represents a morally sanctioned behavior, which runs directly counter the traditional Australian colonial ethos characterized by the values of toughness, gameness, resilience, "die-hardness", comradeship, and good humor (Wierzbicka 1997). As pointed out in Rigotti and Rocci (2005) this kind of culturally shared evaluations evoked by keywords do, in fact, correspond to what the rhetorical tradition calls *endoxa* and play an important role in conversational argument. Thus, the simple mention of the word *whinge* gives access to a traditional Australian endoxon:

Every true Australian knows that: complaining about one's misfortunes instead of confronting them through action is unworthy of a grown-up man (or, in its modern version, man or woman).

The mere presence of the keyword is sufficient to evoke this endoxon as an implicit premise in a conversational argument, as in (1) below:

(1) Perhaps some of the *whingers* should get out there with black bags, paint and paintbrushes and mops and tidy up around [...] (example extracted from *Google*).

Having introduced the *locus* and the *endoxon* as two distinct component of a conversational argument, we can now see how the two parts of the argument hang together in our "ham dispute" example. The entire structure of the two arguments is shown in Figures 27 and 28 in the following pages.

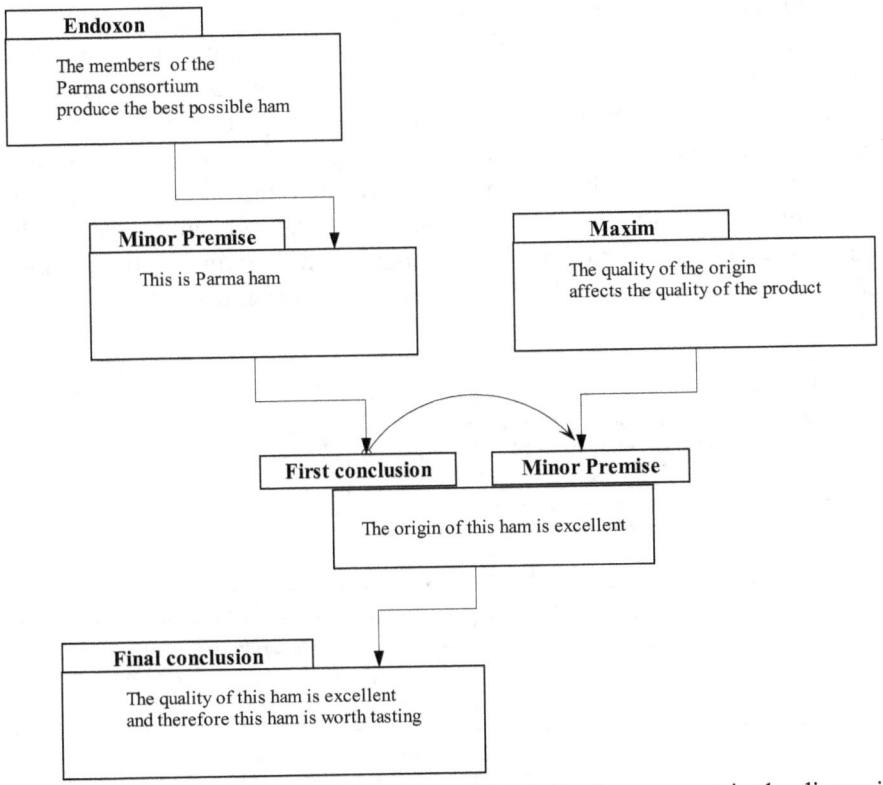

Figure 27. A full fledged reconstruction of the Italian's argument in the discussion *ham* discussion.

If we look at the line of reasoning starting from the endoxon we can see that from the (implicit) endoxon and the (explicit) minor premise, a first conclusion is generated: *The origin of this ham is very good*, which corresponds exactly to the minor premise that the maxim was "looking for". As a consequence, the first conclusion, playing the role of a minor premise, is applied to the maxim of the locus, which plays the role of the major premise. From this second syllogism the final conclusion is derived: *The quality of this ham is excellent*. So it turns out that our argumentation is made of two connected syllogisms, based, respectively, on the endoxon and on the maxim. The two components have distinct and complementary functions: the maxim is responsible for the inferential mechanism and defines a general law, while the endoxon links the argument to a shared opinion in the culture of the community (where, in this case, a shared belief about the quality of the ham can be found).

We could even say that the "maximal" component sets the inferential force, which is universally agreed upon, while the "endoxical" component provides the persuasive effectiveness. In our case, in fact, the Italian and the Spaniard agree on the general principle that the quality of the product is affected by the quality of its origin, but quarrel on what is the best possible origin for a ham (the region around Parma or the Spanish pigs?). Thus, the maxim guarantees the logical consistency of the procedure but if this procedure is not combined with an endoxon, it remains a mere logical mechanism with no hold whatsoever on the persuasion of the discussion partner.

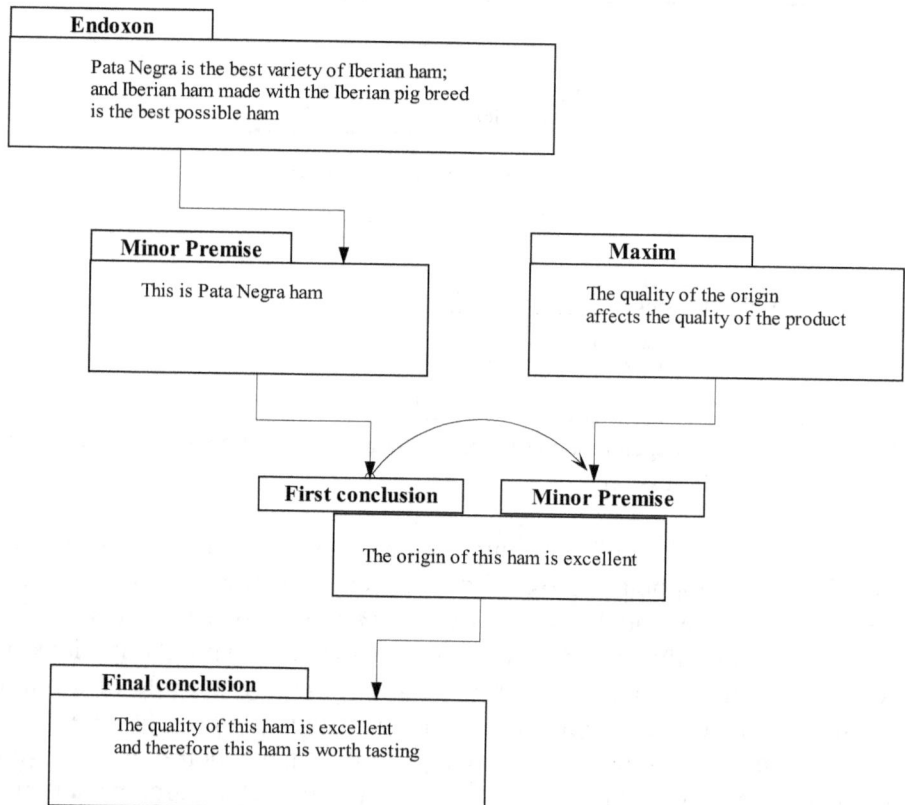

Figure 28. A full fledged reconstruction of the Spaniard's argument in the discussion *ham* discussion.

Indeed, if one does not know of the existence of Parma or Pata Negra ham, he or she would have no logical key to unlocking the ongoing implicit debate. As the argumentation between our hypothetical Italian and Spaniard is about to unfold further, this is in fact what occurs. One of the two Egyptians (C) at the table interrupts the two interlocutors as follows:

> C: It is nice to see what an important issue ham is for the two of you. But it means nothing to us, since we do not eat ham.

C's statement might make the Italian and the Spaniard realize that not even the partial common ground on which their utterances were enunciated is shared by other members at the table. Indeed, they come to the realization that the quality of ham and all its contextualized references (origins, tradition, etc.) is relevant only to them, given their culinary traditions. Without this common ground there are no endoxa that would support the argumentation. The Egyptian (C) uses the very same *locus from the origin* and argues for a completely different conclusion: ham, be it from Italy or Spain, "comes from the flesh of the swine, and therefore is *haram* 'forbidden' according to the teachings of the Holy Quran". The Chinese professor at the table (D) took a different slant on the whole argumentative process, since she assumed a different premise, namely that Chinese pigs are tastier than European ones. But after C's intervention, she tried to understand the situation better, taking into account the arguments made by A and B, along with their logical structure, so as to resolve the situation in her own mind. The other Egyptian at the table (E) tried a different, pragmatic, approach by introducing his own specialty into the argumentation process, lamb with yogurt.

Without going into the hypothetical conversation that might subsequently have unfolded at the table, the purpose of the vignette was to show that the maxim generated by the locus, giving rise to the inferential force of the reasoning, is universally acceptable, while the endoxa, providing the effectiveness of argumentation, vary accordingly with the different cultures, and often must be re-negotiated, and further founded through other arguments. The decipherment of endoxa and other components of the common ground is crucial for any communication to be successful. Neglecting differences and assuming an illusory common ground is a major source of misunderstanding. The *principle of complementarity of cultures* – which has been highligted, in particular, by the scholars of the Tartu-Moscow school of cultural Semiotics (Cf. Gatti

2003) – , makes us discover that the others' values are often values that we also share, but that we did not know to share. So, the different values are not necessarily mutually exclusive. That said, we do sometimes encounter values that we find completely incomprehensible or even unacceptable. For instance, women's role in families and societies seems to be a controversial issue that often emerges in IC. In these cases, again, giving reasons of one's endoxa and always keeping in mind the intrinsically positive nature of each culture as a "human cradle" (Cf. Chapter 4) is the key for enriching one's personal heritage by understanding the other and by reflecting on one's own experience.

8. Intercultural Fallacies

All human argumentative activity is prone to the risk of fallacy. Some fallacies are reasoning errors – like the pseudo-syllogisms lacking a terminus medius that we surveyed in § 4.3 – while other fallacies, like threatening someone (*ad baculum*), sometimes do not involve reasoning at all but a covert or overt adoption of non argumentative means to settle the dispute. The Amsterdam school proposes to view all fallacies as breaches of cooperativity in a critical discussion (van Eemeren and Grootendorst 2004). For various reasons, often because they get carried through by personal interests or emotions, people go overboard and breach cooperativity, manipulating others and often deceiving themselves. Given the complex and intrinsically risky nature of IC, intentional and unintentional fallacies abound in intercultural argumentation.

8.1. Culture or ideology?

One of the problems associated with fallacies is that they are often constructed on the common ground of an ideological system and its particular logical structure. It is true that both culture and ideology fit Lotman's and Uspenskij's (1975) definition of non-genetic information which is transmitted across generations. The modality of the transmission is nonetheless clearly different.

Culture is somehow a "natural" product, emerging from the interaction of human freedom and experience, and is transmitted to the new generations by a free and spontaneous choice of human beings, who give it to their children somehow as a "present". The transmission of natural languages to children is a paradigm of how culture is transmitted. Ideology, on the contrary, is intentionally "built up" by someone who has a precise project, and, when it becomes a dominant ideology, as in the sadly well-know examples of the totalitarian regimes, it is imposed on new generations through an organized system of ideological reproduction. Ideologies are often imposed on people, rather than transmitted through traditions, as evidenced by the histories of totalitarian regimes.

Culture, as discussed in Chapter 4, is a hypertextual system whose constitutive texts are meaningful to the relative community. As such, culture is justified by its past; and its categories, values, expressive forms, assumptions, etc. are passed on through the channels of textual traditions. The beliefs of a culture are, in effect, entrenched in its textual network (in its stories, legends, proverbs, etc.). A text in this system may have economic, political, philosophical, artistic, or religious value or function. Whatever its purpose, it is designed to provide people reared in that culture with a system of values that they come to assume as being true and meaningful. Ideologies are often constructed to assail historical hypertextual systems. Some ideologies involve references to economic and political textualities within this hypertext, attempting to alter them. Most "isms" are, by definition, ideologies. Ideologies do not rely equally on factual information to support beliefs and worldviews; they rely on fallacious argumentation. People who accept an entire ideological system usually reject all other systems.

Perhaps the more distinctive feature of culture is its openness to the individual's verification of principles, values, reasons and traditions through experience. Cultures do not change on the basis of previously established programs; they evolve thanks to the continuous dialogue between the individuals and their experience. On the contrary, ideologies tend to refuse the possible falsification of their axioms through the construction of devices that immunize them from contradiction.

Scapegoating is one of these devices. Hitler, for instance, took the Jews – represented as a single cohesive entity (Rocci 2005) capable of malign will – as scapegoats for avoiding to assume the responsibility for any problem or even any contradiction in the Nazi regime. As every problem was the Jews' fault, no criticism could be leveled at the regime. Moreover, as strategy to avoid the verification of experience, totalitarian regimes based on ideologies aim at constructing closed systems (controlling the people's freedom of travel and communication) and impose a tight control on the media (Wilke 2005): falsity in reporting news and facts, or in avoiding to report something that would be relevant, can be only achieved through a severe control on mass media and other sources of information.

Of specific interest to GL is the use of ideologically-based argumentation in intercultural interaction, which happens when the interlocutors refuse to engage in any argumentative critical discussion with each other, because they perceive each other's premises as ideologically unacceptable. The arguments put forward in any dialogue would thus be perceived as skewed, even if they might in some cases hold water logically speaking. Often, they are perceived as "contaminating," thus precluding any possibility of a reasonable discussion and meaningful intercultural dialogue. As a matter of fact, in today's global village, IC is constantly under threat of ideological discourse. Supposedly intercultural issue are exploited by intra-cultural ideological discourse for purposes that have nothing to do with intercultural understanding: scapegoating is a case-in point.

Indeed, one of the main objectives of GL should be to identify how argumentation in intercultural situations can be structured to avoid ideological manipulations. According to Rigotti (2005b), in general, a message is manipulative if it intentionally attempts to twist worldview to one's ideological objectives, so that an interlocutor can be manipulated into believing that he or she is indeed pursuing some meaningful objective in the conversation (even though this is not the case). Sometimes, an individual who manipulates interlocutors is often himself or herself a victim of self-manipulation, being truly swayed by the distorted vision of the world he or she promotes.

8.2. Stereotyping

Perhaps the most harmful form of fallacious argumentation in IC is the one based on *stereotyping*, which for the present purposes can be defined as the acceptance of unfounded premises about individuals belonging to certain communities or having certain traits. Common false premises include, for example, statements such as:

- Italians are romantic.
- Germans are unfriendly.
- Swiss people are precise.
- Americans are loud.
- etc.

Examples such as these are based on an "irresistible tendency to look for principles having general validity" (Rigotti 2005b), whereby a particular event (having met an Italian or German once), it is assumed as a sign of a more general truth, without taking statistical and probability factors into account. These are the sources of what has been called a process of *hasty generalization* (Walton 1999).

The following e-mails provide examples of how stereotypes could intervene in intercultural settings. They were exchanged by one of the authors of this text (B) and a colleague who lived in a northern European country (A). The reason for the initial e-mail was the fact that the author was late with a submission of proofs to the colleague's scholarly journal:

> A: You know that you are late with the proofs. We need them right away. You know, we in northern countries have a scientific mind; we expect such things to be done with scientific precision. You Italians, being southern, are people of the heart and are more easy-go-lucky. It is time to be scientific, no?
>
> B: Thanks for the reminder. I am attaching my corrections. I got really busy. By the way, I thank you for your attempt at humor. I guess Pythagoras, Archimedes, Galileo, and others like them were really northerners living in the south, no?

Here, of course, A evaluates B's being late with the proof as a cultural sign. A relied on a questionable premise about the difference between people living in northern and southern cultures (one could also challenge where the imaginary boundary between south and north really is, if there is one at all). B found this quite inappropriate, perceiving A's statement as an unfortunate attempt at humor. Indeed, had B not known A, he would have been offended. His retort was intended to point that out without further commentary.

The development of mass communications technologies and mass media have made it possible for various arguments to be spread far and wide. This is especially important for GL, given that Internet has become a key locus within which IC unfolds. On the one hand, the Internet is a very democratic system of communication, because, by reducing the costs of communication it potentially allows any individual to become an interlocutor on a truly world-wide interaction field. Any individual who has access to the Internet is generally free to navigate in it, and to access any type of information that other individuals have provided in it.

On the other hand, the Internet can be a source of stereotyping and the dissemination of fallacious arguments. In this virtual global community, a sort of *ad populum* argumentation is often at work, whose maxim can be formulated as follows:

> If everyone (= many) makes a certain decision, then this decision is likely to be good, or, more specifically, If everyone has access to this content, then this content must be worth accessing.

A primary goal of GL should be to unravel the sources of fallacious argumentation in IC, both intentional and unintentional. To provide a basis for this task, this chapter has presented a means for evaluating argumentative moves pragmatically as contributions to a critical discussion, and logico-semantically as invitations to inference based on certain reasoning schemes. In order to provide an instrument well adapted to tackle IC, we have dwelled on the influence of the socio-cultural context in the shaping of discussion and we have distinguished between the largely stable logical core of arguments (*loci*), and the culture-dependent values and generalizations that are appealed to (*endoxa*).

In many ways this remains a barebones presentation of the fundamentals. We can only hope that it motivates the readers to apply these tools to practical problems in IC.

Chapter 6
Global Linguistics

> *What our eyes behold may well be the text of life but one's meditations on the text and the disclosures of these meditations are no less a part of the structure of reality.*
>
> Wallace Stevens (1879–1955)

1. Introductory remarks

As mentioned several times in this book, Franz Boas's studies of American aboriginal languages led him to discover phenomena that suggested to him a principle that we have called the classificatory principle (Chapter 1, §3.1) — namely, that languages serve people as classificatory devices, allowing them to organize their particular worlds cognitively. For this reason, his work (and that of his students at Columbia University) constitutes a forerunner and a model for what we have been calling Global Linguistics here. Although the context in which Boas carried out his work was not the global village, it showed how crucial it was for the linguist to understand the role of the classificatory principle in guiding human interaction. His investigations of specialized vocabularies in particular were truly ahead of their time. As we saw in Chapter 1 (§3.1), he found, for example, that the Eskimo language had a sophisticated and highly detailed vocabulary for referring to animals such as seals and to natural events such as snowing, while English had a much more restricted vocabulary in these referential domains. The reason, Boas noted, was that seals and snow played a much more important role in Eskimo life than they did in English-speaking American culture. Boas came to the conclusion that by naming things people are putting them into the categories that they require to understand their own lives.

Boas was a founder of American anthropology. One of his students was (as mentioned) Edward Sapir, who continued his teacher's investigations of aboriginal languages. And, also as mentioned, Benjamin Lee Whorf was one of Sapir's students (Chapter 1, §3.1). Whorf gave Boas's and Sapir's use of an implicit classificatory principle in their work a precise and empirically-testable articulation. In this chapter, we will thus consider the so-called Whorfian Hypothesis (WH) in more detail than we have in previous chapters. We believe that the WH provides an insightful framework for studying IC, since it allows the linguist to penetrate the flow of classification-based meanings in conversational interactions and, thus, to detect differences within the flow that could lead to misunderstanding. Essentially, the WH posits that language structures predispose native speakers to attend to certain concepts as being necessary. This does not imply, however, that interlocutors cannot understand each other, as we have seen. Speakers can always use analogies and paraphrases to do so. Nevertheless, it is a fact of IC that problems tend to emerge when people are not aware of linguistic differences.

2. The Whorfian Hypothesis

Boas and his student Sapir were among the first modern-day linguists to carry out extensive field work on native aboriginal languages, examining how they shaped the thought patterns of their users through the particular lexical and grammatical categories that developed within them over time. The following quote from *Language* (Sapir 1921: 75) is a widely-cited one, and is worth repeating here given its obvious relevance to the GL agenda:

> Human beings do not live in the object world alone, nor alone in the world of social activity as ordinarily understood, but are very much at the mercy of the particular language system which has become the medium of expression for their society. It is quite an illusion to imagine that one adjusts to reality essentially without the use of language and that language is merely an incidental means of solving specific problems of communication or reflection. The fact of the matter is that the "real world" is to a large extent unconsciously built up on the language habits of the group.

It was Whorf who gave the Boas-Sapir view a testable articulation by suggesting that the function of language was to allow people to classify experience and, thus, that it was an organizing grid through which people living in a particular society come to perceive and understand the immediate world around them. By extension, the idea has emerged within certain sectors of argumentation theory (previous chapter) that the categories of a language affect argumentation itself. As will be discussed below, the crux to successful argumentation, and thus dialogue and conversation, is what a word implies as an unconscious premise (so to speak). When we refer to *tigers* as *felines*, we are using a cultural taxonomy that classifies *tigers* in the same category as *lions*, *cats*, and other similar mammals. But what happens if a language does not classify them in this way? Then, an argument in which felines are involved may break down.

The language in which Whorf became interested empirically was Hopi, an aboriginal language spoken in the southwest region of the US (Whorf 1956). Two things about the grammar of Hopi—plurals and verb tenses—caught Whorf's attention (SAE = Standard Average European):

1. After comparing plurals in SAE languages and Hopi he concluded that the former have both real and imaginary plurals—"4 people," "ten days." Four people can be counted together in an aggregate. The plural marker in this case refers to a real situation. But ten days cannot be put into an aggregate, since days are notions involving continuation and sequentiality, yet we still pluralize them. The plural marker in this case refers to something imagined, rather than real. SAE uses the plural in this case because, conceptually, it tends to objectify time, treating it as a quantifiable object ("two days, four months," etc.). Hopi, on the other hand, does not have imaginary plurals, since only real aggregates can be counted. It treats units of time as cyclic events, not as measurable ones.

2. SAE languages have three basic tense categories that predispose speakers to view time sequences as occurring *now*, as having occurred *before*, and as occurring *after* in the future. This reflects a view of time as a unit that can be arranged as a point on some linear axis running from the past to the future. Hopi speakers, on the other hand, use verb markers that indicate duration and other characteristics of an action, not its segmentation into units. To use a physical analogy, SAE verbs reflect a classic physics view of time as a distinct dimension of reality, Hopi verbs an Einsteinian (relativity) view of time as a continuous phenomenon relative to other dimensions. Hopi speaks the language of modern physics and always has.

In effect, Whorf discovered that differences in grammar reveal differences in worldview. This is perhaps why physicists attempt to avoid "linguistic relativity effects," or "Whorfian effects" (WEs) as we have called them (Chapter 4, §2.1) by using a supposedly nonverbal language—mathematics. Without going into the debate on mathematical language here, suffice it to say that science has always understood the problems related to the problems that language raises in the study of reality and only since the advent of quantum mechanics has it been able to deal directly with them, rather than avoid them. A WE can be defined simply as the filtering cognitive effect produced by a language. Recall (Chapter 1, §3.2) that whereas a speaker of English sees two distinct time-keeping devices—labeled watch and clock—an Italian would see only one—labeled orologio. This pattern of "seeing" is produced by different WEs.

For some reason, the WH has always been, and continues to be, a topic of fierce debate among linguists (see for instance Pinker 1994 who is fiercely against the WH, Wierzbicka 1997 and Levinson 1997, who defend it). Those opposed to the WH maintain that (1) it does not take into account the fact that languages across the world share the same "deep structure" and that (2) differences in vocabulary are incidental and easily "translated" into appropriate constructs across languages. Both remarks are largely true, but, in our view they do not amount to a counterargument to the WH, if properly construed. The predicate-argument structures that organize meaning (Chapter 2, § 5.1) represent a very plausible candidate to the role of shared deep structure of all languages. That said, it remains that the predicates that are lexicalized or grammaticalized by different languages are widely different. As for the role of translation and paraphrase, Whorf did recognize, as Cantoni (1999) observed, the possibility of translating and of using a language to explicate itself (auto-metalinguistic use).

In fact, the critics have interpreted the WH in a rather extreme fashion, the so-called "strong version" of the WH, referring mostly to those passages in Whorf's texts that seem to authorize this view and discounting other parts of his works that offer a more balanced and nuanced view (Cantoni 1999). According to this view, the "strong WH" postulates a strict linguistic determinism of thinking and culture: the language we speak strictly decides how we reason and determines the kind of culture we create. It is a one-way influence process. In this extreme view different cultures are separated cognitive universes and communication between them is impossible, let alone translation. We think that the "strong WH" is largely a *straw man* construed by the critics. In argumentation theory the *straw man fallacy* amounts to the presentation of a distorted version of the opponent's standpoint with the sole purpose of debunking it.

As observed by Cantoni (1999), a more extensive reading of Whorf's writings would reveal that the American linguist did not think that language completely determines thinking and culture.

According to Cantoni (1999: 323-327) Whorf envisages a complex, two-ways relation between language and the "habitual thought worlds" of speakers. We might summarize this relationship as follows: linguistically encoded categories offer a default set of conceptual tools for making sense of the world and reasoning about it. This conceptual toolbox, however, is not fixed. On the one hand, the existing system of linguistically encoded categories captures the distinctions that are perceived as salient in view of the life experience of the previous generations of a culture. On the other, the categorization system can evolve due to changed living conditions, to the encounter with new, and hence uncategorized, realities (the story of the platypus examined in Chapter 5 is a case-in-point), or simply because of an intercultural encounter. Whorf pays particular attention to the experience of learning a foreign language: initially the beginner will approach the new language, say Hopi, with the unconscious thought categories of her own language, say SAE, but in the long run she will be obliged to gradually abandon them in favor of language's own categories. Interestingly, it is by abandoning the native categories that the speaker will become consciously aware of their existence and articulation: "Then we find that the exotic language is a mirror held up to our own" (Whorf 1956).

In sum, the WH certainly does not claim that the realities of others cannot be understood or even learned. This happens every time we learn a foreign language and this enriching experience casts a new light on our own language and culture.

In a key study (Kramsch 1998:13-14) it has been found that Navajo children distinguish between "picking up a round object," such as a ball, and "picking up a long, thin flexible object," such as a rope, as required by their particular vocabulary. When presented with a blue rope, a yellow rope, and a blue stick, and asked to choose which object goes best with blue rope, Navajo children tend to choose the yellow rope, associating the objects on the basis of their shapes, whereas English-speaking children almost always choose the blue stick, linking the objects on the basis of color, even though both groups of children are perfectly able to distinguish colors and shapes. Such experiments show that speakers tend to sort out and distinguish things according to the categories provided by their languages. However, Navajo children who had studied English and know it functionally tend to choose the blue stick and yellow rope in a fairly equal way. The implications of such studies for the study of IC are obvious. These show that the WH is a useful framework for understanding differences in languages that can lead to misunderstandings.

In actual fact, there is much evidence of this type of file to support the WH. As a case-in-point, consider the empirical work of John Lucy. In one experiment (Lucy 1996), he studied the effect of grammar on memory tasks on English and Yucatec (a Mayan language) speakers. The languages differed as follows:

Table 18. English and Yucatec plural marking

English	Yucatec
Requires an obligatory plural marker for count nouns, including those referring to animate beings (humans, animals) and inanimate objects	Allows for plural marking, but does not require it, except for a small number of nouns
Plural marking is not used with mass nouns (*sugar*, *mud*, *water*, etc.)	Such marking is likely to be used with nouns referring to animate beings, but it is not obligatory

Lucy presented pictures of Yucatec village scenes to both speakers of English and Yucatec, and later asked them to recall the scenes (or aspects of the scenes). He found that English speakers recalled objects in the scenes that involved number marking for animate beings and objects, but had difficulties with those that involved number marking for substances. Yucatec speakers, on the other hand, were better able to recall animate beings, since these were marked for number. In effect, the recall tasks were dependent upon grammar, not pure memory.

2.1. Specialized vocabularies

As mentioned throughout this book, the study of specialized vocabularies is important for GL because these reveal the sources of many WEs that, in turn, affect the flow of argumentation in discourse and conversation. Take again kinship vocabulary as a case-in-point. As discussed in Chapter 4, §3.2, English distinguishes between a *nephew/niece* and a *grandchild*, but this distinction is not encoded in other languages. In Italian, as we saw, *nipote* refers to both "nephew/niece" and "grandchild." This difference reveals that kinship systems are structured differentially. When conversations between individuals who carry in their heads differential kinship systems take place, therefore, such differential structure may lead to misunderstandings. We tend to judge others according to our own categories and thus, may evaluate such things as marriage between people as incorrect depending on how we categorize them on the kinship grid.

As we saw, color terminology is also a common topic of interest to GL because of the potential WEs it might have, since the cognition of color is largely a matter of what words are used to encode it. Names for colors are, often, selections and evaluations of color. They are far too inexact to describe accurately all the colors we actually see. As a result, people often have difficulty trying to describe a certain color. This is why adjectives and other qualifiers, especially metaphorical ones, are used—*lime green, army green,* etc. If one were to segment the visible spectrum of all possible colors into several parts, there would be only a negligible difference in gradation in the adjacent colors at either side of the segmentation line (Figure 29). From violet to red, the spectrum blends smoothly from one color to the next. Yet, a speaker of a language will use his or her specialized color vocabulary with additional resources (adjectives, for example) to distinguish the gradations. These allow the speaker to classify the content of the spectrum in specific ways. There is nothing inherently natural about the color scheme used; it is a reflex of vocabulary, not of Nature. What is a shade of color in one language is a distinct color in another.

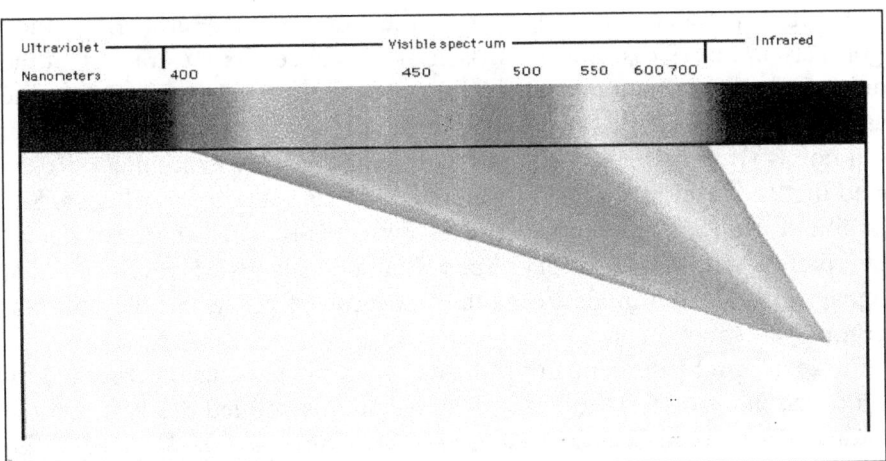

Figure 29. The spectrum.

To test for any WEs in color systems, Verne Ray conducted what has become a classic study in 1953 by interviewing the speakers of 60 different native languages spoken in the southwestern US. He showed his subjects colored cards under uniform conditions of lighting, asking the speakers to name them. He found that color systems varied considerably, and even when the number was the same the terms did not coincided conceptually. For example, in Wishram and Takelma, where there are as many terms as in English, the boundaries were different. Ray concluded as follows (1953: 98): "Color systems serve to bring the world of color sensation into order so that perception may be relatively simple and behavioral response, particularly verbal response and communication, may be meaningful."

As discussed (Chapter 4, § 3.2), Berlin and Kay published a significant study in 1969 that seemed to disclaim the presence of any WEs in color perception. Their study (as mentioned) has become a point of reference in discussing the WH ever since, because it apparently showed that a sequence pattern of color terminology operated across languages. Kay revised the sequence in 1975 in order to account for the fact that certain languages, such as Japanese, encoded a color category that does not exist in English, and which can only be rendered as "green-blue." This category, which Kay labeled *grue*, may occur before or after *yellow* in the original sequence. Since then it has been found that the sequence needs to be either modified, expanded, or even discarded. For example, Russian and Italian do not have a single color term for *blue*, but rather name *light blue* and *dark blue* as distinct focal colors (*azzurro* = blue, *celeste* = light blue, *blu* = *dark blue*). Many pursued the intriguing implications of the Berlin-Kay study vigorously in the 1970s. Eleanor Rosch, for instance, demonstrated that the Dani people of West Irian, who have a two-color system similar to the Bassa system described in Chapter 4, were able to discriminate easily eight focal points (Rosch 1975). Using a recognition-memory experiment, Rosch found that the Dani recognized focal colors better than non-focal ones. She also found that they learned new colors more easily when the color names were paired with focal colors. Such findings suggested to Rosch that languages provided a guide to the interpretation of color, but they did not affect its perception in any way.

But many problems remain to this day with the conclusions reached by such research. In effect, the Berlin-Kay has hardly refuted the WH. On the contrary, it seems to have kindled even more interest in it. Very recently, Paul Kay in a series of experiments carried out jointly with other cognitive researchers (Aubrey, Gilbert, Regier, Kay and Ivry 2005) has found that certain WE in the area of color are indeed observable, but they are limited to the right visual field. Information from the right visual field (RVF) is processed by the left emisphere of the brain and linguistic information is indeed localized in left emisphere. It is therefore plausible that the right visual field is the one more directly affected by the way in which colors are categorized in the language. The results of the experiments show that Whorfian effects are clearly present in the right visual field, but much less so in the left visual field.

For the present purposes suffice it to say that specialized vocabularies would seem to be potential sources of misunderstanding in IC, given the WEs that they seem to produce and, thus, that they should constitute a basic target of GL.

Actually, specialized vocabularies are not cast in stone, and are constantly being altered to meet new need. In a world where color plays a critical role, such as the modern world, there are now color experts who attempt to overcome problems in describing and matching colors by developing new specialized systems of classifying colors. Two widely used ones are: (1) the Munsell Color System, and (2) the CIE System of Color Specification. The former is one of the most popular and useful systems for classifying colors used today. It was developed in the early 1900s by Albert H. Munsell, an American portrait painter. It classifies colors according to basic characteristics of hue. To match a particular color, one must find that color among the samples provided. However, the number of samples in such systems cannot approach the number of colors we are able to distinguish. For this reason, it is sometimes impossible to find an exact match. The CIE System of Color Specification is used by manufacturers of such products as foods, paints, paper, plastics, and textiles who must often match colors precisely. But because of the nature of color, all such systems turn out to be highly limited. The CIE System simply provides a more refined color nomenclature that is based on metaphorical forms. CIE stands for Commission Internationale de l'Eclairage (International Commission on Illumination), an international organization that establishes standards for measuring color.

2.2. Whorfian effects

Understanding how specialized vocabularies and particular grammars encode reality differentially and imparting this to intercultural communities should be one of the practical outcomes of GL analysis. Consider the following stretch of conversation recorded at the University of Toronto during a colloquium of semioticians who came from various parts of the world, but who spoke English as the default among themselves (unless the interaction field determined that other languages could be used). The conversation took place in English between a native speaker of English (A) and a native speaker of Italian (B). The recording was made by one of the two authors of this book who had an open microphone attached to a tape recorder as he stood by and observed the two speakers.

A: These conferences are not always that good.
B: It was only this section, no? No fault of the organizers.
A: Of course.
B: I don't understand.

The two interlocutors did come to an understanding shortly thereafter but the conversation manifested in this segment reveals how a certain mode of expressing a premise affects its comprehension. A's opening statement has the structure *As are not always B*, which does not logically entail that *All A's are not B*. However, in Italian a similar turn of phrase *Questi convegni non sono sempre così belli* would convey a particular conversational implicature (Chapter 2, § 6.3). In Italian, A's utterance implies by innuendo not that, in general, the quality of the conferences is variable, but that the specific one in the present context of interaction is not good. Clearly, this shows a WE, which involves not only specialized vocabularies, but also virtually everything that a language makes available to speakers, from grammatical categories to modes of innuendo (as was the case above). In a phrase, WEs affect the pragmatics of verbal communication. Thus, sifting out what linguistic features affect the pragmatic interpretation of utterances in context and how they do so is a crucial aspect of GL. Once the details of this sifting process have been documented, it will be possible to study particular language vocabularies, grammars, and stylistic codes on the basis of how they realize specific speech acts and discourse strategies that are recognized by addressees who share the relevant linguistic and cultural background.

Consider, as another case-in-point, the distinction between count and mass nouns. To an Italian *grapes* are not countable and thus are assigned to the mass noun category, *uva*, a noun that has no plural form. Vice versa, to an Italian *information* is countable, unless it refers to the general concept itself—that is, if the concept of *information* is indicated, then Italian (like English) assigns it to the mass noun category: *L'informazione è importante* ("Information is important"). But if it refers to "bits and pieces" of information (as one would put it in English, then it is assigned to the count noun category: *Non ho tutte le informazioni necessarie* ("I do not have all the pieces of information that are required"). So, even when vocabularies coincide, their grammatical designations and assignments do not always do so, as this example shows. This too produces WEs. One example of this will suffice. The hypothetical conversation below is, actually, a paraphrase of a true conversation that took place in a classroom of one of the authors several years ago. A is a student of Italian background and B is the instructor (who is bilingual in English and Italian).

A: The informations I received are all wrong
B: You mean the bits and pieces of information you received.
A: No, all the informations.

B subsequently explained the difference to A. But the misunderstanding, as minor as it was, shows how noun categorization can interfere potentially in any discussion. Certainly, a native (non-bilingual) speaker of English would find A's statements awkward. Examples like this abound in the data on conversations and discourse. Most of the examples used in previous chapters could be re-analyzed in this light. The WEs that these systems produce should, thus, constitute a major objective of analysis in any GL approach to IC.

3. Noise versus interference

The discussion of WEs suggests, as mentioned previously (Chapter 4, §4), that a basic methodological orientation of GL should be the same one utilized by contact linguistics, since it entails, ultimately, studying the role of interference in IC and, thus, of the role of specific linguistic and conceptual systems in contact. It is worthwhile distinguishing between *noise* and *interference*. The former is essentially the term used in communication science to refer to any obstruction to the decipherment of a message that can easily be overcome because of the built-in redundancy features in the communicative system itself (Chapter 1, §1); the latter refers to the unconscious linguistic and conceptual transfers and calques from the native language that affect the meaning of an intercultural exchange, which cannot be repaired automatically because of redundancy or any other predictable structural feature in the system.

Overall, it can be claimed that intercultural noise is caused by such momentary aberrations as word mispronunciations and inappropriate greeting protocols. Interferences, on the other hand, are caused by WEs and, thus, are potentially more destructive of interaction.

3.1. Noise

In second language teaching, it is an implicit law of learning that the native language of learners is an ever-present factor in shaping the learning flow and, thus, that it cannot be ignored pedagogically because it largely determines the ways in which students perceive and assimilate the new language. Known generally, as *transfer theory*, it grew out of the common observations of the errors students typically make, along with the predictable difficulties they experience, especially during the early learning stages. Transfer theory led to the development of a new analytical technique called *contrastive analysis* (CA), which teachers continue to use, in one way or other, as the basis for designing textbooks and organizing the teaching syllabus. By "contrasting" the target and native languages, they can thus identify which features of pronunciation, grammar, and vocabulary will require more emphasis and which ones will not. Those that are identical or similar to corresponding native ones will receive less pedagogical emphasis because the transfer process—known as positive transfer—would allow the students to acquire them automatically. Those that differ radically will instead receive much more instructional salience because the transfer process—known as negative transfer—would interfere with the student's efforts to learn the new habits and categories. In this way, positive transfer is maximized and negative transfer minimized through pedagogical means.

Language teachers distinguish between *mistakes* and *errors*. The former are the blunders that students make, but which they can easily correct themselves; the latter are unconscious deviations caused by gaps in linguistic competence and, thus, cannot be corrected by students themselves, requiring pedagogical intervention. Together, these make up communicative noise. An analogous situation exists in IC. Analyses of both student and intercultural discourse have made it obvious that there are two general types of errors: (1) *interlinguistic*, which is caused by negative transfer; and (2) *intralinguistic*, which is caused by inference (generalization, analogy, simplification, etc.). An example of a typical interlinguistic error committed by English-speaking students of Italian is:

Io aspetto per Maria = "I am waiting for Mary." The correct form is *Io aspetto Maria*. The source of this error is *syntactic noise*, that is, the negative transfer of English *for* to the formation of the Italian sentence. In Italian the verb *aspettare* is transitive, whereas in English *to wait* is intransitive (requiring the preposition *for* before the object) (NL = native language, SL = second language):

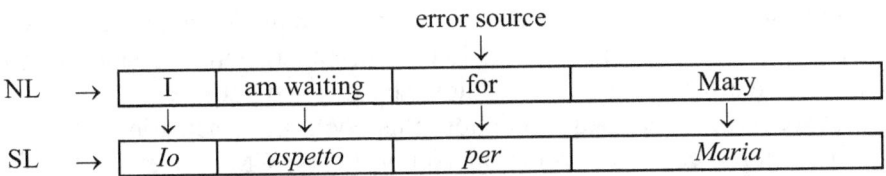

Figure 30. Syntactic noise

This type of error does not usually disrupt communication. It simply introduces a momentary syntactic noise into it. In several studies of IC at the University of Toronto, the authors of this book have found that this type of noise characterizes from 10% to 14% of conversations. We simply collated recordings of IC, conducted randomly, covering over 18 hours of recorded talk. We then counted the instances of noise in them. We identified something as being "noisy" if we detected that the conversation continued on without any significant disruptions to the meaning flow. If a disruption did occur, its trigger was reclassified as an interference. Interlinguistic features require less emphasis in GL analysis than do other sources.

Intralinguistic errors—the second main source of noise identified by second language teachers—are caused by general inferential processes intrinsic to language acquisition in general. They are very similar to the developmental errors that children manifest as they acquire their native language. Thus, for instance, when a non-native student of English produces the form *goed (for *went*), he or she is guessing on the basis of what he or she knows about past-tense morphology (*play* = *played*, *try* = *tried*, etc.). Similarly, when a non-native student of Italian pluralizes *problema* ("problem") as *probleme* (rather than *problemi*), he or she is guessing that the rule *nouns ending in -a are pluralized by changing the -a to -e* applies to *problema*, which it does not. The study mentioned in the previous paragraph revealed that barely 3% of such interferences characterized the sample of IC that we used as a database. Our conclusion is, tentatively, that noise is not only a superficial factor in intercultural breakdowns, but that it is also a statistically unimportant one.

3.2. Interference

The same study revealed that almost 25% of conversational content in the sample contained what we define strictly here as interferences leading to misunderstandings and, in some cases, communication breakdowns. Interferences have a logico-semantic or conceptual source (Chapter 4, §3). They are, in effect, the result of what we have called WEs here.

As we have mentioned throughout this book, the fascinating work that has been going on in conceptual metaphor theory (CMT) over the last few decades is, clearly, of crucial importance to GL since, as we have seen, conceptual metaphors are the source of many interferences in intercultural contact situations. In order to discuss this more broadly, it is useful to revisit some of the central ideas in CMT and Cognitive Linguistics.

In his ground-breaking 1936 book, *The Philosophy of Rhetoric*, the literary scholar I. A. Richards (1893-1979) argued that metaphorical coinages are attempts to understand reality by an associative inferential process. Consider the expression *John is a monkey* which, as we have seen, is one of the products of the conceptual metaphor [people are animals] (§2.4.4). Portraying *John* as a *monkey* forces us to imagine a human person in simian terms. If we were to call John a *snake*, a *pig*, or a *puppy*, then our mental impression of *John* would change in kind with each new vehicle chosen from the [animal] source domain—he would become serpentine, swine-like, and puppy-like in our mind's eye. In other words, we would be painting a different metaphorical picture of his personality in animal terms. The problem in intercultural discourse is not the conceptual metaphor involved, [people are animals], which seems to be universal, but rather the particular vehicle selection from the [animal] source. Calling someone a *monkey* may have non-offensive and purely descriptive effects in one language, but it may be construed as highly offensive in another. In our database (§3.1, above), we found a large number of instances where speakers used a conceptual metaphor correctly cross-culturally, but selected an inappropriate vehicle, leading to rather serious breakdowns in the communication flow. In effect, the interference was not caused by the conceptual metaphor type, but by the vehicle used.

Let's look at this phenomenon a little more closely. The linkage of the target and source domains in a conceptual metaphor produces a concept which suggests that we sense some intrinsic existential link between the two domains. Thus, if an inappropriate source domain is chosen in an intercultural situation, true interference surfaces. This is particularly so, as the database suggests, when it comes to *root metaphors*—metaphors based on sensation. The number of root metaphorical constructions in vocabularies throughout the world is immeasurable. Here is a handful of such constructions in English based on the sensation of vision (Danesi 2004b):

Table 19. English root metaphors based on vision.

– flash of insight	– a shining mind
– spark of genius	– a bright fire in his eyes
– a bright mind	
– a brilliant idea	– sparking interest in a subject
– a flicker of intelligence	
	– words glowing with meaning
– a luminous achievement	
	– flickering ideas

Needless to say, vision is not the only sensory modality people use as a source to name [thinking] processes. The etymology of common words for such processes in English reveals that vision is used alongside touching, grasping, and other sensory analogues to produce root metaphors:

- comprehend (from Latin *prehendere* "to grasp")
- discern (from Latin *dis* + *cerno* "to separate")
- examine (from Latin *ex* + *agmen-* "to pull out from a row")
- idea (from Greek *idein* "to see")
- intelligence (from Latin *intellegere* "to pick, choose")
- perceive (from Latin *-cipio* "to seize")
- speculate (from Latin *speculari* "to look at")
- theory (from Greek *theoria* "view")
- think (from Old English *thincean* "to take, handle")
- understand (from Old English *ongietan* "to see, feel")

In effect, when English speakers refer to thought processes they will tend to invoke sensory ones metaphorically. Problems in intercultural conversations arise when different sensory vehicles are used by speakers leading to what has been called throughout this book, conceptual interference. An example is the following stretch of conversation that took place between an English-speaking student (A) and a Japanese student (B) at the University of Lugano:

A: Can you hear what I am saying? (= Do you understand?)
B: I do not hear well.
A: Are you kidding?
B: No, I hear only your anger.

As this shows, the [hearing] vehicle designates different things in English and Japanese. Speaker A used it for [understanding], but speaker B used the same sense modality for [feelings] because, in Japanese *yoin* ("reverberating sound") is the source domain for portraying "human feelings." As examples such as this one imply, the notion of conceptual interference can now be recast more precisely as a differential selection of culture-specific vehicles in discourse that obstruct communicative exchanges. Clearly, much more research must be conducted in this area if GL is to determine the nature and extent to which this is verifiable and what its various modalities are.

In languages across the world, the human body is also a productive source domain for naming all kinds of things that are abstractions and perceived to be linked to the body. This is why we refer in English to the *bowels of the earth*, to its *heart*, and so on. Again, this is a source of disruptive interference in IC because the body metaphors used may or may not coincide in different languages. A content-based statistical analysis of the differences will be useful in this area, since it is such a constant problem in IC, as we found in our own data. By such analysis we are referring to identifying differential vehicles for referring to the same target domain and then quantifying the differences overall to estimate potential interference rates in actual conversation.

Here are some examples of bodily metaphors in English contrasted with those in Italian. This list gives an indication of the degree to which the two languages might vary (n/a = not applicable).

Table 20. Bodily metaphors in English and Italian.

English	Italian
1. a body of people	n/a
2. a body of water	n/a
3. the body of a work	n/a
4. the eye of a storm	n/a
5. the eye of the needle	n/a
6. the face of a clock	n/a
7. the foot of a mountain	*piede di una montagna*
8. the head of a table	*capo tavola*
9. the head of an organization	*capo di un ditta*
10. the head of the household	*capofamiglia*
11. the leg of a race	n/a
12. holding a meeting	*tenere una riunione*
13. taking things at face value	n/a
14. nosing around	*ficcare il naso*
15. mouthing lyrics	n/a
16. shouldering a burden	n/a
17. knuckling under	n/a
18. going belly up	n/a

The above list shows only 6 of 18 matches and even these show significant differences in how the source vehicles are grammaticalized or lexicalized (assigned grammatical or lexical form), with attendant differential semantic nuances. An analysis of our database, using a similar comparative technique showed that, on average, there was less than 30% consistency of this kind across conceptual categories in IC.

As a strategy for understanding the world, Richards claimed, metaphor is at the core of an individual's worldview. It is a constant source of interference because the constant juxtaposition of source domains in common discourse produces, cumulatively, Idealized Cognitive Models (ICMs) of what people are discussing in the interaction. ICMs are clusters of conceptual metaphors delivering the same concept, allowing people to navigate mentally through the source domains as they speak about certain things and thus understand each other. To see what this means, let's symbolize six source domains for speaking about [ideas], [theories], and other such constructs in English as follows:

S_1 = 'sight'	as in:	*I see what that idea is all about now*
S_2 = 'geometry'	as in:	*Those are parallel ideas*
S_3 = 'plants'	as in:	*That idea has deep roots*
S_4 = 'buildings'	as in:	*Those ideas have a solid foundation*
S_5 = 'food'	as in:	*I can't quite swallow your idea*
S_6 = 'fashion'	as in:	*That idea is really in fashion right now*
S_7 = 'commodities'	as in:	*I don't buy that theory*

The clustering of these source domains make up the ICM of [ideas]. Now, the following utterances can be seen to contain various combinations of these source domains:

(1) I can see (S_1) what you mean with that idea, but it has been passé (S_6) for a while, even though it has deep roots (S_3).
(2) They can't sell me their ideas (S_7) for many reasons; one is that they are not well-founded (S_4); another is that they are diametrically-opposite (S_2) to mine. I just can't digest (S_5) them at all.

An ICM is the clustering of source domains around target domain. If we let a target domain be represented by T_1, T_2, etc., then an ICM has the following general structure:

$T_n = S_1, S_2, S_3, S_4, \ldots S_n$

Research on ICMs has shown that source domains overlap, intersect, and constantly piggyback on each other in the production of discourse. Language, from this standpoint, appears as a network of source domains that crisscross constantly in the construction of communal meanings.
If we go back to our earlier representation of conceptual structure in terms of predicate-argument relations we can say that every culturally stored category, every linguistically manifested predicate is not exhausted by the

translation or paraphrase of its *denotative* content in terms of its entailed semantic components (Chapter 2, § 5.1) , as in discourse and culture predicates are never present as "naked concepts". They carry with them a cluster of connotations that originate from (1) their previous use in culturally significant texts and (2) from the ICM in which they feature as a target domain. In sum, the sources metaphorically attributed to a target are not part of the target's semantic entailments, yet these sources are culturally established "models", ways of seeing the denotatum and understanding it in its relationships with the rest of the material and cultural world. For instance, [war] is not an entailed semantic component of the English predicate *argument / to argue*, but the conceptual metaphor [argument is war] contributes considerably to the connotations of this predicate in English. In English speaking cultures the concept of [war] is used heuristically to infer, or discover *typical* properties of arguments. Interestingly, these connotations and the inferences they bring about carry through only very partially to other languages such as Dutch, French or Italian (Chapter 1, § 4.2).

It is clear that the notion of ICM raises crucial questions for GL: Which ICMs are more or less productive in a culture? For example, is the concept of *love* more or less productive than, say, *ideas*? That is to say, does the concept of *love* surface more often in texts, in discourse, and in social rituals than does the concept of *ideas*? Which concepts are more or less productive cross-culturally?

By simply counting the number of source domains associated with the ICM of some concept, we can get an idea of the productivity of that concept with relation to others. For example, as we saw above, in English [ideas/thinking] concept was rendered by such source domains as [food], [people], [fashion], [buildings], [commodities], [vision], and [geometry]. How many more are there? We were able to find at least 89 source domains. On the other hand, we were able to come up with only 36 source domains for the ICM of [love]. Common ones are [physics] ("There were sparks between the two"), [health] and [disease] ("Their relationship has become sick"), [insane symptoms] ("He's gone mad over her"), [magic] ("She has bewitched her lover"), among others. Our estimates suggest that in English [love] is a less productive concept than [ideas]. Needless to say, our estimates were rough ones based primarily on introspection. Readers may come up with more (or less) source domains in both cases. It is unlikely, however, that they will find many more (as one of the authors discovered by giving this very task as an assignment to several of his linguistics and semiotics classes a few years ago).

What does this imply? It suggests, arguably, that in English culture [thinking] is a concept that is given much more cognitive and representational salience than [love] is. This does not mean that the latter is not important, but simply that there are fewer ways to talk about it and, thus, to think about it. When we compared the English ICMs to Italian ones, we found that most of the source domains used to deliver the concept of [thinking] were identical—92 in total. However, we came up with 99 source domains for the Italian ICM of [love], suggesting that it is probably a more productive concept in Italian culture.

Such differential ICM structures produce WEs in IC. As our database of recorded discussions shows, this occurs around 30-35% of the time. In effect, as speaker A navigates (as a native speaker) through an ICM in a conversation, a non-native speaker, B, will have difficulty following the "thread of thinking." Speakers who do not possess knowledge of S_2 ([geometry]) as a source domain will experience conceptual noise in not being able to understand that [ideas] is the target of discourse; but when they use their own source domains that have a different function in the default language, they risk being misunderstood, as the following stretch of a conversation between a speaker of English (A) and one whose native language was Chinese (B) shows. It was recorded during a conversation at the University of Toronto:

A: I don't see why you like her.
B: Why not?
A: She's kinda square.
B: No, she's very round.
A: Ha, ha.
B: Why are you laughing?

A's laughter was caused by his interpretation of B's use of *round* as a humorous remark. But clearly this was not B's intent who understood A's use of *square* in similar metaphorical terms, but seemingly as a reference to physical appearance.

In our database we found that some of figurative expressions are less likely to be understood cross-culturally than others, even though the same target domains might exist. As a starting point for GL, it might be worthwhile to list here all those English expressions an idioms that we found to be particularly resistant to cross-cultural understanding, since it will give a sense of how extensive the potential base of conceptual interference might be in IC. Indeed, we invite the reader who speaks another language to attempt to translate these in that language:

Table 21. English tropes resistant to cross-cultural understanding.

Color	
in the red	not enough money
out of the blue	a surprise
in black and white	written down, confirmed
red tape	bureaucracy
feeling blue	feeling unhappy
green light	consent
green with envy	very envious
in the black	solvent
red carpet	swanky
white lie	lie avoiding embarrassment
Food	
apple of one's eye	favorite person
baloney	nonsense
cream someone	defeat someone brutally
fishy	suspicious
go bananas	become insane
in a pickle	in difficulty
lemon	something defective
nuts	crazy
peanuts	nothing
piece of cake	easy
Numbers	
forty winks	snoozing
in seventh heaven	ecstasy
of two minds	unsure
on cloud nine	bliss
on second thought	hesitation, doubt
put two and two together	conclude logically
second nature	habit, tendency
second to none	the best
six of one, half a dozen of the other	the same, no difference
sixth sense	hunch

Table 21 (Cont.)

Body	
big mouth	talks too much
by heart	by memory
cost an arm and a leg	cost very much
have a sweet tooth	like sweets
head over heels in love	deeply in love
long face	sadness, seriousness
nosey	prying
pain in the neck	nuisance
pull someone's leg	deceive, tease
see eye to eye	agree
People	
jack of all trades	one who can do many things
keep up with the Joneses	to be like others
real McCoy	the real thing
smart aleck	joker
Tom, Dick, or Harry	any common person
wise guy	joker
Animals	
blind as a bat	someone who cannot see
quiet as a mouse	very silent
bookworm	booklover
copycat	imitator
chicken	cowardly
early bird	one who arrives before the time
eat like a horse	eat abundantly
pigheaded	stubborn
smell a rat	detect a conspirator
talk turkey	to tell the truth
work like a dog	overwork
Movement	
back and forth	intermittently, unsmoothly
ins and outs	details
right and left	in every way

Table 21 (Cont.)

Geography	
dirt cheap	very economical
down-to-earth	practical
go downhill	decline
make a mountain out of a molehill	exaggerate
out of the woods	out of trouble
over the hill	old
tip of the iceberg	only the start, only visible part
up the creek	in trouble
win by a landslide	total victory
Recreation	
get a kick out of something	to be thrilled
go fly a kite	leave me alone
good sport	good person
in the same boat	same predicament
keep the ball rolling	continue on
no dice	not possible
off base	skewed
on the ball	sharp
put one's cards on the table	reveal everything
right off the bat	right away
sink or swim	succeed or fail
Objects	
sharp as a tack	attentive, smart
bury the hatchet	stop fighting, make up
flash in the pan	pass quickly
have a screw loose	a little wacky
on pins and needles	tingling
pan out	develop
sponge off	take credit
throw in the towel	surrender
wet blanket	spoiler

Table 21 (Cont.)

Medicine/Anatomy	
bitter pill to swallow	unpleasant, but to be accepted
cough up	give
feel it in one's bones	sense it
blood is thicker than water	kinship ties take precedence
fly in the ointment	drawback
get burned	be defeated, chastised
taste of one's own medicine	receive similar treatment
have a lot of nerve	courage
hold one's breath	hope
sick and tired	unhappy
take pains	make an effort
Plants	
bark up the wrong tree	err
beat around the bush	be equivocal
hit the hay	go to bed
in a nutshell	briefly
last straw	limit
nip something in the bud	stop something early on
through the grapevine	gossip
turn over a new leaf	new life
up a tree	in trouble
Clothing	
be in someone else's shoes	in another's situation
dressed to kill	dressed provocatively
feather in one's cap	attainment
handle someone with kid gloves	treat someone very delicately
hot under the collar	indignant
keep one's shirt on	do not get upset
keep something under one's hat	control
lose one's shirt	become poor
on a shoestring	meagerly
tied to someone's apron strings	strongly attached

Table 21 (Cont.)

Time	
big time	success
call it a day	stop doing something
for the time being	in the meanwhile
high time	the moment has come
in no time	immediately
in the nick of time	barely
kill time	pass the time
make time	catch up
spur of the moment	spontaneously
Weather	
break the ice	initiate
a breeze	easy
come rain or shine	no matter what
full of hot air	boasting, bragging
have one's head in the clouds	unrealistic
rain cats and dogs	pour
save something for a rainy day	preserve for the right moment
snowed under	extremely busy
under the weather	off color
weather a storm	avoid a problem
House/Buildings	
bring down the house	entertain with laughter
down the drain	lost, missed
drive someone up the wall	make someone really upset
get one's foot in the door	initial opportunity
hit home	affect personally
hit the ceiling	get angry
on the fence	undecided
on the house	free
on the shelf	aside
under the table	illicitly

Conceptual interference can, of course, have other kinds of figurative sources, such as metonymy and irony (Chapter 3, §4.2). Indeed, A's laughter in the conversation above was evoked by the fact the he thought B was being ironic, which was not the case. Irony and metonymy are, in fact, regularly considered separately from metaphor in CMT. Metonymy entails the use of a conceptual entity within a domain to represent the entire domain:

(1) She loves *Nietzsche* (= the writings of Nietzsche).
(2) There are new *faces* in class today (= people).
(3) My brother doesn't like *nose rings* (= people with nose rings).
(4) They bought a *Mazda* (= car named Mazda).
(5) The *trains* are on strike (= train conductors).
(6) The *Church* does not condone such behavior (= theologians, priests, etc.).

The use of the part to represent the whole, or vice versa, is known more specifically as *synecdoche*. In analogy with the notion of conceptual metaphor, the term *conceptual metonym* can be used to refer to generalized metonymical concepts such as [face = person] (Danesi 2004b):

(1) That actor is just another handsome *face*.
(2) Look at all the new *faces* in the audience.
(3) We should hire some new *faces* around here.
(4) You have to talk to each other *face* to *face*.

Conceptual metonyms are interconnected to discourse flow in the same way that conceptual metaphors are, forming ICMs of their own. Here are some other examples of conceptual metonyms as they occur in utterances:

[body part = person]
(1) Put your *brains* to work!
(2) The Yankees need a *stronger arm* at third base.
(3) We don't hire *baggy pants*.

[manufacturer's name = brand product]
(4) I'll have a *Stella Artois*.
(5) We bought a *Saab*.
(6) He's got a *Coca-Cola* in his office.

[object = object's user]
(7) My *cello* is off key today.
(8) The *steak and potatoes* is a lousy tipper.
(9) The *buses* are on strike.

[institution = people in the institution]
(10) *Shell* has raised its prices again.
(11) The *Church* made its opinion known rather clearly.
(12) I don't approve of the *White House's* actions.

Irony constitutes a discourse strategy whereby words are used to convey a meaning contrary to their literal sense. It is designed to highlight a concept through opposition, antithesis, or antonymy. If the sentence "I love torture" is uttered by a masochist, then it would hardly have an ironic meaning. But if it is uttered by someone who is obviously in some sort of pain or distress, then it constitutes irony. Our analysis of the recorded data reveals that metonymy and irony are two of the most destructive sources of interference in IC. As mentioned in previous chapters, the source of the problem is, usually, that a metonymic or ironic statement is taken at face value, rather than conceptual value, and thus creates semantic conditions that destroy discourse flow. One of the most important areas of research for GL, consequently, is to study figurative discourse in IC in a systematic and in-depth fashion.

4. Intercultural Competence

It is obvious that the traditional notions of linguistic competence and communicative competence are not sufficient to tackle the analysis of problems that characterize IC. Indeed, the notion of *intercultural competence* can be tentatively proposed here as a target of future research and understanding. Even though similar notions have been put forward in the relevant literature, ours is restricted to covering the logico-semantic and conceptual dimensions of IC discourse.

4.1. The notion of competence

Throughout this book we have made use of various models and typologies of competence, from Saussure's *langue* versus *parole* distinction to such notions as communicative and discourse competence. However, we have not defined the notion itself. In the relevant literature, it is used generally to refer to "knowledge" of language, including its rules of word-formation, pronunciation, and so on. In essence, it refers to what the Germans call *Sprachgefühl*, or a feeling for how one's native language is put together structurally and how it can be used for communication and other purposes. In effect, to be "competent" in a language is to know how it works and how it can be used. Competence is, by and large, unconscious in native speakers.

As mentioned, there are two main types of competence distinguished by linguists—linguistic (*langue*) and communicative (*parole*). Linguistic competence is knowledge of the language system in itself. It is comprised of various subcompetencies, the chief ones being *lexico-semantic, syntactic, morphological, phonological,* and *graphological* (writing). Lexico-semantic competence involves knowing the meanings of language forms. It manifests itself in discourse as the ability to select forms and structures to match discourse flow appropriately. Syntactic competence involves the ability to organize language forms for physical delivery in speech. This includes knowledge of basic phrase structure, of the ordering of the words within phrases, of agreement between structures (number and gender, subject and verb, etc.), of case structure (position and function of a word within a sentence), of the function of sentence types (negatives, interrogatives, etc.), and so on. Morphological competence involves the ability to recognize and inflect forms. Essentially, this entails knowing what constitutes a word and what units smaller than words (morphemes) convey meaning. Phonological competence is the ability to articulate sounds and utilize the sound system for expression in an appropriate fashion; and graphological competence is the ability to use the graphic system (alphabet characters, pictograms, etc.) to decipher and construct appropriate verbal texts.

Communicative competence is defined as the ability to apply language to interactional and representational situations in an appropriate manner. Its main subcompetencies include *pragmatic, strategic,* and *stylistic* ones (as we have seen). Pragmatic competence involves the ability to recognize and produce speech forms to fit a situation (saying hello, criticizing, etc.). Strategic competence is the ability to use language to carry out certain social interactions in a strategic way: for example, cajoling, persuading, etc. This competence is also called *discourse competence*. However, the term strategic is probably more precise since it focuses on how discourse is used to obtain some objective. Stylistic competence is knowledge of which register or style (formal, casual, etc.) is appropriate in a given situation or medium. As Hymes (1971) showed, linguistic and communicative competencies are hardly autonomous psychological phenomena. The two are intrinsically intertwined, as previously discussed (Chapter 2, §2.1). To maintain the smooth flow of meaning in speech acts, it is necessary to know how to filter out repetitions in them by using anaphoric, cataphoric and other kinds of devices, among other such things.

In this book, we have also used the term *conceptual competence*. We can define it as the ability to reason with the categorical distinctions operated by a culture. It consists of three main subcompetencies, which can be called simply *semantic, figurative* and *reflexive*.

Semantic competence involves the grasp of the semantic implications (entailments) of the predicates that lexicalize the categorical distinctions recognized in the culture. This competence involves the ability to paraphrase, to gloss and to translate cultural meanings in more cross-culturally transparent terms (such as Wierzbicka's conceptual primes and universals). It aslo involves the ability to harness this knowledge of cultural concepts and their entailments to construct arguments that are convincing in a given culture. Without semantic competence, the "hooking" of an argument to the standpoint (Chapter 5, § 7.1) is compromised (Rigotti and Greco 2006).

Figurative competence is the ability to use the ICMs of a language in speech. This entails the ability to recognize and exploit the connotative aura associated with specific predicates within a culture because of the ICMs that are used in connection with these predicates. It also involves directly exploiting ICMs in argumentation through a specific *locus* called *argument from figurative analogy* (Garssen 2008).

Reflexive competence involves the ability to transform concepts into language categories (syntactic, morphological, etc.). This is called reflexive because the view espoused here is that language encodes concepts by mirroring them in some formal way. For instance, the [time is money] conceptual metaphor is reflexivized differentially as follows:

As a verb: We *spent* way too much time on that project.
As an adjective: His time is more *valuable* than you think.
As a noun: What *price* did they pay for her time?

Overall *competence* in a language, or simply *language competence*, involves the ability to utilize all three competencies in an integrated, interdependent fashion—conceptual competence entails knowing what to say in a certain situation; communicative competence what that situation is and how to respond to it verbally; and linguistic competence how to realize the message in terms of the forms a language makes available.

4.2. Intercultural competence defined

The above discussion of competence makes it possible to understand where and how intercultural discourse breaks down. In effect, a non-native speaker of the koiné may have acquired varying degrees of linguistic and even communicative competence, but may not know how to integrate this with conceptual competence in order to carry out various arguments. In such a case the person "speaks" with the memorized formal and communicative structures of the koiné, but "thinks" in terms of his or her native conceptual system: that is, he or she will use the words and communicative protocols of the koiné as "carriers" of his own native language concepts (§4.3).

Intercultural competence, thus, involves for a non-native speaker the ability to navigate among all three competencies associated with the koiné, without unconsciously resorting or defaulting to his or her own native-language competencies. For native speakers of the relevant koiné – be they native speakers of English or of another language functioning as a koiné in IC (Chapter 1, § 3) – intercultural competence involves an awareness of the pitfalls of blind reliance on the default models of the world provided by the categorical distinctions ingrained in the language. These models may not be shared or even understood by members of other cultures. For both, intercultural competence involves an awareness that the default models offered by one own native language are not to be identified with reality. In view of the goal of building a solid intercultural competence, the Whorfian hypothesis can be translated, as suggested by Cantoni (1999: 328), as an invitation to adopt a critical attitude and not let our own language "impose" us a view of the world to be accepted uncritically as reality.

At the same time one should be aware that all linguistically based models are, as we stressed in Chapter 4, respectable hypotheses about reality which have proven *good enough* to sustain the lives of people for generations within their respective communities. They did contribute to provide the *cradle* that allowed the members of such a culture to grow up and live in a human community. They are not set in stone, nor they are inscribed in human genes. They have always changed through the ages and they will continue to change through intercultural contact and cross-fertilization in the Global Village. Our hope is that this ongoing process of reciprocal cultural redefinition will be based more on reasonable argumentation rather than on violence and coercion.

Attaining intercultural competence is a long and arduous task, since it involves the study of culture-based meanings and of how meaning affects argumentation through the WEs it produces. It is not the goal of GL to impart such competence. That is, and always has been, the goal of language teaching. In a sense, GL and applied linguistics have the same basic goal — to make IC fluid, smooth and, especially, free of breakdowns. The difference between the two is essentially that, in the present global village, the goal of GL is to document and analyze IC, while that of applied linguistics is to apply the findings of GL to impart intercultural competence.

As observed by Cowley and Hanna (2005), in the practical teaching of intercultural communication "non-language-based" courses are the norm in many institutions. Failing to combine the teaching of IC and language teaching could represent a serious limitation for both in today's Global Village.

The integration of IC and applied linguistics is important in two respects. First, in the teaching of a koiné language, the complex intercultural implications of its use as a global means of communication should play an important part. Second, the study of *any* second language — be it a global lingua franca spoken by billions of people, a national or regional language, or an endangered language with a few hundred speakers — is a valuable experience in developing an intercultural competence. Rigotti (2005a: 316) reports a dictum of the semioticians Lotman and Uspenskij according to which one needs at least two languages in order to distinguish clearly between language and reality. In a study on bilingual children, Swiss linguist Georges Lüdi (1998) reports the results of a series of experiments on the children's reasoning abilities. The experiments show that bilingual children are more "independent from words", which results in better metalinguistic abilities: they are able to better explain, gloss or paraphrase their meanings. They also excel in constructing novel concepts from experience. According to Lüdi, this means that these children have learned to distance themselves from language, and have become aware of the relativity of the categorical grid used by each language to verbalize the world.

The rewards of encountering other languages and cultures are enormous. Perhaps, one of the most important and least apparent is an increased self-understanding of the participants. By entering conversation with other languages and cultures we become more fully aware of the richness of our own culture. At the same time, by addressing *our own* questions to the "foreign" cultures we reveal new aspects of these cultures, new meanings and implications that were previously unknown to the members of the other cultural community. This kind of process has been analyzed in depth by Bakhtin (1986: 6-7). The Russian scholar observes that immersion is only an initial phase of intercultural understanding:

> There exists a very strong, but one-sided and thus untrustworthy, idea that in order to better understand a foreign culture, one must enter into it, forgetting one's own, and view the world through the eyes of this foreign culture. This idea, as I said, is one-sided. Of course, a certain entry as a living being into a foreign culture, the possibility of seeing the world through its eyes, is a necessary part of the process of understanding it; but if it were the only aspect of this understanding, it would be merely duplication and would not entail anything new or enriching.

A fuller, truly "creative", understanding requires that we do not forget our own culture – the "cradle" we come from – and that we bring it to the dialogue with the other cultures. According to Bakhtin, one should be aware of the fact that one's own culture provides a valuable *outside perspective*, for the self-understanding of the other and for the creation of new shared meanings:

> A meaning only reveals its depths once it has encountered and come into contact with another, foreign meaning: they engage in a kind of dialogue, which surmounts the closedness and one-sidedness of these particular meanings, these cultures. We raise new questions for a foreign culture, ones that it did not raise itself; we seek answers to our own questions in it; and the foreign culture responds to us by revealing us its new aspects and new semantic depths. Without *one's own* questions one cannot understand anything other or foreign (but, of course, the questions must be serious and sincere).

5. Concluding remarks

The purpose of this text has been to show that language plays a key role in IC and that a science for studying this role, which we have designated Global Linguistics, is necessary in today's globally interconnected world. As such, it should be based on the study of those aspects of human interaction that relate language structure to its uses. It thus should draw not only from traditional linguistic method, especially contact linguistics, but also from pragmatics, conceptual metaphor theory, and argumentation theory.

Ultimately, the goal of GL is to promote understanding among people of different cultural backgrounds, by showing that all languages are products of the universal need of humans to understand the world and each other.

Through fieldwork and the systematic comparison of languages, the global linguist can gain insight into how intercultural competence can be achieved and what kinds of problems emerge according to the backgrounds of speakers. Our final comment on GL is, however, cautionary. No matter how scientific or theoretically sound a linguist's account of the connection between language, culture, and discourse might appear or might be purported to be, no science can ever truly account for the remarkable phenomenon that we call language and the many vagaries of human interaction. We might be able to describe what the basic patterns are, *in certain specific situations* and how they mesh together, *in those situations*; but we will never be able to put into a theory or model all there is to know about how people talk to each other and make sense of the encounter.

In a sense, GL analysis should be conceived as a process akin to solving a jigsaw puzzle. The goal of the puzzle-solver is to figure out how the pieces of the puzzle fit together to produce the hidden picture that they conceal as disconnected pieces. But solving the jigsaw puzzle tells the solver nothing about why such puzzles exist in the first place, and thus what relevance they have to human life. Analogously, the global linguist should seek to figure out how the bits and pieces cohere into the flow of IC. But having described this flow, he or she is still left with the dilemma of figuring out what it all means in human terms.

GL shows that diversity is the norm, but that diversity only reflects differentiated attempts to solve similar problems across the world. It shows how we go about tackling the same problems of classification and understanding, coming up with different solutions according to situation, time, and place. The fact that we can understand each other nonetheless shows how much we are really all one race, equal and seeking similar objectives and outcomes to the experience of existence.

References

Abdulaziz-Mkilifi, M. H.
    1972   Triglossia and Swahili-English Bilingualism in Tanzania. *Language in Society* 1(1).

Allan, K.
    2004   Politeness, orthophemism, euphemism and dysphemism. *International Journal of the Humanities*, 2/1 (entire issue).
    2005   The pragmatics of connotation. Paper presented at the 9th International Pragmatics Conference: http: // www. arts. monash. edu. au/ling/staff/allan/docs/Pragmatic-Connotation.pdf (December 2005).

Allwood, J. and P. Gärdenfors
    1998   *Cognitive Semantics: Meaning and Cognition.* Amsterdam: John Benjamins.

Alpher, B.
    1987   Feminine as the unmarked grammatical gender: Buffalo girls are no fools. *Australian Journal of Linguistics* 7: 169-187.

Aristotle.
    1952   *Rhetoric.* In: W. D. Ross (ed.), *The Works of Aristotle*, Vol. 11. Oxford: Clarendon Press.

Arnheim, R.
    1969   *Visual Thinking* :Berkeley: University of California Press.

Austin, J. L.
    1962   *How to Do Things with Words.* Cambridge, Mass.: Harvard University Press.

Bakhtin, M. M.
    1981   *The Dialogic Imagination.* Trans. by C. Emerson and M. Holquist, ed. by M. Holquist. Austin: University of Texas Press.
    1986   *Speech Genres and Other Late Essays*, trans. by V. W. Mc Gee, ed. by C. Emerson and M. Holquist. Austin: University of Texas Press.

Bakhtin, M. M. and V. N. Voloshinov.
    1986   *Marxism and the Philosophy of Language.* Cambridge, Mass.: Harvard University Press.

Baudrillard, J.
    1998   *The Ecstasy of Communication.* St. Louis: Telos Press.

Bazerman, C.
    2004   Intertextuality: how texts rely on other texts. In: C. Bazerman and P. Prior (eds.) *What writing does and how it does it. An introduction to analyzing texts and textual practices.*, 83-96, Mahwah (N.J.): Lawrence Erlbaum.

Benedict, R.
   1934   *Patterns of Culture*. New York: New American Library.

Benveniste, E.
   1969   The semiology of language. *Semiotica* 1: 1-12 and 127-135.

Berlin, B. and P. Kay.
   1969   *Basic Color Terms*. Berkeley: University of California Press.

Best, A.
   1975   The comedians' world: Three methods of structural analysis for free association data. Paper presented at the *Southeastern Psychological Association Meeting*, Atlanta, March 1975.

Bettoni, Camilla.
   2006   *Usare un'altra lingua. Guida alla pragmatica interculturale*. Bari: Laterza.

Betz, W.
   1949   *Deutsch und Lateinisch: Die Lehnbildungen der althochdeutschen Benediktinerregel*. Bonn: Bouvier.

Biggam, C., P. Kay, J. Christian and N. Pitchford
   2006   *Progress in Colour Studies*, 2 volumes. Amsterdam: John Benjamins.

Bigi, S.
   In press Keywords. Proceedings of the VI ISSA Conference on Argumentation Theory, Amsterdam, June 2006.

Bloomfield, L.
   1933   *Language*. New York: Holt.

Boas, F.
   1940   *Race, Language, and Culture*. New York: Free Press.

Bonvillain, N.
   2008   *Language, Culture, and Communication: The Meaning of Messages*, 5th edition. Upper Saddle River, NJ: Pearson Education.

Bovay, C.
   2004   *Le paysage religieux en Suisse*. Neuchâtel: Office fédéral de la statistique.

Brown, G. and G. Yule
   1983   *Discourse analysis*. Cambridge: Cambridge University Press.

Brown, P. and S.C. Levinson.
   1978   Universals in language use: politeness phenomena. In: E. Goody(ed.) *Questions and politeness. Strategies in social interaction* (pp. 56-289). Cambridge: Cambridge University Press.

Brown, R. W.
   1958   *Words and Things: An Introduction to Language*. New York: The Free Press.

Bruce, L.
    1984   *The Alamblak Language of Papua New Guinea (East Sepik)*. Canberra: Australian National University.

Cantoni, L.
    1999   Benjanin Lee Whorf ed Emile Benveniste. In: G. Bettetini, S. Cigada, S. Raynaud, E. Rigotti (eds.) *Semiotica I. Origini e fondamenti*. Brescia: La Scuola.

Cantoni, L. and S. Tardini
    2006   *Internet*. London and New York: Routledge.

Casad, E. H.
    1996   *Cognitive Linguistics in the Redwoods: The Expansion of a New Paradigm in Linguistics*. Berlin: Mouton de Gruyter.

Chambers, J. K. and P. Trudgill
    1998   *Dialectology*. Cambridge: Cambridge University Press.

Cherry, C.
    1957   *On Human Communication*. Cambridge, Mass.: MIT Press.

Chomsky, N.
    1957   *Syntactic Structures*. The Hague: Mouton.
    1965   *Aspects of the Theory of Syntax*. Cambridge, Mass.: MIT Press.
    1975   *Reflections on Language*. New York: Pantheon.
    1982   *Some Concepts and Consequences of the Theory of Government and Binding*. Cambridge, Mass.: MIT Press.
    1986   *Knowledge of Language: Its Nature, Origin, and Use*. New York: Praeger.
    1995   *The Minimalist Program*. Cambridge, Mass.: MIT Press.
    2000   *New Horizons in the Study of Language and Mind*. Cambridge: Cambridge University Press.
    2002   *On Nature and Language*. Cambridge: Cambridge University Press.

Clark, H.
    1996   *Using Language*. Cambridge: Cambridge University Press.

Cohen, E. and N. Avieli
    2003   Food in tourism: attraction and impediment. *Annals of Tourism Research*, 31/ 4: 755–778.

Cole, K. C.
    1984   *Sympathetic Vibrations*. New York: Bantam.

Conklin, H.
    1955   Hanonóo color categories. *Southwestern Journal of Anthropology* 11: 339-344.

Connor, U.
    2004   Intercultural rhetoric research: beyond texts. *Journal of English for Academic Purposes*, Vol. 3: 291-304.

Constitution of the Russian Federation
    1993   English translation available at http://www.constitution.ru/en/10003000-01.htm (Last consulted: 08.10.2008)

Cowley, P. and B. E. Hanna
    2005   Cross-cultural skills – crossing the disciplinary divide. *Language and Communication*, 25: 1-17.

Crystal, D.
    2003   *English as a Global Language.* Second Edition. Cambridge: Cambridge University Press.

Danesi, M.
    2000   *Semiotics in language education.* Berlin: Mouton de Gruyter.
    2002   *The Puzzle Instinct: The Meaning of Puzzles in Human life.* Bloomington: Indiana University Press.
    2003   *Second Language Teaching: A View from the Right Side of the Brain.* Dordrecht: Kluwer Academic Publishers.
    2004a   *Poetic Logic: The Role of Metaphor in Thought, Language, and Culture.* Madison: Atwood Publishing.
    2004b   *A Basic Course in Anthropological Linguistics.* Toronto: Canadian Scholars' Press.
    2007   *The Quest for Meaning: A Guide to Semiotic Theory and Practice.* Toronto: University of Toronto Press.

Deacon, T.
    1997   *The Symbolic species: The coevolution of language and the brain.* New York: W. W. Norton.

Demel, W.
    1992   Wie die Chinesen gelb wurden: Ein Beitrag zur Frühgeschichte der Rassentheorien. *Historische Zeitschrift* 255: 625-666.

Dirven, R. and M. Verspoor.
    2004   *Cognitive Exploration of Language and Linguistics.* Amsterdam: John Benjamins.

Dressler, W. U. and L. Merlini Barbaresi
    1994   *Morphopragmatics. Diminutives and Intensifiers in Italian, German and Other Languages.* Berlin/: Mouton de Gruyter.

Eckhouse, B.
    1999   *Competitive Communication: A Rhetoric for Modern Business.* Oxford: Oxford University Press.

Eco, U.
    1999   *Kant and the Platypus: Essays on Language and Cognition.* San Diego/New York/London: Harcourt-Brace.

Eder, D.
1990 Serious and playful disputes: Variation on conflict talk among female adolescents. In: D. Grimshaw (ed.) *Conflict Talk*, 67-84. Cambridge: Cambridge University Press.

Edie, J. M.
1976 *Speaking and Meaning: The Phenomenology of Language*. Bloomington: Indiana University Press.

Egner, I.
2006 Intercultural aspects of the speech act of promising: Western and African practices. *Intercultural Pragmatics*. 3-4: 443–464.

Emantian, M.
1995 Metaphor and the expression of emotion: The value of cross-cultural perspectives. *Metaphor and Symbolic Activity* 10: 163-182.

Fauconnier, G. and M. Turner
2002 *The Way We Think: Conceptual Blending and the Mind's Hidden Complexities*. New York: Basic.

Ferguson, C.
1959 Diglossia. *Word,* 15: 325-340.

Fillmore, C. J.
2003 Topics in lexical semantics. In: C.J. Fillmore, *Form and Meaning in Language*. Stanford (CA): CSLI Publications.

Fischer, J. L.
1958 Social influences in the choice of a linguistic variant. *Word* 14: 47-57.

Fisher, R. and W. Ury
1981 *Getting to Yes. Negotiating Agreement Without Giving In*. Boston: Houghton Mifflin Company.

FitzGerald, H.
2002 *How Different Are We? : Spoken Disocurse in Intercultural Communication*. Clevedon/Buffalo/Toronto/Sidney: Multilingual Matters Ltd.

Foley, W.
1997 *Anthropological Linguistics: an introduction*. Oxford: Basil Blackwell.

Foucault, M.
1971 *L'ordre du discours. Leçon inaugurale au Collège de France*. Paris: Gallimard.

Frye, N.
1981 *The Great Code: The Bible and Literature*. Toronto: Academic Press.

Garssen, B.
2008 Comparing the incomparable: Figurative analogies in a dialectical testing procedure. In: Frans H. van Eemeren & Bart Garssen (eds.). *Pondering on Problems of Argumentation. Twenty Essays on Theoretical Issues.* New York: Springer.

Gatti, M C.
2003 Pratiche di analisi semiotica in Jurij Lotman e Boris A. Uspenskij. In: G. Bettetini Cigada, S. Raynaud E. Rigotti (eds.), *Semiotica II. Configurazione disciplinare e questioni contemporanee*, 23-45. Brescia: La Scuola.

Geeraerts, D.
2006 *Cognitive Linguistics.* Berlin: Mouton de Gruyter.

Gibbs, R.
1994 *The Poetics of Mind: Figurative Thought, Language, and Understanding.* Cambridge: Cambridge University Press.

Gilbert, L., T. Regier, P. Kay, and R. B. Ivry
2005 Whorf hypothesis is supported in the right visual field but not the left. *Proceedings of the National Academy of Sciences.* 103: 489-494.

Goatly, A.
2007 *Washing the Brain: Metaphor and Hidden Ideology.* Amsterdam: John Benjamins.

Goddard, C. and A.Wierzbicka
1997 Discourse and culture. In: *Discourse as Social Interaction.* Edited by Teun A. van Dijk. London: Sage Publications. 231-257.

Goffman, Erving.
1967 On face-work: an analysis of ritual elements in social interaction. In E. Goffman (ed.) *Interaction ritual: Essays in face-to-face behavior* (pp. 5-45). Chicago: Aldine.

Greco Morasso, S.
2006 Towards a multidisciplinary context-dependent model of mediation practice. *Studies in Communication Sciences.* 6/2: 281-292
2007 The covert argumentativity of mediation. Developing argumentation through asking questions. In: F.H. van Eemeren, J.A. Blair, Ch.A. Willard, B. Garssen (eds.). *Proceedings of the 6th Conference of the International Society for the Study of Argumentation.* Amsterdam: SicSat.
2008 The ontology of conflict. *Pragmatics and Cognition.* 16/3: 540-567.
2009 *Argumentative and other communicative strategies of the mediation practice.* Ph.D. Thesis Thesis. Faculty of Communication Sciences. University of Lugano.

Grice, H. P.
    1991   Logic and conversation. In: S. Davis (ed.) *Pragmatics: a Reader.* Oxford: Oxford University Press. (Reprint of the paper originally presented in the William James Lectures at Harvard University in 1967 and circulated as a typescript).

Gumperz, J.
    1982   *Discourse Strategies.* Cambridge: Cambridge University Press.

Halliday, M. A. K.
    1975   *Learning How to Mean: Explorations in the Development of Language.* London: Arnold.
    1985   *Introduction to Functional Grammar.* London: Arnold.

Harré, R.
    1981   *Great Scientific Experiments.* Oxford: Phaidon Press.

Haugen, E.
    1950   The analysis of linguistic borrowing. *Language* 26: 210-231.

Hewitt, H.
    2002   How we pay: transactional and interactional features of payment sequences in service encounters. In: *Proceedings of the Postgraduate Conference 2002.* University of Edinburgh. Department of Linguistics and English Language. Text available online at: http://www.ling.ed.ac.uk/~pgc/archive/2002/pgc02-proceedings.html (Last consulted: 1/8/2009).

Holm, J. A.
    1989   *Pidgins and Creoles.* Cambridge: Cambridge University Press.

Honeck, R. P. and R. R. Hoffman.
    1980   *Cognition and Figurative Language.* Hillsdale, NJ: Lawrence Erlbaum Associates.

Hornikx, J.
    2006   *Cultural Differences in the Persuasiveness of Evidence Types in France and the Netherlands.* Nijmegen: F&N Boekservice.

House, J.
    2003   English as a Lingua Franca: A Threat to Multilingualism? *Journal of Sociolinguistics* 7/4: 556-578.

House, J., G. Kasper and S. Ross
    2003   *Misunderstanding in Social Life: Discourse Approaches to Problematic Talk.* London: Pearson Education.

House, J. and J. Rehbein
    2004   *Multilingual Communication.* Amsterdam: Benjamins.

Hurford, J.R.
    2003   The neural basis of predicate-argument structure. *Behavioral and Brain Sciences.* 26: 261–316.

Hymes, D.
    1971   *On Communicative Competence*. Philadelphia: University of Pennsylvania Press.

Jackendoff, R.
    1983   *Semantics and Cognition*. Cambridge (Mass.): MIT Press.
    1997   *The Architecture of the Language Faculty*. Cambridge (Mass.): MIT Press.

Jacobs, S.
    2000   Rhetoric and Dialectic from the Standpoint of Normative Pragmatics. *Argumentation* Vol. 14: 261-286.

Jacobs, S. and S. Jackson
    2006   Derailments of argumentation: It takes two to tango. In: P. Houtlosser, and A. van Rees (eds.). *Considering Pragma-Dialectics: A Festshrift for Frans H. Van Eemeren*. Mahwah: Lawrence Erlbaum.

Jakobson, R.
    1960   Linguistics and poetics. In: T. A. Sebeok (ed.), *Style and Language*, 34-45. Cambridge, Mass.: MIT Press.
    1963   *Essais de linguistique générale*. Paris: Éditions de Minuit.

Janssen, T. and G. Redeker
    2000   *Cognitive Linguistics: Foundations, Scope, and Methodology*. Berlin: Mouton de Gruyter.

Jaszczolt, K. M. and K. Turner
    1996   *Contrastive Semantics and Pragmatics*. Oxford: Elsevier.
    2003   *Meaning through Language Contrast*. Amsterdam: John Benjamins.

Jespersen, O.
    1924   *The Philosophy of Grammar*, London.

Johnson, M.
    1987   *The Body in the Mind: The Bodily Basis of Meaning, Imagination and Reason*. Chicago: University of Chicago Press.
    1989   Image-schematic bases of meaning. *Semiotic Inquiry* 9: 109-118.
    2007   *The Meaning of the Body: Aesthetics of Human Understanding*. Chicago: University of Chicago Press.

Jones, R.
    1982   *Physics as Metaphor*. New York: New American Library.

Joos, M.
    1967   *The Five Clocks*. New York: Harcourt, Brace and World.

Kaplan, R. B.
    1966   Cultural thought patterns in intercultural education. *Language Learning*. 16: 1-20.
    2001   Contrastive Rhetoric and Discourse Analysis: Who writes what to whom? When? In what circumstances?. In: S. Sarangi and M. Coulthard (eds.) *Discourse and Social Life*. London: Longman.

Kay, P.
  1975   Synchronic variability and diachronic change in basic color terms. *Language in Society* 4: 257-270.
Kay, P. and L. A. Michaelis
  to appear   Constructional Meaning and Compositionality. In: C. Maienborn, K. von Heusinger and P. Portner (eds.). *Semantics: An International Handbook of Natural Language Meaning.* Berlin: Mouton de Gruyter.
Kerbrat-Orecchioni, Catherine.
  2005   *Le discours en interaction.* Paris: Armand Colin
Kirch, Max S.
  1979   Non-Verbal Communication across Cultures. *The Modern Language Journal*, 63/8: 416-423.
Klyukanov, I. E.
  2005   *Principles of Intercultural Communication.* Boston: Pearson Education.
Komlósi, L. I., P. Houtlosser and M. Leezenberg
  2003   *Communication and Culture. Argumentative, Cognitive and Linguistic Perspectives.* Amsterdam: Sic Sat.
Kövecses, Z.
  1986   *Metaphors of Anger, Pride, and Love: A Lexical Approach to the Structure of Concepts.* Amsterdam: John Benjamins.
  1988   *The Language of Love: The Semantics of Passion in Conversational English.* London: Associated University Presses.
  1990   *Emotion Concepts.* New York: Springer.
  2002   *Metaphor: A Practical Introduction.* Oxford: Oxford University Press.
Kramsch, C.
  1998   *Language and Culture.* Oxford: Oxford University Press.
Kroeber, A. L. and C. Kluckholn
  1963   *Culture: A Critical Review of Concepts and Definitions.* New York: Vintage.
Labov, W.
  1966   *The Social Stratification of English in New York City.* Washington, DC: Center for Applied Linguistics.
  1967   The effect of social mobility on a linguistic variable. In: S. Lieberson (ed.), *Explorations in Sociolinguistics*, 23-45. Bloomington: Indiana University Research Center in Anthropology, Linguistics and Folklore.
  1972   *Language in the Inner City.* Philadelphia: University of Pennsylvania Press.

Lakoff, G.
- 1987　*Women, Fire, and Dangerous Things: What Categories Reveal about the Mind*. Chicago: University of Chicago Press.

Lakoff, G. and M. Johnson
- 1980　*Metaphors We Live By*. Chicago: Chicago University Press.
- 1999　*Philosophy in the Flesh: The Embodied Mind and Its Challenge to Western Thought*. New York: Basic.

Langacker, R. W.
- 1987　*Foundations of Cognitive Grammar*. Stanford: Stanford University Press.
- 1990　*Concept, Image, and Symbol: The Cognitive Basis of Grammar*. Berlin: Mouton de Gruyter.
- 1999　*Grammar and Conceptualization*. Berlin: Mouton de Gruyter.

Laroche, P.
- 2007　*On Words: Insight into How our Words Work and Don't*. Oak Park, Ill.: Marion Street Press.

Lawn, B.
- 1993　*The Rise and Decline of the "Quaestio Disputata". With Special Emphasis on its Use in the Teaching of Medicine and Science*. Leiden/ New York/ Köln: BRILL.

Leech, G.
- 2004　Review of David Crystal *English as a Global Language*, second edition. *Journal of Pragmatics* 36: 2077-2080

Levine, R.
- 1997　*A Geography of Time: The Temporal Misadventures of a Social Psychologist or How Every Culture Keeps Time Just a Little Bit Differently*. New York: Basic.

Levinson, S. C.
- 1979　Activity types and language. *Linguistics*, 17: 365-399.
- 1997　From outer to inner space: linguistic categories and non-linguistic thinking. In: J. Nuyts and E. Pederson,(eds.), *With language in mind: the relationship between linguistic and conceptual representation*, Cambridge: Cambridge University Press (pp. 13–45).

Lotman, Y.
- 1991　*Universe of the Mind: A Semiotic Theory of Culture*. Bloomington: Indiana University Press.

Lotman, Y. M. and B. A. Uspenskij
- 1973　Il problema del segno e del sistema segnico nella tipologia della cultura russa prima del XX secolo. In: Yuri M. Lotman and Boris A. Uspenskij. *Ricerche semiotiche. Nuove tendenze delle scienze umane nell'URSS*. Torino: Einaudi.
- 1987　Sul meccanismo semiotico della cultura. In: Yuri M. Lotman and Boris A. Uspenskij. *Tipologia della cultura*. Milano: Bompiani.

Lucy, J.
- 1996 The scope of linguistic relativity: An analysis and review of empirical research. In J. Gumperz and S. Levinson (eds.), *Rethinking Linguistic Relativity*, pp. 37-70. New York: Cambridge University Press.
- 1997 Linguistic Relativity. *Annual Review of Anthropology*, Vol. 26: 291-312.

Lüdi, G.
- 1998 L'enfant bilingue: chance ou surcharge? In: Lorenza Mondada, Georges Lüdi (eds.), *Dialogues entre linguistes. Recherches en linguistique à l'Institut des langues et littératures romanes de le l'Université de Bâle* (Acta Romanica Basiliensia 8): 13-30. Also available online at the URL : http://sprachenkonzept.franz.unibas.ch/Annexe_8.html (Last consulted: 08.10.2008).

Lüdi, G. and I. Werlen
- 2005 *Le paysage linguistique en Suisse*. Neuchâtel: Office fédéral de la statistique.

Lyons, J.
- 1995 *Linguistic Semantics. An Introduction.* Cambridge: Cambridge University Press.

Maclaury, R. E., G.V. Paramei and D. Dedrick
- 2007 *Anthropology of Color*. Amsterdam: John Benjamins.

Malinowski, B.
- 1922 *Argonauts of the Western Pacific*. New York: Dutton.
- 1929 *The Sexual Life of Savages in North-Western Melanesia*. New York: Harcourt, Brace, and World.

Mallery, G.
- 1972 *Sign Language among North American Indians Compared with That among Other Peoples and Deaf-Mutes*. The Hague: Mouton.

Mathiot, M.
- 1962 Noun classes and folk taxonomy in Papago. *American Anthropologist* 64: 340-350.

McLuhan, M.
- 1951 *The Mechanical Bride: Folklore of Industrial Man*. New York: Vanguard.
- 1962 *The Gutenberg Galaxy*. Toronto: University of Toronto Press.
- 1964 *Understanding Media*. London: Routledge and Kegan Paul.

McNeill, D.
- 1992 *Hand and Mind: What Gestures Reveal about Thought*. Chicago: University of Chicago Press.

Mead, M.
   1939   *From the South Seas: Studies of Adolescence and Sex in Primitive Societies.* New York: Morrow.
   1950   *Coming of Age in Samoa.* New York: North American Library.

Mel'chuk, I.A.
   2004   Actants in semantics and syntax. *Linguistics* 42: 1-66.

Moeschler, J.
   2004   Intercultural pragmatics: a cognitive approach. *Intercultural Pragmatics,* 1-1: 49–70.

Morris, Desmond et al.
   1979   *Gestures: Their Origins and Distributions.* London: Cape.

O'Keefe, D. J.
   2002   *Persuasion: Theory and Research.* London, New Delhi: Sage Publications, Thousand Oaks.

Palmieri, R.
   2008   Reconstructing argumentative interactions in M&A offers. *Studies in Communication Sciences* 8/ 2&3: 279-302

Pavlenko, A.
   2006   Russian as a Lingua Franca. *Annual Review of Applied Linguistics* 26: 78-99.

Pateman, T.
   1980   How to do things with images. An Essay in the pragmatics of advertisements. *Theory and Society* 9: 603-622.

Peirce, C. S.
   1931-1958   *Collected Papers of Charles Sanders Peirce*, Vols. 1-8, ed. by C. Hartshorne and P. Weiss. Cambridge, Mass.: Harvard University Press.

Petty, R. E. and J:T. Cacioppo
   1986   Communication and Persuasion. Central and Peripheral Routes to Attitude Change. *Springer Series in Social Psychology*, Springer-Verlag New York, Berlin, Heidelberg, London, Paris, Tokyo.

Pinto, R. C.
   1996   The relation of argument to inference. In: J. van Benthem, F.H. van Eemeren, R. Grootendorst and F. Veltman (eds.). *Logic and argumentation.* North-Holland: Amsterdam.

Plümacher, M. and P. Holz
   2007   *Speaking of Colors and Odors.* Amsterdam: John Benjamins.

Polanyi, L.
   1989   *Telling the American Story.* Cambridge (Mass.): MIT Press.

Poplack, S., D. Sankoff and C. Miller
   1988   The social correlates and linguistic processes of lexical borrowing and assimilation. *Linguistics* 26: 47-104.

Princen, T.
1992   *Intermediaries in International Conflict.* Princeton: Princeton University Press.

Pustejovsky, J.
1995   *The Generative Lexicon.* Cambridge (Mass.): MIT Press.

Radcliffe-Brown, A. R.
1922   *The Andaman Islanders.* Cambridge: Cambridge University Press.

Radden, G. and R. Dirven
2007   *Cognitive English Grammar.* Amsterdam: John Benjamins.

Ray, V.
1953   Human color perception and behavioral response. *Transactions of the New York Academy of Sciences,* Volume 16 (entire issue).

Reddy, M.J
1979   The conduit metaphor. a case of frame conflict in our language about language. In: Andrew Ortony (ed): *Metaphor and Thought.,* 284-324. Cambridge: Cambridge University Press

Richards, I. A.
1936   *The Philosophy of Rhetoric.* Oxford: Oxford University Press.

Rigotti, E.
2000   On semiosis, human freedom and education. In P. Perron, L.G. Sbrocchi, P. Colilli e M. Danesi (eds.). *Semiotics as a Bridge between the Humanities and the Sciences,* New York/Ottawa/Toronto: Legas.

2005a   Plurilinguismo e unità culturale in Europa. In: C. Cambiaghi, C. Milani and P. Pontani (eds.), *Europa plurilingue: comunicazione e didattica.* Milano: Vita e Pensiero.

2005b   Towards a typology of manipulative processes. In: L. De Saussure and P. Schulz (ed.s), *Manipulation and Ideologies in the Twentieth Century,* 61-84, Amsterdam: Benjamins.

2005c   Congruity theory and argumentation. In: M. Dascal, F.H. van Eemeren, E. Rigotti, S. Stati and A. Rocci (eds.) *Argumentation in Dialogic Interaction.* Special Issue of *Studies in Communication Sciences*: 75-96.

2009   Can classical topics be revived in the modern theory of argumentation? In: F.H. van Eemeren and B. Garssen (eds.). *Pondering on Problems of Argumentation,* 157-178. New York: Springer.

Rigotti, E. and S. Cigada
2004   *La comunicazione verbale,* Milano: Apogeo.

Rigotti, E. and S.Greco Morasso.
- 2006 The argument generator. In: E. Rigotti E. et al., Argumentation Skills for Financial Communication. *Argumentum eLearning Module*, www.argumentum.ch.
- 2009 Argumentation as object of interest and as social and cultural resource. In: A.N. Perret-Clermont and N. Müller-Mirza (eds.). *Argumentation and Education. Theoretical Foundations and Practices*. New York: Springer.

Rigotti, E. and A. Rocci
- 2001 Sens – non-sens – contresens. *Studies in Communication Sciences*, 2: 45-80.
- 2003 "Categorie nascoste in prospettiva interlinguistica". In: L. Mondada and S. Pekarek Doehler (eds.). *Plurilinguisme/ Mehrsprachigkeit/ Plurilingualism : Enjeux identitaires, socio-culturels et éducatifs. Festschrift pour Georges Lüdi*. Tübingen: Francke: 277-294.
- 2005 From argument analysis to cultural keywords (and back again). In: F. H. Van Eemeren, P. and Houtlosser (eds.). *Argumentation in Practice*. Amsterdam: John Benjamins.
- 2006a Denotation vs connotation. In: K. Brown (ed.). *The Encyclopedia of Language and Linguistics*, 2nd Edition, Amsterdam: Elsevier.
- 2006b Towards a definition of communication context. In: Colombetti, M. (ed.) *The Communication Sciences as a Multidisciplinary Enterprise, Studies in Communication Sciences* 6/2 (Anniversary Issue): 155-180.
- 2006c Le signe linguistique comme structure intermédiaire. In : L. de Saussure (ed.). *Nouvelles perspectives sur Saussure. Mélanges offerts à René Amacker*, Publications du Cercle Ferdinand de Saussure, Genève : Droz. (pp. 219-247).

Rigotti, E., A. Rocci and S. Greco
- 2006 The semantics of reasonableness. In: P. Houtlosser, and A. van Rees (eds.). *Considering Pragma-Dialectics: A Festshrift for Frans H. Van Eemeren*. Mahwah: Lawrence Erlbaum.

Rocci, A.
- 1996 Funzioni comunicative della posizione dell'aggettivo in italiano. *L'analisi Linguistica e Letteraria*, III /1: 220-284.
- 2005 Are manipulative texts coherent? Manipulation, presuppositions, and (in-) congruity. In: L. Saussure & P. Schulz (eds.). *Manipulation and Ideologies in the Twentieth Century: Discourse, Language, Mind. (Discourse Approaches to Politics, Society and Culture,* 17) Amsterdam/Philadelphia: Benjamins. (pp. 85-112).
- 2006 Pragmatic inference and argumentation in intercultural communication. *Intercultural Pragmatics*, 3-4: 409–442.

    2009   Doing discourse analysis with possible worlds. In: Jan Renkema (ed.) *Discourse. Of course!* Amsterdam: Benjamins.

Rosaldo, M.
    1982   The things we do with words: Ilongot speech acts and speech act theory in philosophy. *Language and Society* 11: 203-237.

Rosch, E.
    1975   Cognitive reference points. *Cognitive Psychology* 7: 532-547.

Rubagumya, C. M.
    1991   Language Promotion for Educational Purposes: The Example of Tanzania. *International Review of Education*. Vol. 37, No. 1: 67-85.

Sacks, H., E. Schegloff and G. Jefferson
    1974   A Simplest Systematics for the Organization of Turn-Taking for Conversation. *Language* 50: 696-735

Sapir, E.
    1924   The grammarian and his language. *American Mercury*. 1: 149-55.

Saussure, F.
    1916   *Cours de linguistique générale*. Paris: Payot.

Schmandt-Besserat, D.
    1978   The earliest precursor of writing. *Scientific American* 238: 50-59.
    1992   *Before Writing*, 2 vols. Austin: University of Texas Press.

Schulz, P.
    2001   Rationality as a condition for intercultural understanding. *Studies in Communication Sciences*. 1/2: 81-100.

Scollon, R. and S.W. Scollon
    2001   *Intercultural Communication*. New Jersey: Blackwell Publishing.

Scotton, C., M. Myers and J. Okeju
    1973   Neighbors and lexical borrowing. *Language* 49: 871-889.

Searle, J. R
    1969   *Speech Acts: An Essay in the Philosophy of Language*. Cambridge: Cambridge University Press.
    1995   *The Construction of Social Reality*. London: Penguin Books.
    2001   *Rationality in Action*. Cambridge, Mass.: MIT Press.

Sebeok, T. A.
    2001   *Global Semiotics*. Bloomington: Indiana University Press.

Seuren, P. A. M.
    1985   *Discourse Semantics*. Oxford : Blackwell.

Shannon, C. E.
    1948   A mathematical theory of communication. *Bell Systems Technical Journal* 27: 379-423.

Sperber, D. and D. Wilson
    1986   *Relevance: Communication and Cognition*. New Jersey: Blackwell Publishing

Stalnaker, R.
- 1973 Presuppositions. *Journal of Philosophical Logic 2*: 447-457
- 2002 Common Ground. *Linguistics and Philosophy* 25: 701-721

Stubbs, M.
- 2008 *Three concepts of keywords* . Paper presented to the conference on *Keyness in Text* at the Certosa di Pontignano, University of Siena. Preprint available at http://www.uni-trier.de/fileadmin/fb2/ANG/Linguistik/Stubbs/stubbs-2008-keywords.pdf.

Tannen, D.
- 1989 *Talking Voices. Repetition, dialogue and imagery in conversational discourse.* Cambridge: Cambridge University Press.

Taylor, D. M.
- 1977 *Languages of the West Indies*. Baltimore: Johns Hopkins.

Tillemans, T. J. F.
- 2008 Introduction: Buddhist Argumentation. *Argumentation*, 22:1–14.

Tolmach Lakoff, R.
- 2001 Nine ways of looking at apologies: The necessity for interdisciplinary theory and method in discourse analysis. In: D. Schffrin, D., Tannen, and H. E. Hamilton (eds.). *The Handbook of Discourse Analysis.* Blackwell Publishing: Oxford.

Tylor, E.
- 1871 *Primitive Culture*. London: Murray.

Uspenskij, B.
- 2001 *La pala d'altare di Jan van Eyck a Gand: La composizione dell'opera (la prospettiva divina e la prospettiva umana).* Milano: Lupetti.

U.S. Census Bureau
- 2007 *Selected Social Characteristics in the United States.* Available online at http://factfinder.census.gov (Last consulted: 22.02.2008).

van Eemeren, F. H. and P. Houtlosser
- 1999 Strategic Manoeuvring in Argumentative Discourse. *Discourse Studies.* 1/4: 479-497.
- 2005 Theoretical construction and argumentative reality: An analytic model of critical discussion and conventionalised types of argumentative activity. In: D. Hitchcock (ed.). *The Uses of Argument: Proceedings of a Conference at McMaster University, 18-21 May 2005, Hamilton* (pp. 75-84). St. Catharines, ON: OSSA.

van Eemereen, F. H. and R. Grootendorst
- 2004 *A systematic theory of argumentation. The pragma-dialectical approach.* Cambridge: Cambridge University Press.

van Eemereen, F. H., R. Grootendorst and F. Snoeck Henkemans
    2002   *Argumentation. Analysis, Evaluation, Presentation*. Mahwah (New Jersey): Lawrence Erlbaum.

van Eemeren, F. H. , B. Garssen and B. Meuffels
    2003   The conventional validity of the freedom rule. In: van Eemeren F., Blair H., Willard C. et alii. (eds.), *Proceedings of the fifth conference of the International Society for the Study of Argumentation* , Amsterdam : Sic Sat.: 278-280.

van Rees, A.
    1994   Analysing and evaluating small-group decision making discussions. In: L.Waes, E. Woudstra and P. van den Hoven (eds.) *Functional Communication Quality*. Amsterdam: Rodopi.

Van Valin, R. D.
    2005   *Exploring the Syntax-Semantics Interface*. Cambridge: Cambridge University Press.

Vendler, Z.
    1963   The grammar of goodness. *The Philosophical Review*. 72/4: 446-465.

Vygotsky, L. S.
    1962   *Thought and Language*. Cambridge, Mass.: MIT Press.
    1978   *Mind in Society*. Cambridge, Mass.: Cambridge University Press.

Voloshinov, V.N.
    1986   *Marxism and the Philosophy of Language*. Translated by L. Matejka and I.R. Titunik. Cambridge (Mass.): Harvard University Press.

Walton, D. N.
    1998   *The New Dialectic: Conversational Contexts of Argument*. Toronto: University of Toronto Press.
    1999   Rethinking the fallacy of hasty generalization. *Argumentation* 13:161-182.
    2006   *Fundamentals of critical argumentation*. Cambridge: Cambridge University Press.
    2007   *Dialog Theory for Critical Argumentation*. Amsterdam: Benjamins

Weinreich, U.
    1953   *Languages in Contact*. New York: Linguistic Circle of New York.

Wescott, R. W.
    1978   Visualizing vision. In: B. Rhandawa and W. Coffman (eds.), *Visual Learning, Thinking, and Communication*, 21-37. New York: Academic.
    1980   *Sound and Sense*. Lake Bluff, Ill.: Jupiter Press.

Whorf, B. L.
    1956   *Language, Thought, and Reality*, J. B. Carroll (ed.). Cambridge, Mass.: MIT Press.

Wierzbicka, A.
- 1988 What's in a noun? (or: How do nouns differ in meaning from adjectives?) In: *The Semantics of Grammar*. Amsterdam: John Benjamins.
- 1996 *Semantics: Primes and Universals*. Oxford: Oxford University Press.
- 1997 *Understanding Cultures through their Key Words*. Oxford: Oxford University Press.
- 1999 *Emotions Across Languages and Cultures: Diversity and Universals*. Cambridge: Cambridge University Press.
- 2003 *Cross-Cultural Pragmatics: The Semantics of Human Interaction*. New York: Mouton de Gruyter.

Wilke, J.
- 2005 Press instructions as a tool to manipulate the public under the German Nazi government. In: L. Saussure & P. Schulz (eds.). *Manipulation and Ideologies in the Twentieth Century: Discourse, Language, Mind*. (*Discourse Approaches to Politics, Society and Culture*, 17) Amsterdam/Philadelphia: Benjamins.

Winner, E.
- 1988 *The Point of Words: Children's Understanding of Metaphor and Irony*. Cambridge, Mass.: Harvard University Press.

Wittgenstein, L.
- 1921 *Tractatus logico-philosophicus*. London: Routledge and Kegan Paul.
- 1953 *Philosophical Investigations*. New York: Macmillan.

Wolf, H. G. and R. Dirven
- 2006 *Cognitive Linguistics Bibliography*. Berlin: Mouton de Gruyter.

Ye, Zhengdao
- 2004 Chinese categorization of interpersonal relationships and the cultural logic of Chinese social interaction: an indigenous perspective. *Intercultural Pragmatics*, 1-2: 211-230.

Yoon, Kyung-Joo
- 2004 Not just words: Korean social models and the use of honorifics. *Intercultural Pragmatics*, 1-2: 189-210.

Zipf, G. K.
- 1935 *Psycho-Biology of Languages*. Boston: Houghton-Mifflin.
- 1949 *Human Behavior and the Principle of Least Effort*. Boston: Addison-Wesley.

Subject index

Abduction, 183-184
Action, 105-106
Argument (argumentation theory), 184-189
  In context, 200-203
  Argument (semantics), 70-75
  Vs proof, 189-193
Argumentation, 30-32, 173-174,
  Culture-bound and universal components of, 203-204

Calque
  Conceptual, 157-158
  Lexical, 158-160
  Metaphorical, 160-161
Categorical adequacy, 195-199
Common Ground, 84-88
Communicative competence, 52-55
Compositionality, 75-77
Conceptual interference, 79-82
Conceptual Metaphor Theory (CMT), 80-82, 230-243
Congruity Theory, 22, 68, 74-82, 126-129, 167
Connotation, 77-78
Contact linguistics, 5, 227, 248
Contextualization, 88-90
Conversation, 49, 50-52
Cultural diversity, 139-144
Culture, 138-139
  And cognition, 153-157
  And perception, 149-153
  As grammar, 144
  As hypertext, 144-149

Deduction, 183-184
Denotation, 77-78
Desires, 106-110
Dialogue, 46
Diglossia, 12

Discourse, 49, 55-57
Discussion
  Freedom in, 174-177
  Plausibility in, 177-181
  Relevance in, 177-181
  Responsibility in, 174-177

Endoxon (*pl.* endoxa), 206-207

Fallacies, 212

Human nature, 139-144

Idealized Cognitive Models (ICM), 233-243
Ideology, 212
Induction, 183-184
Inference
  Conversational, 90-93
Interaction, 99, 113
  Benevolent, 122-124
  Competitive, 120-122
  Cooperative, 114-120
  Transactive, 114-120
Intercultural communication, 3-5
Intercultural competence, 243
  Defined, 246-248
Intercultural contact, 161
Interference, 5-6, 227, 230-243

Jakobson's model, 58-63
Joint action, 103-105

Keywords, cultural, 207-212
Koiné, 2

Language, 11-13
  Language vs. speech, 25-30
Language design, 17-24
Lingua franca, 2

Linguistics, 33-34
Loanwords, 162-163
Locus (*pl.* loci), 204

Maxim, 204-206
Meaning, 67-69
Metaphor, 79-82, 230-243
Multiglossia, 12
Multilingualism, 12-13
    In Switzerland 169-172

Needs, 106-110
Noise, 227, 228-230

Politeness, 130
    Theories of, 131-136
Predicate, 70
    Pragmatic, 126-129

Reasonableness, 193-195

Reasoning, 181
Relational Communication, 129-130

Specialized vocabularies, 222-225
Speech, 24-25
Speech acts, 63-67
Speech functions, 57
Stereotyping, 214-216

Translation
    As textual borrowing, 164-169

Utterance, 82-83

Verbal communication, 124-126

Whorfian effect, 225-227
Whorfian Hypothesis, 218-222

www.ingramcontent.com/pod-product-compliance
Lightning Source LLC
Chambersburg PA
CBHW071405300426
44114CB00016B/2185